TEACH YOURSELF TO SKI

TEACH YOURSELF TO SKI

This book was originally published in France by ARTHAUD
under the title

POUR APPRENDRE SOI-MÊME A SKIER

**Translated from the French
by Sim THOMAS**

ASPEN SKI MASTERS

The photographs, the photomontages, and diagrams are by Georges JOUBERT.
Printed by SADAG, BELLEGARDE (AIN) FRANCE.
The cover is by Richard RAILLET
and Joël PICAUT

PUBLISHERS ENGLISH EDITION
ASPEN SKI MASTERS
P. O. BOX 3071
ASPEN, COLORADO 81611 USA
0-9600570-1-3

BY
Georges JOUBERT
President of the Grenoble University Club
Technical Director and Coach of GUC-SKI
President of the Association of University Skiers (A.U.S.)

In collaboration with
The Coaches of the Grenoble University Club and the Members of the A.U.S.

Participation in teaching experiments by
THE GRENOBLE UNIVERSITY SKI CLUB
THE GRENOBLE UNIVERSITY SKI SCHOOL
THE ASSOCIATION OF UNIVERSITY SKIERS
THE GRENOBLE SKI SCHOOL

Foreword by
Curt CHASE
Director, Aspen Ski School

Translated from the French
by
Sim THOMAS
Head Coach, Aspen Ski Club

Annie FAMOSE, A Good Model to watch

World champion in Portillo, several time collegiate world champion, Annie Famose
started summer training with the Grenoble University Club when only thirteen
years old. Today, she is a champion and also a professor of physical education.
Her charming anatomy and solid technique make her an excellent model.

Patrick RUSSEL and Avalement

This movement, which is still unusual for the average skier, illustrates perfectly the latest technical element used by virtuoso skiers, *avalement*. Jean Vuarnet and I were the first to analyze and name this movement in our book, *How to Ski the New French Way*. Jean-Claude Killy used it from time to time unknowingly in slalom or in moguls. With Patrick Russel I was able to make the movement the basis of a technique which has been assimilated by all international racers. A field of moguls is the most natural place for a good skier to learn *avalement* through the suggestions in this book.

The Ultimate in Pleasure Skiing : Powder

Skiing powder is the most intoxicating pleasure open to a skier. Contrary to widespread opinion, powder technique conflicts neither with packed slope skiing nor with competitive technique. Only an abusive use in the past of certain technical elements like forward pressure could have given credence to his belief. The best racers become the best powder skiers very quickly. Here, Patrick Russel shows how *avalement,* which relates to the seated position required in downhill, can be effective in pulling the tips of the skis out of deep powder.

TABLE OF CONTENTS

FOREWORD

In 1958, the book SKI ABC *first brought Georges Joubert to the attention of English speaking skiers. He was firmly endorsed at that time by another great French ski technician and former World Champion, Emile Allais, as a prophet whose conceptions of ski technique were the most exact. Allais also hopefully predicted that Joubert's work would lead to the disappearance of the differences between the various national schools, and to the flowering of a universal method to which all skiers would pay tribute.*

Since 1958, Joubert has emerged as one of the most astute ski technicians of all time. We have been made aware, through the publication of several more books, of Joubert's uncanny ability, not only to analyze precisely the essential movements of a rapidly developing sport, but to reduce them to a remarkably simple method of instruction.

It has been my privilege to ski with Georges Joubert, and to study him at work, as well as to edit this, his latest book. In introducing it to English speaking readers, I can now only agree with Allais. Georges Joubert's conceptions of ski technique are still the most exact. I am also convinced that, although perhaps not totally accomplished, his work has contributed significantly to the understanding of that universal method of which Allais spoke so long ago. Today the various national ski schools are fairly well agreed on the concept of teaching a basic elementary turn that employs the same principles and fundamental movements of the most advanced turns. Teaching systems are increasingly geared to the development and refinement of the basic skills of skiing. This, very simply, is the Joubert doctrine.

Does it work? I can assure you that it does. For many years I have worked with the Joubert approach to ski teaching. Today it is in fact the basis of the Aspen Ski School system. In over twenty years of ski teaching, no technical development has escaped my attention. In my opinion the Joubert way is the most simple, most direct and most effective.

As Joubert tells us in his Preface, he has written a "Teach Yourself To Ski" book. It contains words of wisdom for skiers of all levels, beginner to International class racer. In studying "Teach Yourself To Ski", it has become obvious to me that Joubert has accomplished much more than he set out to do. For ski teachers he has produced perhaps the best guide to teaching method ever written. For ski coaches he has produced a bible. Teach Yourself To Ski *is a book no skier should be without.*

Curt Chase, Director
Aspen Ski School
Aspen, Colorado

PREFACE

I have tried to produce a practical guide for the use of all those desiring to learn to ski or to improve their skiing.

You will think perhaps that I have been pursuing this unoriginal goal for a long time. In collaboration with my friend, Jean Vuarnet, I have in fact written five books concerning ski technique. Why write a sixth?

I will have to return briefly to the past. In 1956 in publishing Ski Technique Moderne *written exclusively for good skiers, our goal was to jostle French teaching dogma established twenty years before by Emile Allais and Paul Gignoux and to try to lead the ski schools along with us. The evolution beginning too slowly, we then published* Ski ABC *in 1958, then* Ski Moderne *in 1960. Two things occurred to us as a result.*

Ski schools are very ponderous establishments in which the evolution is necessarily very slow and in which the finality is more commercial than pedagogical. The best way for us to influence the ski schools was to pursue our own evolution and to publish the results of our research. We soon realized that thanks to this approach our influence could spread to ski schools of all nationalities including even Austrian ski schools.

Our original intention, to change the ski schools, led us to develop in our own turn what is called in skiing a technique, that is a coherent, logical construction built around a radical new idea and seemingly closer to a pseudo-

scientific dogma than to a simple teaching method. Well, the tenacious survival of circular projection, outgrowth of Emile Allais' rotation, proved to us the danger of dogma. In 1956 the slopes were ravaged by battles similar to the Wars of Religion due to our radical idea of twisting-angulation (vissage-angulation).

It was, then, as an experiment that we launched a collection of technical recipes based on entirely new analyses, Savoir Skier, *in 1963. The success of this book proved that a new path was opened to us : the pursuit of a direct contact with non-professional skier-readers without the intermediary teacher or an interested amateur capable of digesting a method developed for specialists and redistributing it around him in simpler terms. This pursuit of a direct contact transformed not only our writing style, but also our approach to technique. It was no longer a question of describing movements seen from the outside, but one of transmitting basic sensations, principles susceptible to making our readers feel the movement, and creating for them the mental, motor image which must always precede the conscious execution of the new movement.* How to Ski the New French Way, *published in 1966 in France, used this new idea. It has already become a milestone in sports books written for the non-specialist. Many readers have communicated to me their enthusiasm for this new concept in teaching. I would like to thank them. In this new book I try to adapt even better to this teaching method. Other readers have complained of becoming lost in the involved suggestions and of having difficulty finding the material which applied particularly to their level. I therefore attempt to provide more clarity in the design and presentation of this book so that each individual can quickly find what he is looking for and only what he is looking for. In a desire for more clarity and a closer adaptation to the needs of the reader, I have also decided to separate the teaching sections for the self-taught skier from those intended for the experienced skier who wants to remodel and correct his skiing. In addition, I have separated the explanations, analyses, and technical and pedagogical considerations which concern only those interested in understanding the why of our method or in acquiring knowledge helpful in teaching their children, friends, or pupils.*

Concerning the technique of movements, How to Ski the New French Way *was not a step into, but a bet on the future. I was lucky enough six years ago to foresee an extraordinary evolution, almost a revolution in the movements of the greatest champions. Most of the illustrations in the book chosen four years ago showed a young citadin racer of the Grenoble University Club practising a technique which we had worked on together and which was being used only occasionally by some inspired racers. Time proved me right. Today, these movements form the basis of the technique of almost all of the great champions. The young, unknown citadin racer, Patrick Russel, whose positions were criticized in 1966, won the World Cup in slalom in 1969 and 1970. Winning this bet was not all : it remained to be seen how this new concept of a more effective technique could be used to improve the* movements of advanced, intermediate, and even beginning skiers. From systematic observation, deduction, and imagination it was necessary to move to experimentation, and I would like to thank my many collaborators at the University of Grenoble and the Association of University Skiers who helped experiment with a large number of technical and pedagogical elements, some of which proved valuable in improving ski teaching.

In effect, I think this new book is as original in the teaching of beginners (about which it seemed everything has been said) as in the teaching of good skiers. Since 1963 I have proposed the wide stance and steering, that is the simultaneous pivoting of both skis by leg action, to beginning skiers. 20 to 30 % of my readers have succeeded in this exercise and moved directly to parallel skiing, but the others had to undergo the normal progression with the traditional stem. This weakness has now been overcome with the help of my collaborator Désiré Rossi. We have discovered how the stem can be closely associated to steering, and give way at any time to parallel skiing. I was again caught in one of those deep ruts which prevent technicians from moving straight in the direction of progress. I do not pretend on the other hand to have solved all the problems posed by ski technique and teaching method. This book itself is only another step...

I can affirm that no suggestion, no hint has been included in this book without having been experimented with over a long period. My only concern has been the continued increase in effectiveness of my skier-readers. It is from this point of view that my method can be understood and not in the exactness of a captivating theoretic construction perhaps insufficiently associated with reality. The only criticism I would like to receive would be that of skiers and teachers who have tried carefully to apply my suggestions. Their aid would then become part of the immense effort of renovation in technique and teaching which seems to have been laid out by all ski technicians as a group.

Georges JOUBERT.

Classic and Acrobatic

Braquage is a pivoting of both feet beneath the body from a wide stance. It is a great help to beginners... as well as to the more experienced skier. Here, Jean-Claude Killy uses it to check abruptly and Alain Penz uses it for pivoting his skis rapidly after being thrown in the air by a bump.

Braquage

The Stem

There is nothing dishonorable about using a stem as this young racer competing in the F.I.S. World Championships demonstrates. The stem is an important technical tool for the virtuoso as well as for the beginner.

BEGINNERS LET'S GET STARTED

This advice will seem absurd to all those who believe blindly in a traditional teaching method. On the other hand, it will fascinate those who have understood that the essence of learning is the effort of self-discipline one must make in order to memorize and learn to feel new movements, and in order to overcome one's laziness or fear. It is for these people that I intend the following. Not only will they be able to learn as fast, if not faster, than with a good instructor, but they will also have the satisfaction of disciplining themselves and of working alone to acquire a new skill.

Readers, I will not give you useless theoretical discussions. I will give you a predigested, immediately assimilable, on-the-slopes lesson.

Have confidence in me and in a few days you will improve beyond the level of a beginning skier.

17

Choose your run carefully

Your start in skiing will be a success or failure depending on whether or not you have chosen an area where there are real beginner slopes. I am not referring only to the slopes where you will make your first straight runs but also to those where you will use the tow for the first time and where you will ski for mileage in order to practice your first turns. Many areas do not provide this kind of run because the needs of the beginner are not well known and because the ski schools do not call for them. Moving in an orderly fashion under the careful direction of the instructor, ski school classes do not require the vast, wide open runs needed by the independent beginning skier, voracious devourer of slopes. Two ski areas in France which offer exceptionally good runs for the beginner are l'Alpe d'Huez and Courchevel. (In the U.S. there are Buttermilk in Aspen, Colorado; Mount Snow in Vermont;...)

Much talked about recently is the "Graduated Length Method" or "GLM" based on a progression in the lengths of the skis used. I would like to propose a second graduated method, the "GSM" or Graduated Slope Method based on a progression in the steepness of runs. First level : a run allowing a maximum speed in a straight run ("Schuss" is the expression in skiing jargon.) of 10 to 15 mph. Second level : maximum schuss speed of around 25 mph, in wide turns 7 to 15 mph. Third level : maximum schuss speed of 40 mph, in wide turns 10 to 20 mph. Take a child, put him on each slope successively for one or two days without any instruction : He will not only learn to ski, but as in probably eighty per cent of the cases, he will learn to ski parallel. Obviously, you do not have the ability to adapt as easily as a child, but you do have more

self-control, more will-power, and more method. You can do just as well. Let's return to the slope where you are going to make your first straight runs. It should be almost flat, just steep enough for you to slide at the speed of a man walking or running slowly. First, slide twenty, then thirty, then forty or fifty yards before stopping. Ideally the slope should end in a flat. If this is not the case, you must resign yourself to sitting down on the snow. You will see that there is nothing terrible about sitting down in the snow if you first assume as low a position as possible, and then sit down to the side of your skis.

Use appropriate skis for beginners

Careful! Good skis for beginners are not necessarily short skis. In the 130, 160, and 175 centimeter lengths there are bad skis for beginners just as there are in the 200, 205, and 210 centimeter lengths. Perhaps fewer bad pairs, but they do exist. Skis for beginners should be, before anything else, "easy" skis, that is skis which sideslip and turn easily. Since you are not capable of judging whether or not a pair of skis is "easy", have an experienced friend check to see if your skis are warped, too stiff, too concave, or if they have too much camber, if the edges are sticking above the base, or if they have too many nicks in the edges so that they will not slide properly.

I will not discuss your boots, safety bindings, and poles at length. At your level you will have to place your confidence in the ski shop where you will be equipped. Be careful, however, not to get boots which are too stiff for you or which hurt your feet. You should feel comfortable and confident with safety bindings adjusted a little looser than normal.

Ready, take off !

You have already put on your skis on the flat, put your hands through the ski pole straps correctly, and you are now taking your first steps. The first strange feeling you experience is caused by the fact that your heels are held down. Relax your ankles, let them free wheel, and discover for yourself how to walk on skis. Climbing the flat slope where you plan to

The Natural Body Position in a Wide Stance

experience your first exploits poses no problem. Supporting yourself on your ski poles prevents you from sliding backwards. Again, by holding yourself with your poles you can put your skis across the slope in order to catch your breath, and then face downhill ready to plunge into the unknown. Holding yourself against your poles planted obliquely downhill, *spread your skis eight to sixteen inches apart, and flex (bend) your legs slightly (a little more if you are robust). Feel the undersides of your feet stick to the innersole of your boots from toes to heels, and "cast off"*! Nature has endowed you with a reflex system perfect enough to keep you in balance on your skis if you do nothing to interfere with it. If the slope does not end in a flat and if you do not stop automatically, assume as low a position as possible, then sit down on the snow to the side of your skis.

Your number one enemy, fear

Ninety per cent of a beginner's falls are due to fear, either an instantaneous panic which makes him shriek and which cuts his legs from under him causing him to take a dangerous fall, or a fear caused by a lasting rapid acceleration which forces the poor beginner into inventing outrageous contortions in hopes of slowing down or changing trajectories. I do not think that you will have this problem if you have chosen your slope properly, if you have made gradually longer runs (first from ten yards upslope, then fifteen, then twenty or thirty), and especially if you have made up your mind to end your runs by sitting down if there is no flat to stop on. There is another important way of controlling your speed which should be mentioned here. On any continuous slope a skier very rapidly attains a speed which no

High Body Position for the Less Athletic or the Tall, Slim Skier

Low Body Position for the Hardy Skier

longer increases. If you have chosen your slope correctly, you will feel yourself reach this ceiling speed, and when you do, your confidence and your relaxation will increase tenfold.

Your enemy number two, stiffness

Did you know that, even when you are standing in a stationary position on both feet, your body is oscillating continuously forward, backward, and from side to side? Hundreds of muscle fibers act like the stays of a sailboat contracting and releasing in order to maintain your balance. The same action will occur while you are skiing if you allow your muscles to work naturally, but not if you lock your arms, your back, or especially, your legs into a fixed position. During

your straight runs concentrate on one

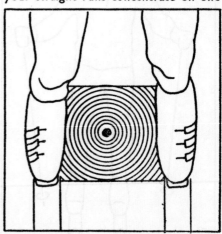

Skis spread four to eight inches apart, your support base is wide, and your center of gravity can oscillate freely between your skis without making you lose your balance.

idea : Relax, allow your skis to move freely. If you feel them "float" laterally, good. That's ideal. Turns and sideslipping will come easily to you. If on the other hand you hold your skis too firmly and if they catch in the snow, look out. They may take off, each ski toward the outside, or worse, they might cross! Try not to force with your feet; try to feel with them. Feelings in skiing are the only source of the balancing reflexes open to the beginner.

Try the stepped turn at the end of your straight runs

Stepped turn, that's asking a lot! When you reach the flat part of the slope where you plan to stop, if you decide to move toward your left, for example, concentrate, and legs slightly flexed, pick up your left ski a little and put it down again opening its tip outward slightly, that is, to the left. Immediately pick up the other ski, and place it parallel to the first. Wait a little while, and repeat the same movement, then repeat it several times, and your direction of travel will change. Move your skis very little but quickly and without doing anything special with your upper body. Later, when you have acquired better balance, you will balance on one ski, then on the other. You will be able to throw yourself from one ski to the other while skating. However, you are not there yet, and you must understand that in order to improve quickly, you must not be too impatient.

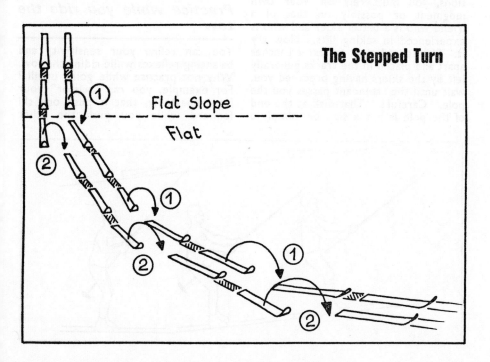

The Stepped Turn

Flat Slope

Flat

Take the pomalift

As soon as you can ride your skis in a straight run and make a timid stepped turn, you are ready to take the beginner's tow. It is not always easy to recognize these tows, and I would like to propose that an international agreement be made to post a distinctive sign near them. A colored disk, for example, such as those used to mark the difficulty of trails, could indicate "very easy", "easy", "intermediate", or "difficult". The slope of the terrain would not be the only factor of concern but also the speed, the abruptness of the start, possibly the lateral inclination of "side hills", and the condition of the arrival area. (For children, by the way, there is also a risk of being lifted off the snow). Lacking these indications, you must rely on your own judgment or possibly on that of a friend who is a better skier and who is experienced in taking lifts. Now try it. Skis spread eight to sixteen inches apart and placed in the tracks generally left by the skiers having preceded you, wait until the attendant passes you the pole. Careful! That disk at the end of the pole is not a seat but simply a comfortable support which will pull you up the hill. To begin with, ignore this support. Take the pole in both hands, absorb the shock of the start with your arms, and let yourself be pulled by the arms while balancing on your skis as you did in your straight runs. If you do not feel very confident and if it is not too difficult for you, continue to hold on with your arms until you reach the top platform, then let go. If on the other hand everything goes well, twenty or thirty yards after the start, let five or six inches of the pole slip through your hands, and you will feel the disk push firmly against your seat and haul you up to the top. Having reached the upper platform, pull the pole from between your legs, and let it go. If the tow is a "T" bar for two, insist on going up alone.

Practise while you ride the tow

You can refine your sensitivity and balancing reflexes while riding the tow. Why not practise while going uphill ? For example, you can "scissor" your legs repeatedly, that is push one ski forward while you push the other

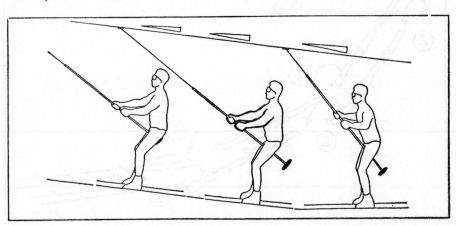

An Exercise

keep you warm and allow you to dive back into action as soon as you reach the top.

Chair lifts

Getting on the chairlift poses no problems. Take your poles in one hand, move into the spot indicated, turn to watch the approaching chair, catch the elbow rest with your free hand, and sit down. On many chairlifts there is a protection bar which you then pull down in front of you while a transverse bar comes up underneath for a footrest. The difficulty occurs at the end of your ride where you encounter a ten to fifteen yard ramp down which you must slide in order to leave your chair behind. First hint, when you have a partner, choose the outside seat. Before the arrival area, push up the protection bar, and grab a pole in each hand. As soon as your skis touch the snow, stand up, and slide. If the snow is slow, you can even push with your poles. Take the precaution of telling your partner that you are a beginner so that he is prepared for a possible, but not catastrophic fall.

back, then the inverse. You can lift one ski for a fraction of a second, then the other. You can even lift one ski and displace it laterally, then lift the other and put it next to the first and, next, do the same to the opposite side. These two exercises will prepare you for the stepped turn. Later, you can open your skis into a gliding snowplow, then close them, open one ski into a stem and try to slow down with it, then close. You can try to balance on one ski, then on the other. These exercises are not only good practice, but they also prevent your legs from becoming stiff during the ride. They

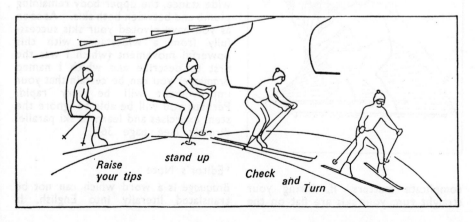

Raise
your tips

stand up

Check and Turn

If you are hardy and dynamic, the natural stop

Slide straight down a smooth, well packed slope in a slightly wider stance and lower position than normal. Wait until you pick up good speed and feel the support over the full length of the soles of your boots, particularly on your heels. Make up your mind to slide your skis instantaneously across the hill. I will not explain that it is necessary to push your knees, pivot your legs, etc. You should simply make your skis pivot, that is make your feet pivot without trying to

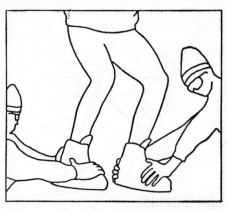

Braquage, *the pivoting of both feet in a wide stance, is a very powerful movement. Have some friends hold your feet while you verify the power of this movement.*

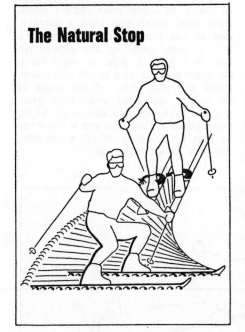

The Natural Stop

snow, if you do not hesitate and if you use enough force to pivot your feet, your skis will pivot across the slope and, God willing, you will keep your balance. After a few other attempts you will keep in balance fairly easily because the whole movement is made in a low position, in a wide or very wide stance, the upper body remaining plumb and between both skis. As soon as you have pivoted your skis successfully from a widestance with this powerful movement (which I was the first to describe and which I named *Braquage*) you can be certain that your improvement will be very rapid. Perhaps you will be able to ignore the stem exercises and learn to ski parallel directly (see page 36).

*Editor's Note

Braquage is a word which can not be translated literally into English. It

complicate matters. If, during your straight run, your skis are flat on the

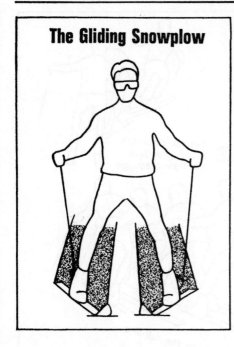

The Gliding Snowplow

implies an abrupt and simultaneous pivoting of the feet and legs, combined with a vigorous cranking movement of the knees. The action produces what has been called "the Hockey Stop" in American ski schools.

To slow down, the gliding snowplow

How do you open a snowplow? It is very simple : spread your feet first slightly wider than usual, then weighting your heels, push them outwards. Try to keep your skis as flat as possible on the snow. The ideal would be to let them slide freely enough to float slightly.

This snowplow will slow you down very little, but if you are using the very flat slopes which I recommended to you, it will be adequate to slow your speed noticeably. If you are afraid, the gliding snowplow, even when your skis are almost flat on the snow, will give you a certain feeling of security, perhaps because of your perception of the fairly obvious braking action of your skis which reminds you vaguely of the solid ground beneath you.

The natural stop from a gliding snowplow

If you were not able to do the preceding natural stop and if you feel much more at ease in a gliding snowplow than in a parallel stance, try this exercise. Slide in a fairly narrow plow, with well flexed legs, until you attain a certain speed. Make an abrupt effort to pivot both feet across the hill. You will then be as far along in the progression as those who were able to do the natural stop without a preliminary stem. Try also to slide diagonally down the slope rather than straight. Your *braquage* will be made even more easily.

The Gliding Snowplow into a Natural Stop

25

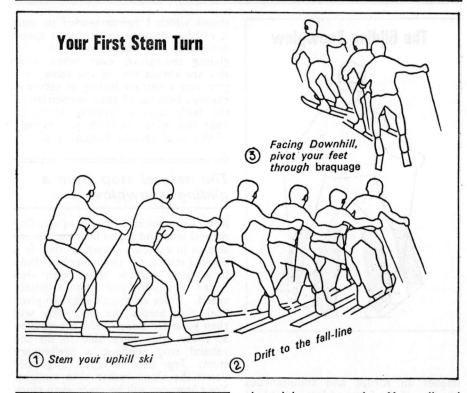

Your First Stem Turn

③ Facing Downhill, pivot your feet through braquage

① Stem your uphill ski

② Drift to the fall-line

The three phase stem turn

As soon as you can slide more or less relaxed at a speed similar to that of a man walking hurriedly, you will be ready to make downhill turns on the wide, flat runs where you should be practising. What do you do ? It will be extremely simple if you follow these suggestions :

1) Sliding across the hill, displace your uphill ski (the highest ski on the slope) to the side and open it into a stem by pushing on your uphill heel. If you feel the heel catch in the snow and if you have trouble opening it into the stem, push your uphill knee inward slightly in order to flatten the ski on the snow. The tail of the ski will then slide more easily. You will end up in a slightly uncomfortable position, but you remedy that immediately by weighting both skis equally as in the gliding snowplow which you used in straight running. 2) Let your skis go. They will start a long curve, and soon you will be facing downhill. 3) At this instant pivot your skis forcefully, especially the inside ski, but being careful not to do anything in particular with your upper body. After a few yards, your skis will be across the slope and more or less wide spread. Your turn is then finished.

In your first attempts the first two phases will be the most important. *Open your uphill ski*, not your downhill ski or both skis. We will see why later on. *Let yourself drift downhill*

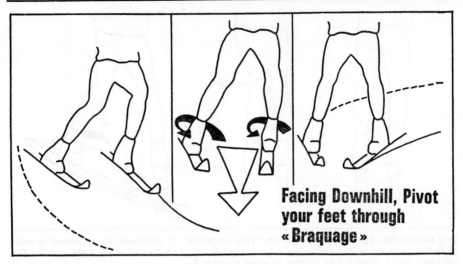

Facing Downhill, Pivot your feet through « Braquage »

When you reach the fall-line, you are in a favorable position for pivoting your skis with braquage *which brings your skis back parallel to one another.*

without forcing on your skis, without doing anything voluntarily, not a movement of the arms, nor of the upper body, nor of the hips or knees. The importance of this turn derives from this sliding, passive phase. It will not matter very much if you are not immediately able to do the third phase, the pivoting action while facing downhill. If your natural cautiousness makes you avoid gathering enough speed, or if you open too wide a stem, you may finish the turn perhaps by remaining in the stem. This is nothing to worry about. After a few attempts you will discover the precise instant when it is easiest to pivot your skis and finish the turn holding them parallel.

Use a steeper traverse in the turn

In the preceding paragraph I directed you as you made a complete downhill turn, that is a turn for the ultra-cautious, a turn starting and finishing with an almost horizontal traverse. Obviously, if you start by facing partly downhill (closer to the fall-line, the line of greatest slope) you will have to turn less. To be sure, you will gain

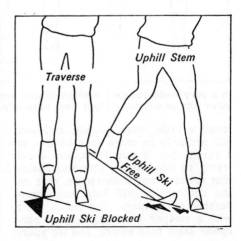

Traverse

Uphill Stem

Uphill Ski Free

Uphill Ski Blocked

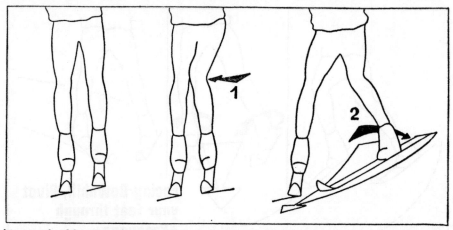

In a semi-wide stance *in order to stem your uphill ski: 1) push your knee inward in order to flatten your ski on the snow and edge it slightly; 2) push the tail of your ski uphill. The ski can also be lifted for an instant in order to stem it.*

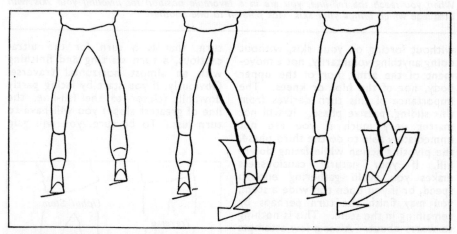

In a very wide stance : *A simple inward push of the knee is enough to initiate the turn either with or without a slight stem, especially if you are close to the fall-line.*

speed a little more quickly, and you will probably be more apprehensive as a result, but if you relax and avoid trying to slow down, you will notice that speed is not bothersome, that on the contrary it will help you considerably in turning. Therefore, start with a steeper traverse, open a narrower stem than before, and let yourself be pulled into the hill while remaining between your skis in good balance and security. When you are facing straight downhill, pivot both skis just enough to turn them across the hill slightly. Repeat the movement then until you reach the bottom of the run, and quickly take the lift back to the top. Practise this turn. It can develop into a parallel turn very quickly if you are talented enough. *Most important, do not think that you are ready for steeper slopes. That would be a big mistake.*

Move toward parallel skiing

When you have succeeded in making both turns just described, you will realize that initiating a turn with an uphill stem from a steeper traverse makes it possible on the one hand to use a narrower stem and on the other hand to pivot both skis more easily out of the fall-line. This pivoting is no longer a problem; it happens all by itself. *With a bit of daring you will be able to discard the uphill stem.* In fact, the importance of the uphill stem lies in the fact that the ski is flattened on the snow or even tipped onto its inside edge. The closer you remain to the fall-line, the easier it will be to obtain this position of the ski. You

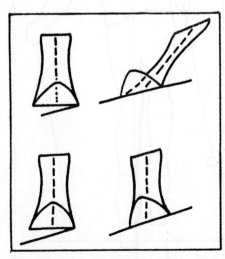

Because of the sidecut of your skis, when you edge them you get a stemming effect even when they are parallel.

simply push your knee inward slightly. Try to make this turn on a very flat slope but with lots of speed. Change your direction only very slightly from the fall-line. Once you have felt how the movement works, try to turn a little farther. You can cheat a little too : a slight stem, if very gradual and if it only serves to flatten the ski on the snow, is not noticeable and is therefore actually part of parallel skiing. I will mention this type of turn again in the chapter on competition as it is common to racers who "ride a flat ski".

29

Learn first to make your skis « hold » in a traverse on hard snow

On the flat beginner's slopes where you have been practising until now, you have had no difficulty sliding in a traverse, that is across the slope. Perhaps you pushed your uphill ski forward and put more of your weight on your downhill ski instinctively, but if you did not do so, that's not impor-

tant. Soon you will be confronted with slightly steeper slopes on which you will feel such a rapid acceleration that you will not dare make the stem turn even when starting from an almost horizontal traverse. Perhaps it is wrong to send you to a slope that necessitates checking your speed. I would prefer seeing you ski in an area like Alpe d'Huez (or Buttermilk in the U.S.) on flat slopes which are miles long and on which you will refine your balancing reflexes to the point that, later, you would be able to make up three times

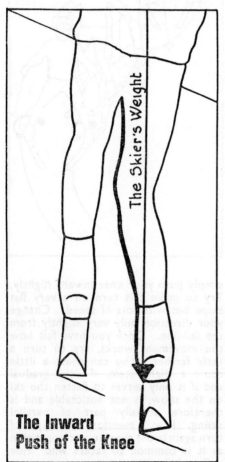

The Skier's Weight

The Inward Push of the Knee

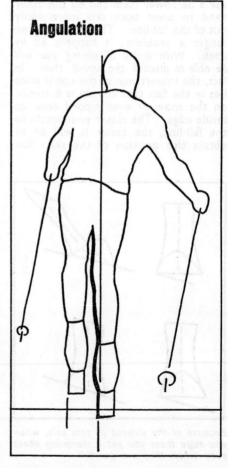

Angulation

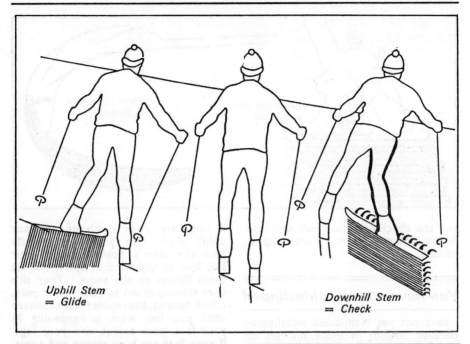

Uphill Stem
= Glide

Downhill Stem
= Check

the time lost. But since that is what you want, I will try to prepare you for steeper and possibly hard frozen slopes. *Do you lose all confidence because you do not feel your skis bite into the hill?* This is not very surprising because you must know what to do in order to make them bite. You will have to tip your downhill ski onto its inside edge. In order to do so, you must put all your weight onto the inside of your downhill foot. An inward movement and position of your knee, that is a lateral displacement of your knee, and sometimes even a lateral displacement of your hip, are the results. However, you should not always push your hip uphill. The important thing is to press with the inside of your foot and to put all of your weight on it while taking all of the weight off the other. This is how you will acquire stability in a traverse. The most common error is to lean uphill, and thus to weight the uphill ski.

In traverses, slow down with a downhill stem

Memorize these equations :
- **Uphill stem = flat ski for sliding**
- **Downhill stem = edged ski for checking**

You already know what to do when you have trouble making your skis hold or when you have trouble in a traverse on a hill which is a little too steep for you and which is frozen hard. To "check", to slow down, the process is almost the same. Stem your downhill ski, then weight the inside edge of your downhill foot in order to make the inside edge of the ski bite into the snow as much as possible. Because the ski is moving transversally, crosswise to your direction of travel, the braking action of the ski is maximal. Decrease the amount of stem or the amount of pressure on the inside edge,

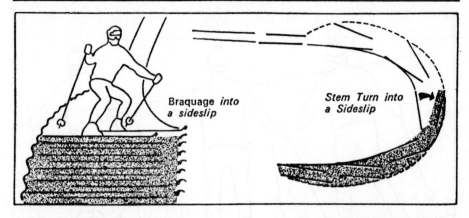

Braquage *into a sideslip*

Stem Turn *into a Sideslip*

and the checking action will decrease. Repeat the movement, release, repeat, release,...

You have already sideslipped

I have not yet mentioned sideslipping because nothing is more difficult on the flat slopes where you have been practising. But just as the man spoke, you have alreadysi deslipped. Indeed, in the stem turn once you reached the fall-line, you had to initiate a sideslip. If you were able to steer your skis into a natural stop, you had to sideslip before stopping once your skis were across the hill. Thus, your balancing reflexes for sideslipping are already developing, and you will be able to do the following exercises very quickly.

Sideslip between your poles

On the steepest portion of the slope even if it is only a few yards square, plant both poles, one uphill and slightly forward, the other downhill and to the side. Leaving your poles planted, move up and down between them in order to smooth the snow

if necessary, then climb up to your uphill pole. Flex your legs slightly into the skier's position, hold your skis four to eight inches apart, and let them flatten on the snow. Your skis then sideslip down to your lower pole. Climb back up, and repeat the manoeuvre until you feel what is happening in your feet, your ankles, and your legs. If your legs are very strong and tonic, your knees might have to move downhill in order to allow your skis to slip. If you are tall and loose jointed, everything will happen in your ankle. Do not

worry too much about the details; your skis should simply flatten on the snow and sideslip.

Check with a downhill stem, then sideslip

If you were able to slow down with a downhill stem in a traverse, you will learn to sideslip from a traverse very quickly. Push your downhill ski into a stem, and balance on its inside edge, then pivot your other ski parallel to it. You are now sideslipping despite not flattening your skis. This is another, more brutal way of sideslipping, that is to pivot your skis slightly across your direction of travel. Your sideslip in this case slows you down, and you stop within a few yards. To learn to sideslip better, to master side-slipping, try to decrease the bite of the edge of your downhill ski. Flatten it on the snow. Thus, through side-slipping you will develop the balancing reflexes indispensable to the higher speed turns that you will be learning soon.

Note that the downhill stem places your upper body in a particular position relative to your stemmed ski. I will discuss this position (the position of angulation and anticipation) later. It is the best means for balancing in a sideslip. Your upper body faces the direction of travel, and only your legs fastened solidly to the skis, pivot slightly uphill relative to their normal traversing position. Avoid the common error resulting from stiffness. When you start sideslipping, do not face your ski tips. Only your legs move. You will feel this movement more easily in the following sideslip exercise.

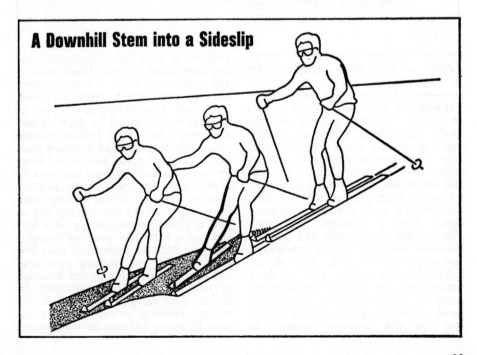

A Downhill Stem into a Sideslip

«Braquage» from a Traverse into a Sideslip

From a traverse steer into a sideslip

Through this exercise, you will be able to practise sideslipping even on relatively flat slopes. You must simply build up a little speed *before sideslipping*. If you were able to do the natural stop, that is the brutal steering of the skis across the fall-line from a straight schuss to a stop, you will not have any trouble with the same steering action from a traverse. You must simply steer less brutally and put less pressure on your heels; otherwise, you would tend to do a "three-sixty". If you have not been able to do a natural stop, this exercise can help you learn it. Start in a wider stance than usual. Take a slightly lower position, and feel the pressure under the

bottoms of your feet distributed over the inner soles of your boots, especially under your heels. Once you have built up good speed, pivot both feet. You have a considerable amount of force at your disposal for pivoting and a maximum amount of balance because your body is positioned between your skis. Your skis pivot, and carried along by your momentum, you continue to slide in your original direction, but in a sideslip. Try to avoid holding with your edges. Make the sideslip last as long as possible by relaxing your ankles and legs a little and even by straightening up little by little from your low position. Try also to keep your head and upper body facing in the direction of your displacement by looking far ahead. Just as you did before for straight running, you must now allow your balancing reflexes for sideslipping

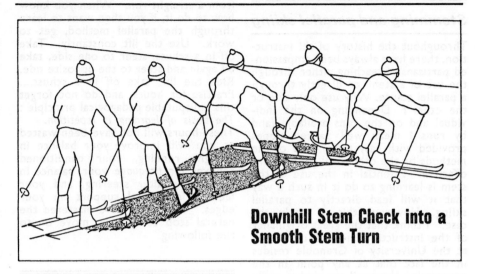

Downhill Stem Check into a Smooth Stem Turn

to develop. They will be necessary for your balance during turns.

Turn with security

If you are going too fast and if you know you will need to slow down during the stem which turns you to the fall-line, never try to turn as I have already taught you, that is by a simple uphill stem. The same recommendation is true if you encounter what is a steep hill for your level of skiing. Your improvement would come to a complete halt. Instead, slow down with a down-hill stem as described on page 31. Nothing is simpler. Put pressure onto the inside of your downhill foot, on the heel in particular. Stem the downhill ski, and weight the inside edge of this ski as much as possible. Once you have slowed down, stem your uphill ski, weight both skis equally, and let the slope pull you into the fall-line. It might seem to you that your speed is increasing too quickly

during the turn, however, under no circumstances should you check. Be confident. You now know that even if you reach the next traverse going too fast, you will be able to slow down easily by sideslipping or by stemming your downhill ski. In this kind of turn as in all stem turns performed at reduced speed, wait until you reach the fall-line before trying to "tighten" the turn (that is before shortening its radius). The fall-line phase is in effect the most favorable instant for pivoting both skis through *braquage*. Resist the impulse to steer beforehand.

The advantages of this exercise are numerous. It is the only one which can help you to avoid checking during the turn or to develop the very common, serious bad habit of stiffening the outside leg. In addition, the exercise prepares you for the movements necessary to initiate more advanced turns, wedeln, and racing turns. For the present, try to develop the correct checking methods even if the run does not require them.

35

Stemming and parallel skiing

Throughout the history of ski instruction, there have always been empassioned partisans of teaching either through the use of a stem, or directly through a parallel stance. Why use only one or the other ? Depending on the individual and on the runs available (and by runs I mean well packed slopes provided with easy tows), one of the methods or the other will prove more effective. Essential in the use of the stem is learning to do it in such a way that it will lead directly to parallel skiing. However, this is rarely the case. I think that the great originality of the instruction method developed at the University of Grenoble resides in the fact that at any point in the progression the pupil can change easily from stem to parallel skiing. The more talented can learn parallel from the very beginning through the same technical principles as their less talented friends, at the same time and on the same slopes. *The parallel method requires easy slopes and, if possible, long and easy slopes* mainly because the pupil must work close to the line of greatest slope (the fall-line) at higher speeds than the stemmer, but nevertheless at beginner's speeds. If you feel capable of learning through the parallel method, you must resign yourself to spending a long time on fairly flat slopes until you have mastered the movements which I am about to suggest.

Improve your natural stop

I explained this movement on page 24 where I also suggested you try it from a traverse if you had trouble. If this is the case, repeat the natural stop dozens of times from a traverse, then from a straight run. When you know how to do it, if you then want to learn through the parallel method, get to work. Use the lift constantly. Take off in a schuss, steer to one side, take off again and steer to the opposite side. Ride the lift, take off in a schuss,... Practise for hours, and do not forget this indisputable pedagogical principle : *The basis of learning is repetition.*
These hours will not have been wasted as you will improve your balance in straight running, your conditioned reflexes for *braquage* your balance in sideslipping after steering, and your feelings for lateral support on your edges. When you have mastered the natural stop completely, move on to the following.

Zigzag down the fall-line through braquage

Start a straight run down a fairly flat slope. Build up speed, then very incisively pivot both skis as in the natural stop, but with less force. Do not pivot your skis more than ten or fifteen degrees, and make your straight run in a slight traverse. When you have built up your speed again, hup ! Steer to the opposite side. It is a little more difficult than from a straight downhill run, but if you have followed directions, if you have practised hundreds of natural stops, and if your stance is wide enough, you should overcome this difficulty. *A slight down motion at the instant you steer will help.* In addition, it is obvious that the smaller your zigzags, the less difficulty you will have with the exercise. A fairly talented beginning skier should be able to displace his skis approximately fifteen degrees from the fall-line. You can judge this angle from the accompanying diagram.

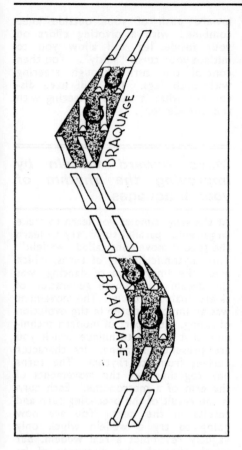

Make your braquage smoother

If you were able to zigzag down the fall-line, you have made the second step. You will now spend a few hours practising on the slope you previously worked over with your natural stops. However, now you are going to try to smooth your relatively abrupt, angular changes in direction, to try to make them rounder and to transform them little by little into real turns. To do so, here are two hints.

First, start your braquage just as sharply as before but as soon as your legs start to pivot, slow it down.
Feel yourself control the movement. Try to spread the effort over a longer period of time in order to continue the turning of your skis. Your skis will turn too far from the fall-line to permit another *braquage* turn, but you can let them run and gradually steepen their traverse. When you have felt what it means to control the steering movement, move on to the next step.
Second, initiate your braquage more softly. To soften your effort would seem contradictory because until now you have relied on your strength and decisiveness in order to steer. However, the time has come. You have been able to skip a lot of exercises because of your dynamism, but now you must learn to work softly because the basic essential in skiing is *glissement,* the ability to keep your skis sliding rapidly on the snow without undue shocks or edging. Even the wilder, more athletic looking international class racers are only working for one thing : "*la glisse*", fast, "flat" ski. You must learn to avoid the shock which results from the way you initiate your *braquage.* You will not be able to do so unless you have repeated the previously described zigzag and *braquage* exercises many, many times. You will have felt little by little the fact that your outside leg (the leg to the outside of the turn) must do most of the work. This is normal because your speed in the turn results in centrifugal force, which pushes you outward, and which you resist mostly with your outside leg. You have felt that in order to resist, you support yourself on the inside edge of your outside ski by pushing your knee laterally inward, that is toward the inside of the turn. If you have not experienced these feelings, repeat the zigzag exercise until you are conscious

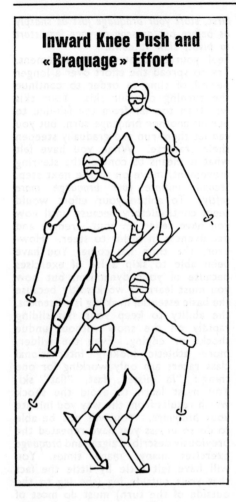

Inward Knee Push and « Braquage » Effort

inward push of your outside knee combined with a pivoting effort on your inside leg will allow you to initiate your turns "softly". You then control the turn through steering with both legs. You will have discovered what is called "steering with the outside leg".

Move toward wedeln by improving the rhythm of your braquages

At the same time as you learn to make large-radius parallel turns, try to learn the special movement called "wedeln". This rhythmic linking of turns, which gives the impression of dancing, was the dream of a whole generation of skiers unable to do it. The movement was an important step in the evolution of skiing. It is part of modern technique, that is, the technique which you are presently learning. Its character derives from its rhythm. The turns link together like the movements of the arm of a metronome. Each turn is the result of the preceding turn and results in the next. You are now going to try a wedeln which only vaguely resembles a real wedeln, but which through the discovery of its rhythm will help your improvement considerably.

How do you learn this rhythm ? From a straight run, steer your legs first in one direction then in the other. Try to lose as little time as possible between successive *braquages* until you feel that making one of them helps in initiating the next. When you feel one steering movement result in the next, you will have learned a rudimentary wedeln. To discover the rhythm you must be inspired. If you do not get it right away, work on something else for a while, then try again. On a beautiful

of them. Only if you have very bowed legs, will you not feel this lateral knee movement. If this is your case, you must refer to page 183.

Once you have felt the knee movement, try to combine it with or substitute it for the *braquage* of both legs with which you have initiated your turns. Try several times. Very quickly, you will feel that a simple

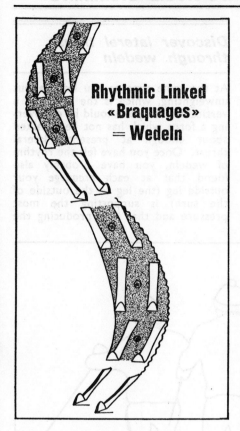

Rhythmic Linked «Braquages» = Wedeln

up motion between *braquages*. Due to the uninterrupted linking of the turns, you will begin to feel one *braquage* start while you straighten up following the preceding *braquage* You

Wide Stance Wedeln with Unweighting

Unweighting and Braquage

Unweighting and Braquage

bright sunny day on good snow when you really feel like skiing, you will be touched by the hand of God...

Learn to unweight through wedeln

Each time you steer them, your legs bend a little. You will realize very quickly that if you do not straighten up slightly between steering movements, you will end up sinking into a lower and lower position. Therefore, once you have discovered the wedeln rhythm, make an effort to amplify the are on the right track. Keep going, but be careful that your straightening movement does not become too great. Your legs should never straighten completely. Little by little, you will feel your *braquages* become easier to make, necessitating less vigorous pivoting efforts with your legs. Your skis are no longer fully weighted during the straightening phase, (more exactly at the end of the straightening movement), but are partially, or completely unweighted when you begin to pivot them. This fact is not difficult to understand. It is as if you were skipping rope with small linked hops.

Discover lateral thrust through wedeln

At the same time as you learn about unweighting, which is the result of a vertical thrust, you should be discovering a force which has not been talked about enough at present : lateral thrust. Once you have felt the rhythm of wedeln, you have probably also found that at each *braquage* your outside leg (the leg to the outside of the turn) is supporting the most pressure and that it is producing the

Use Lateral Thrust for Wedeling

Wedeln with a Stem

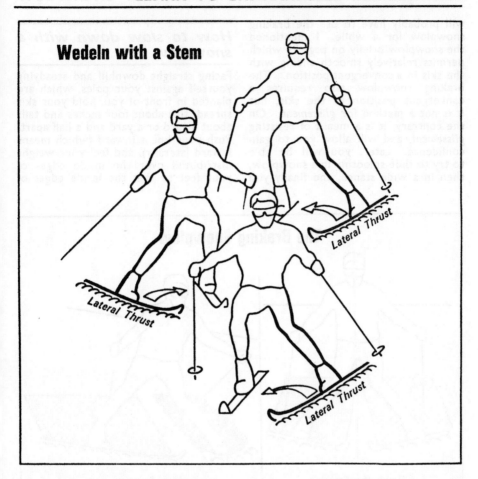

most work. Right leg, left leg, right, left, etc... During your straightening movement between two *braquages* you move from a predominant support on your right leg to a predominant support on your left leg, each change accompanied by a lateral thrust. Try to become conscious of this thrust at the end of each *braquage*. It is directed both upward (vertical thrust resulting in unweighting) and laterally, and it is part of the technique of the true skier. If you have trouble feeling these

lateral supports, try to emphasize them by stemming your downhill ski slightly at the end of each *braquage*. You will then find the support on the inside edge of your outside ski more easily, and it will push you into the next turn. (I will discuss this exercise at greater length on page 60.)

If you were scared to death as soon as you felt that the ground was sliding under your skis, if while discovering the stem you felt like a drowning swimmer finding a life preserver, you will probably have to use the braking snowplow for a while. I mentioned the snowplow briefly on page 24 which permits relatively smooth sliding with the skis in a convergent position. The braking snowplow also requires a convergent position of the skis, but it is not a method for *glissement*, On the contrary, it is a means of resisting *gilssement,* and will allow you to gain confidence. Later, you will be able to try to slide smoothly in a snowplow, then in a wide stance, and finally you

How to slow down with a snowplow

Facing straight downhill and steadying yourself against your poles, which are planted in front of you, hold your skis spread, tips about four inches and tails about a yard or a yard and a half apart. Push your knees inward (which means inward laterally), and feel your weight distributed over the inside edges of your feet so that the inside edges of

The Braking Snowplow

Down the Fall-line   *In a Traverse*

will be able to follow the instructions given in the preceding pages, but at a slower rate. Above all, do not consider the braking snowplow your final goal.

your skis will bite into the snow. Lift your ski poles out, and decrease the bite of your edges if your skis do not slide. You will then feel the need to push outward hard with your heels so that your skis will not cross one over the other, and so that they will continue to slow you down. You will also feel that in order to slow down more, it is enough to simply press your knees inward (pressing them together and pushing downward so that the edges will bite harder into the snow). In order to slide faster, just push your knees outward slightly, and the skis will flatten on the snow.

How to turn

The mechanical principle of the snow-plow turn is simple. When one ski holds (bites into the snow) more than the other, its direction of travel is imposed on the other which then follows... sometimes resisting. For your first snowplow turn start with a straight run in a snowplow. If you

decide to turn to the left, for example, push your right knee inward and make its inside edge hold. Under this ski you will feel a great increase in pressure which you must resist. You will then turn to the left. Next push your left knee inward, and make the left ski hold. You turn to the right. All your effort and all your movement occurs in your legs. Your arms, trunk, and hips have nothing to do with the mechanism. Concentrate on feeling the work of your feet on the skis.

If you are very strong and if you have tonic joints, your inside ski might catch and tend to cross over the outside ski during your snowplow turn. Try to flatten this ski on the snow by pushing your inside knee outward as the turn begins.

A Turn from the Fall-Line

The occasional snowplow

Why I discourage the use of the snow-plow is obvious. Ninety-nine out of

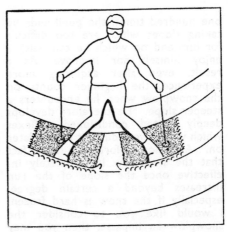

From a braking snowplow down the fall-line it is enough to push a knee inward in order to turn. If you push the outside knee outward, the turn is made more easily.

The snowplow is valuable in hollow cat-tracks

The Downhill Snowplow Turn

one hundred times, the pupil ends up taking slopes which are too difficult for him and on which he can neither enjoy himself nor improve. As a result, even after acquiring more experience, the beginner counts on the snowplow when he encounters a steeper slope. He therefore develops deeply seated conditioned reflexes which will be very difficult to lose later on. And most unfortunate is the fact that the snowplow is completely ineffective once the slope of the run increases beyond a certain degree, especially if the snow is hard frozen. I would like you to consider the snowplow an impasse, then you may learn and use it from time to time when nothing else works : in hollow cat tracks or in narrow, badly prepared ski lift entrances.

The child's snowplow

Fortunately, because of the great flexibility of their joints and their boots, and because of their rounded steel edges and light weight, children do a gliding snowplow naturally. *Glissement* is natural for them. Because of this fact, three times out of four, children move easily into wide track parallel. But what a pity, those long lines of snowplowing youngsters (each trying to avoid running into the one ahead) which we see once in a while in some areas. They remind me of chain gangs. An intelligent choice of slopes will allow the instruction of children without the use of the snowplow, without the braking snowplow in particular. It might even be said that a well placed tow could replace the best of instructors.

Why shortskis ?

This question merits discussion because it is not by chance that the lengths of skis have become standardized over the last forty years. However, it might be considered that due to the improvements in their design, skis could be made shorter and still hold well on hard snow. In addition, in this era of the snowcat and other packing machines we are almost always skiing on packed slopes where skis, even short ones, do not sink in. The current popularity of skiing as a fashionable sport attracts many unathletic people. The widespread development of secondary residences in the mountains encourages all the members of a family to participate in skiing, even those who might be better off back in the lodge. A new level of participation without ambition has developed, the "head-of-the-family technique", without effort and without danger. This situation has created a demand that must be satisfied. All of these reasons, plus the need for promotion for certain ski areas and for certain ski manufacturers, have resulted in the development of short (160 to 175 centimeter) and even very short (130, 100, or 75 centimeter) skis.

The « GLM » method with instructor

The "Graduated Length Method" is so called because of the use of successively longer skis from 100, 130, 150 centimeters to full length. The aim is to avoid developing fear reflexes in the pupil by having him progress from walking on skis little longer than his boots to the use of normal length skis without the difficulty of major readjustments. It is as much a psychological as a technical action, and this is why the presence of an instructor is indispensable to GLM.

The goal of GLM is relatively easily attained up to the level of what I call "intermediate skiers" in this book. Afterwards, shortskis, in my opinion, do not permit a faster improvement than do normal length skis for the majority of skiers. However, for the older skier or the skier who has important responsibilities, shortskis are justified as they definitely do cause fewer accidents. They are also justified for the overcautious whose speeds are always too low for normal length skis. There is, in fact, an undeniable relationship between the speed and the useful length of skis for an optimum skier balance. It is not by chance that racers have slalom skis X centimeters long, giant slalom skis $X+5$ to 8 centimeters long, and downhill skis $X+10$ to 15 centimeters long. Shortskis, however perfect, do not allow the higher speeds possible on longer skis with the same amount of security. They hold comparably well on ice, but they do not perform as well in soft or deep snows where they sink in too far. They allow the very good skier to thread his way more easily through the enormous, frozen moguls which transform some slopes into real nightmares. However, they decrease the forward-backward balance of any skier schussing over rollercoaster type bumps or even riding a tow under similar conditions. But we have lost our subject. Would you like to learn to ski on shortskis ?

GRADUATED LENGTH METHOD

You can teach yourself on 130 or 160 centimeter skis

If you are small, light, and in addition very cautious, choose the 130's. If you are big and strong or, especially, if you are bold, try 160's or 175's. But careful! Get 175's made for adults not those which are made for children and which would be too flexible and too fragile for you.

As soon as your skis are on, go walking, everywhere. Walking will be ten times easier on these skis than on 200's or 210's. You will wake up your balancing reflexes and quickly become accustomed to having your foot imprisoned. This will make it easier for you once you begin your straight runs. As for a progression of exercises, it is exactly the same as that already proposed for the skier using normal length skis. In general, the exercises will be easier for you if you use the same speed as the beginners on normal length skis, but you might not be able to handle this speed as easily as they because your balance will not be as good. At slower speeds you will encounter the same problems as other beginners, but it will be easier for you to keep your skis parallel. Even if you use the stem exercises, you will not have to emphasize the stem as much, and it will soon transform into a wide parallel stance. Finally, you will tend not to use the snowplow as much because it is not very effective with shortskis. Think about it; perhaps that will be a considerable advantage in your particular case.

GET IN SHAPE

tl is not necessary to be an athlete in order to ski, but you will certainly profit more from the ski season, or at least from your winter vacation, if you make the effort to exercise about a dozen times beforehand. First of all, you will feel better from the very first time you ski. Very often the apprehension you feel about skiing results from a feeling of being too weak to move around with heavy skis and boots on your feet. Next, you will last longer without tiring, and you will be able to enjoy yourself all day long. Finally, you will risk fewer accidents which occur so often because the skier is not strong enough to react correctly to avoid them.

I am referring to a dozen sessions of pre-season dryland training for skiing, spread over a period of one month. However, regular weekly participation in a physical activity like physical conditioning, ballet or modern dance, tennis, fencing, volleyball, jogging, bicycling,.... will be sufficient. If you live on the tenth floor and if you run downstairs four times a day, you can also consider yourself physically well prepared. Physical conditioning sessions for skiing are organized more and more frequently by clubs and physical conditioning centers. These sessions are more or less effective depending on the competence of the instructor who organizes them. They are always beneficial.

I do not intend to compete here with the professionals in physical conditioning. I simply want to offer something to those of my readers who are not able to participate in an organized conditioning program. I will suggest four exercises and some variations for breaking the monotony. They should be performed for fifteen or twenty minutes, two or three times a week, for a month before the season. This is very little, but I know that I would discourage many by suggesting more. You are free to do better.

First exercise : Warm up and loosen up your legs

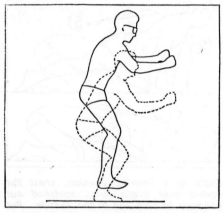

At least once in your life you have skipped rope. You hopped on both feet, rebounding like a rubber ball. Now, you can dispense with the rope, but I would like your feet to leave the ground by four to six inches. You should establish a smooth rhythm, your feet landing softly. Your muscles must supplely absorb their stretching caused by flexing and act to propel you back upwards without effort.
If these hops are easy for you, try to adapt

them to skiing : 1) Hop while holding the low skier's position constantly. 2) Hop without extending your feet. In other words, try to keep the bottoms of your feet constantly parallel to the ground just as you are obligated to do when skiing. Be careful to hold your feet parallel to one another also, not pointed outward.

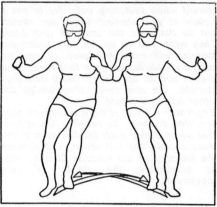

To vary the exercise, hop two, three, or four times on one foot, then switch to the other, and continue. You can also hop laterally from one foot to the other, jumping about two or three feet to each side. If you are particularly strong, jump in a lower position. Hop fifty times, then rest a while and repeat. Do so five or ten times. You can control your rhythm by checking your pulse. It should increase to 120 during the exercise, then fall to 100 while you rest, then increase again to 120...

Second exercise : For your abdnominal muscles

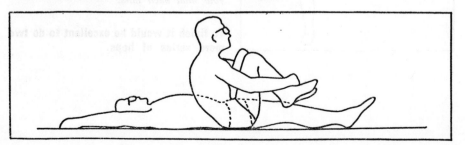

The goal is not to develop your stomach muscles but simply to reawaken them to the fairly violent efforts required by skiing. Lying flat, arms stretched above your head, sit up quickly onto your seat, flexing your legs and grabbing your ankles. Stretch out again, sit up, etc... Use a rhythm that will make the movement easy for you. Breathe out energetically when sitting up; breathe inward when stretching out. Try to put a hollow in your stomach when you stretch out by flattening the small of your back. Thus when you sit up, all your abdominal muscles will come into play. If you are naturally athletic, wedge a foot under your dresser and sit up while holding both legs straight. Do one series, then wedge the other foot and repeat.

Begin with a series of eight repetitions, then ten, then twelve... to twenty. Do at least five series during each session even if you must shorten the last series, and increase the intensity of the exercise little by little by accelerating the rhythm of your movements.

Third exercise : Build your hip muscles

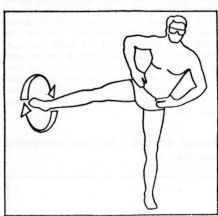

Standing up, hands on hips, lift one leg as high as you can to the side, and make five circles from eight to twelve inches in diameter with your big toe. Do the same exercise next with the other leg. Repeat until your hips become tired. This exercise is an essential preparation for skiing.

Fourth exercise : Build your shoulder, thoracic, and back muscles

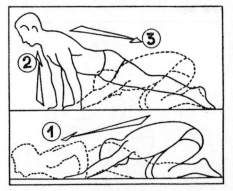

Begin in a kneeling position, chest flat against your thighs, arms stretched out obliquely forward and to the outside. Put weight on your hands and slide your chest along the ground. Then when you are completely stretched out, push upward by straightening your arms. You can either keep your knees in contact with the ground if you are not very strong, or lift your whole body which you stiffen from the back of your neck to your toes. Next, push your seat backward until you are holding the same position you started with. Repeat. Do three series of this exercise going to your limit each time.

To finish it would be excellent to do two more series of hops.

a wide stance, trunk remaining between
eir skis, children do not worry about
nether they are using *braquage* or a stem.
ey do both at the same time, and get
ong very well. It would be absurd to
ant them to ski like adults. However,
is interesting for adult beginners to
derstand how children learn to ski so
ickly...

**The Universal
Children's
Technique**

Gustavo THOENI

This young Italian, who worked his way to the top of international competition in just two years, illustrates perfectly the current tendencies in ski racing.

The use of Wide Stance and Knee Push in Initiating Turns

Patrick Russel and Barbara Cochran, both great international slalom specialists, use the wide stance and inward knee push (which I call *braquage* of the outside leg) in initiating turns while maintaining maximum *glissement*.

BEGINNERS CORRECT YOUR BAD HABITS

The state of being a beginner is, in ninety per cent of the cases, a transitory stage through which one passes during a vacation or a few weekends. In order for the stage to last longer, there must be particular reasons. Certain reasons are normal and make technical improvement a slower process : age, excessive weight, weakness, notable awkwardness, or a morphological error uncompensated for. Other reasons are not normal. Many beginners run into one mistake which halts their improvement completely. I intend the following pages for them.

Have you been skiing a long time without being able to stop snowplowing ? Your case is common, but before giving you any suggestions I must take a closer look.

Are you snowplowing because you are afraid of sliding faster than a man walks ? Do you slow down in spite of yourself ? If this is the case no particular technical suggestion can help you. Go to very, very easy slopes, and try straight runs holding your skis parallel or at least in a gliding snowplow, following the suggestions I have made for true beginners.

Do you use the braking snowplow only when you want to turn ? Then that is not as serious a problem. In a few sessions you will be able to use a flatter ski, and you will begin to improve at a normal rate again.

Feel the difference between the braking snowplow and the gliding snowplow

Choose an easy, smooth slope. Start in a straight run, build up speed, then open a snowplow : your speed decreases. Try then to spread your knees outward and to avoid making your inside edges hold on the snow : your speed then increases as your skis flatten. Slow down again with a snowplow, then spread your knees once again feeling your skis flatten almost completely on the snow. Repeat the exercise again until you feel the difference between the braking and gliding snowplow perfectly. The difference is actually as great as that between a traverse and a sideslip.

Feel the difference between an uphill sliding stem and a downhill checking stem

In a traverse, first stem your uphill ski and flatten it as much as possible on the snow so that it slides easily, then pull it in parallel to your other ski. Repeat this movement several times. Next, stem your downhill ski, and make the inside edge bite as you normally do. Repeat. You should learn once and for all that when you stem the

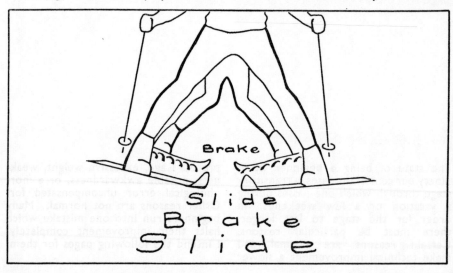

In Traversing on a Steep Slope

Snowplow = an error   Downhill Stem = a check   Uphill Stem = Glissement

uphill ski, it is not to slow down but to slide toward the fall-line, and that when you must slow down a stem while you are in a traverse, you should do so with your downhill ski.

Avoid useless upper body movements

If you have tried these turns before having clearly felt the above differences, you will certainly fall back into your old mistake, this enormous mistake which results in the snowplow and which thousands of skiers retain throughout their lives : checking while turning.

Perhaps you were taught "perfected" snowplows with ample trunk movements. Perhaps, like many of the hardworking beginners I see on the slopes, you are trying to improve the effectiveness of your leg movements through these upper body movements. Forget them, and concentrate on your feet, knees, and legs. Nine times out of ten, the badly performed upper body movement gets in the way of good leg action. Try to stabilize your pelvis completely or, in simpler terms, watch that your seat remains constantly between your skis. Thus, you will be able to find the maximum mobility and effectiveness in your legs.

Eliminate Useless Trunk Movements

51

Do not stiffen your outside leg

"You're turning with your outside leg stiff! Bend your outside leg during the turn!" How often do we hear these useless corrections shouted across the slope. Fifty per cent of beginning skiers, or rather any skiers already capable of skiing on easy slopes, have visibly stiff outside legs. And it is almost always for the same reason. They try to force on the outside leg in order to turn, but it does not work. They then force even more and more awkwardly until they look like they are turning on a wooden leg. If this is your case, let's try to see why.

1) Maybe you have been told, or you have imagined that it is necessary to turn your upper body in order to turn your skis. This case is the most common. The upper body pivots, the seat is pushed to the outside, the skis do not follow, and the skier forces with his outside leg and stiffens it. You will not correct this problem unless you try to turn with your legs and not your upper body. Repeat the

instructions for the sliding stem turn on page 26 and for *braquage* turns.

2) Perhaps you learned to turn through the snowplow, and you have retained the habit of forcing on your outside leg in order to turn. When you skied at slow speed, that was all right, but at higher speeds the ski, that you hold firmly across your direction of travel, "chatters" on the snow, and you are shaken by the least change in relief. To improve, try to open less of a stem or snowplow at the beginning of the turn. If that does not work, go back to the sliding stem turn.

3) Maybe your outside leg is stiff because you are carrying all or most of your weight on your inside ski. Try to feel if this is your case. Perhaps the useless stiffening of your outside leg gives you the impression that you are weighting the leg properly. This is a very common error. To correct it, with a lot of will power try to weight both skis during the whole turn. *Feel your seat remain between both skis.* This may be enough to correct your problem without requiring you to review an entire movement.

The Number One Error : A Stiff Outside Leg

You turn your Upper body Excessively

You stem your Outside Leg Excessively

You Balance on Your Inside Ski

You are having trouble with stem turns

You think that you have improved beyond the snowplow, and when snow conditions are good on an intermediate slope, you can sometimes make a stem turn at low speed. However, most of the time you get into trouble, and you would like to know what to do. *If you fall on your backside when your skis plunge into the fall-line,* there are many possible explanations. Perhaps you are trying to ski slopes which are too difficult for your level. When you turn into the fall-line, your skis accelerate too quickly, and you fall. Maybe you slow down too much before turning into the fall-line. To check you must sit back onto the tails of your skis, and when they accelerate, you fall. Possibly you are simply afraid of the slope, and once you reach the fall-line your legs go weak. If this is the case, make long straight runs at moderate speeds on easy or moderate slopes in a sliding stem. *If you are having trouble pulling your skis into a parallel stance during the* turn, if they tend to cross, you could be making several mistakes.

1) First, you might be opening too wide a stem. After a certain degree of opening you are certainly supporting yourself on the inside edges of both skis, and when you want to pull them toward each other, they catch. 2) You might be trying to hold your seat over your outside ski in order to weight it more. Your inside leg straightens, tipping the ski onto its edge which catches in the snow, when you want to pull your skis toward each other. 3) Maybe you have not felt the favorable instant for sliding your skis from a stem into a wide parallel stance. At slow or moderate speeds this instant occurs as you reach the fall-line. Earlier in the turn, your weight is mainly on your downhill ski which is therefore difficult to pivot. Later, even if you did not want it to do so, your weight has shifted mainly to the outside ski of the turn which becomes the downhill ski. The chances are good that due to this fact you have straightened your inside leg, edging your ski, and thus causing the trouble you have bringing it parallel to the

Stem Turn Errors

Catching an Edge

| You check Excessively with a Snowplow | You Use too Wide a Stem | You Throw your Outside Hip over Your Outside Ski |

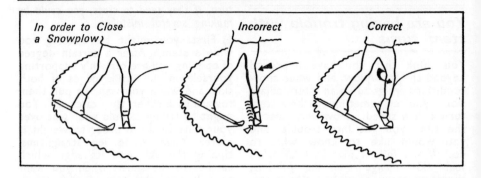

In order to Close a Snowplow

Incorrect

Correct

other. 4) Finally, maybe you have not understood *the movement involves not so much a pulling together of the skis as a pivoting of the inside ski so that it becomes parallel to the other.* These two movements involve different, even opposite, knee action. The first results in a greater angle of edgeset; the second, in a flattening and pivoting of the ski.

You are afraid

While skiing, do you feel terribly awkward and stiff ? Do you lose control of your movements because you are afraid ? Perhaps you do not feel clearly, consciously afraid, but maybe inside you feel an almost organic fear that you are unable to control. Your case is rare, but it does exist. A good remedy for you, perhaps, would be to find a good instructor who would know how to build your confidence by programming your instruction so as to insure your success at each stage. I know a young man who taught his (very timorous) fiancée how to ski by holding on to her hand through straight running, sideslipping, then through turns. He would turn around her and then vice-versa. In a week she was skiing, making downhill turns on an intermediate slope... Without going so far as to try to become engaged to an instructor or instructress, you should be able to find one able to give you a great deal of confidence. The use of short-skis for a few days of walking and slow speed schussing would probably be very beneficial for you as well. 160's or 175's would probably be best for you during the first season at least.

The choice of ski areas and of runs in these ski areas is also of primary importance. Many ski areas do not offer real runs or real lifts for beginners. Some runs have such a reduced surface area and are so cluttered with obstacles that a beginner would have to be a slalom specialist to ski there. I am surprised that this problem has not been better understood, especially, now that so many winter vacationers are not very athletic.

Once your fear has been partially overcome, start our instruction method from the beginning. It requires only flat slopes which should pose no problem for you. It also is an attempt to teach you feelings and reflexes so that you will avoid the neuromuscular blocks which may have resulted from poor instruction, or from bad habits which you have been trying to force upon yourself.

INTERMEDIATE SKIERS IMPROVE

What is an intermediate skier ? He is a skier who is no longer a beginner in that he can ski on almost any run, but who cannot be called a good skier because he lacks the facility and assurance of more experienced skiers who can ski any run with just as few cares as in driving a car.

If you belong below this last level, if for example you have just been able to do the exercises I have suggested for beginners, then this chapter is for you. If on the contrary you are an "old hand", perhaps you will profit more from the next chapter, "Intermediate Skiers, Correct Your Bad Habits". At any rate, I do not think that reading this chapter will do you any harm.

Through speed, modify your stem

To become a "good skier" means to learn to use speed. This is not to say that you should go faster than your present ability permits, but simply that you should consider a certain amount of speed as an ally and not as an enemy. Instead of using your stem to avoid speed, use the speed to make your stem easier, to refine it, and even to transform it into parallel skiing.

On a moderate or easy slope start a traverse, and build up a little more speed than you normally do. *First step:* Open your uphill ski into a flat sliding stem. *Second step:* As in the elementary stem turn described on page 26, try to weight both skis equally by displacing your upper body laterally. (You should have the impression that you are bringing your seat to a position between both skis.) Be careful! Do not perform this movement brutally because you will soon feel a very great increase in pressure under your uphill ski. This is normal. Since you have placed this ski slightly crosswise to your direction of travel, it begins to turn and creates, because of your speed, a centrifugal force which you resist with your outside ski by a reflex action. *Third step:* Use this solid support under your outside ski to balance on and immediately pivot the other ski in order to pull it in parallel in a wide stance. I have not asked you to balance entirely on the outside ski in order to pick up your inside ski and pull it in parallel. No, this would be too difficult for you. Weight both

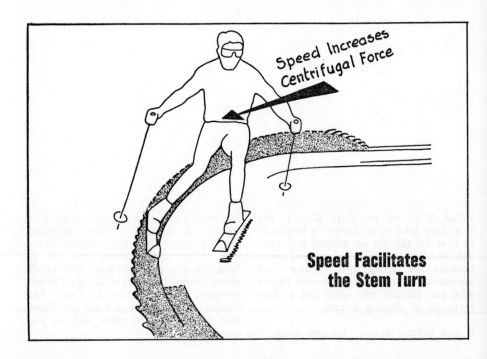

Speed Increases Centrifugal Force

**Speed Facilitates
the Stem Turn**

skis, and use the pressure exerted under your outside ski only to feel a solid support while you pivot the other ski. As soon as your skis become parallel, your turn continues by itself. Simply continue to balance mainly on the support of your outside ski.

Move from the stem to parallel skiing

You will have two ways of making this transition.

On an easy, moderate slope make the same turn as that described above but from a wider stance, opening a narrower and narrower stem and trying to feel as early as possible the support created by centrifugal force on your outside ski. Thus, you will be able to pivot the inside ski of the turn parallel to your other ski earlier and earlier in the turn. Your stem will thus become less and less perceptible and increasingly smoother. Soon, only a widening of your track will be observable at the beginning of the turn. You will be "parallel skiing".

On an easy slope for you where you can go fast enough and remain close enough to the fall-line to do the widestance parallel turns I suggested for the talented beginner on page 37, start with a very shallow traverse and build up your speed. Before starting the turn, widen your stance a little, then weight the inside edge of your outside ski by pushing your knee inward. Next, flatten your inside ski on the snow by displacing your corresponding knee and possibly by pushing the ski forward slightly. You will immediately feel your outside ski start a long turn. Do not turn too far. Do not "complete" your turn, but take off again in a slight traverse to the opposite side, and start over again.

« Braquage » of the Outside Leg

Two elements facilitate your change from stem to parallel : speed and remaining close to the fall-line. Braquage of the outside leg can be substituted for the stem. This is an inward push of the knee with a gradual pivoting effort of the same leg.

When you are able to do this exercise at will, instead of simply edging your outside ski by pushing your knee inward emphasize the inward knee push and transform it into a true *braquage*. In this way, you will discover the parallel turn which depends on a steering of the outside leg. This *braquage* is not a brutal movement, it is performed gradually. The knee is pushed not only inward but also forward.

The stem platform turn

All skiers, even the greatest slalom skiers, use a turn with a check preparation under certain circumstances. They do so in order to slow down without having to slow down in the turn where it would be dangerous to try. It so happens that these checks can become an intimate part of the following turn, make it easier, and improve its effectiveness. This is what I am going to try to make you feel. Traversing with a certain amount of speed, give yourself the impression of falling downhill by opening your downhill ski into a stem. Immediately weight the inside edge of the ski, and try to make it hold as much as possible by using the inside of your foot and your corresponding knee. Your downhill leg flexes while you feel the ski slow down, and as soon as your ski bites, you have the impression that your compressed leg springs you back uphill. Profit from

this recoil, and emphasize it by opening a slight uphill stem, then weighting both skis equally (your seat ending up between both skis). To begin with you will not feel the recoil help the beginning of your turn very much, but little by little you will feel it help, and you will not even need to use the uphill stem. After the weighting of your downhill ski when the recoil helps you weight both skis, you will feel the skis move into the turn by themselves. Once you dare try this turn at a higher speed, you will have to balance quickly on your uphill ski at the beginning of the turn after the downhill platform. You will have encountered the same phenomenon that I described previously when discussing the advantage of using speed in the stem turn. Once you have felt the support of the stem, try to plant your downhill pole to the side at the same instant that you make the platform. Your balance will increase at the delicate instant during the beginning of the turn.

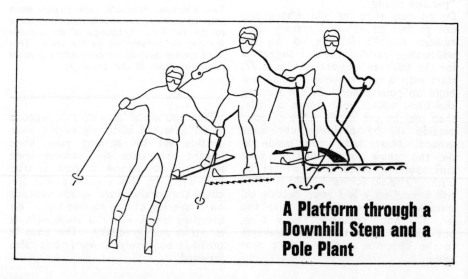

A Platform through a Downhill Stem and a Pole Plant

A Platform through Widening the Stance and Planting the Pole

The parallel turn with a downhill platform

Being a talented beginner already skiing parallel, or having improved your stem to the point of skiing almost parallel, you should learn this next turn. It is related to the platform stem turn just described. Especially its rhythm and mechanism are similar, so that knowing the stem in this case would be an advantage even to the parallel beginner. Having been able to do the final form of this preceding turn, that is a stem platform and recoil to a widestance turn, you are now going to try a platform turn without a stem. Starting in a traverse, you fall slightly downhill and catch yourself on the inside edge of your downhill ski which you have also displaced slightly downhill. Feel this ski bite into the snow, force your knee inward in particular. When you have felt the ski holding, recoil back uphill, and weight both skis while pivoting

them into a downhill turn (see *braquage* page 24). A pole plant at the same time as the platform increases the effectiveness of this turn a great deal.

A Platform into Braquage *of the Outside Leg*

Having felt a solid lateral support with pole plant, you can try to make very short turns by linking a pivoting braquage effort to the platform. You should feel as if the thrust exerted on your downhill foot resulted in a recoil transmitted directly to your uphill foot.

59

For strong skiers wedeln through braquage

The talented, bold skiers, who learned to ski parallel directly, have already done a rudimentary wedeln. (In our film "Learn to Ski in Seven Days", two beginners use a rudimentary wedeln on their second day on skis.) Nevertheless, these skiers should repeat the wedeln exercises indefatigably until they feel all the mechanisms I have mentioned.

These mechanisms are described on pages 36 to 41. From a rudimentary, brutal form, they improve into smoothly linked, rhythmical movements. Due to the rhythm, you will discover unweighting and lateral thrust which permit the recoil from one turn into the other. By trying to learn this lateral thrust, which they have already recognized as helpful in the preceding stem platform turns, the less talented skiers will also be able to learn to wedel.

For the others wedeln through stemming

Start a straight run in a slight gliding snowplow, skis flattened as much as possible on the snow, legs flexible (not stiffened as they are in the braking snowplow). Let yourself fall to the right, for example, stemming the right ski more, then check this displacement by making the edge bite (force on the inside of your right foot, and push your corresponding knee inward). Once

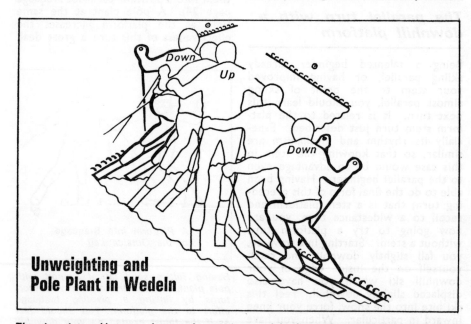

Unweighting and Pole Plant in Wedeln

There is no interval between down and up motions, and this fact is the source of the expression "down-up motion". It is a sort of slow motion rebound. The pole plant at the end of the down motion and beginning of the up motion helps establish rhythm of wedeln.

you feel your ski hold, balance on it, then push off onto both skis which pivot and begin the turn. You might possibly accentuate this pivoting by a slight *braquage* of both feet. Do not turn too much, however. If possible, just turn as far as the fall-line remaining in a sliding stem, and repeat the same movement to the opposite side. Let yourself fall to the left, etc. At first, it will take you a certain amount of time to move from the thrust on the right ski to the thrust on the left ski, etc..., but if you practise the movement hundreds of times remaining closer and closer to the fall-line, you will discover a continuous rhythm : down motion and thrust with the right leg, slight up motion as the skis pivot smoothly, down motion and thrust with the left leg. *Once the down and up motions link together smoothly, you will be wedeling. The poleplant will help you to this rhythm.* As in platform turns, try to plant your downhill pole to the side at the same time that you make each lateral thrust.

From stem wedeln to widestance wedeln

Here, I am referring to the stem wedeln described above and not to the phony wedeln you may have invented yourself. Each turn is preceded by a stem check (which corresponds with the lateral platform of the turn described on page 58) and not by an uphill sliding stem at the beginning of the turn. If you are using the uphill stem, you will never learn to wedel with skis parallel. You will always retain a small stem like many good skiers who have not mastered wedeln. If you do the stem wedeln well, emphasize weighting your outside ski before and during the platform. Your inside ski will begin, little by little, to move parallel to your outside ski. You will have reached your goal.

I do not want you to angulate, that is to push your uphill hip up the hill, so that you will take on a modern look.

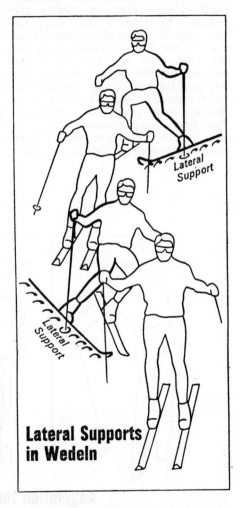

Lateral Supports in Wedeln

The lateral supports are felt most easily in wedeling with a stem, but they also exist in parallel wide stance and semi-wide stance wedeln. The pole plant also adds to lateral support and lateral thrust.

You have already noticed that what happens between your skis and the snow is of more interest to me, and as a result I pay much more attention to your feet than I do to your upper body. Here again, the problem concerns your feet. In guiding the beginner to slopes a little steep for him, page 30, I have already mentioned the trouble he will have making his skis hold. You will now encounter the same problem on yet steeper slopes but you are now better prepared to resolve the problem. You are more familiar with your body positions. You have more correct feelings in your knees and hips, and you are more relaxed because your balance is better.

How to hold on a hard frozen, steep slope

You already know that in order to hold a traverse you must balance on your downhill ski. You also know that in order to hold you must make the inside edge of your ski bite by weighting the inside of your foot through an inward push of your knee (that is, a lateral displacement of the knee toward the mountain). This inward push increases the angle of the ski to the snow, but it should not interfere with putting all of your weight on that ski. In other words, you must angulate, that is, displace your upper body downhill. Your trunk is, as it were, in balance on the head of the femur (thigh bone) of your downhill leg. *This is what you should feel in order to hold in a traverse*

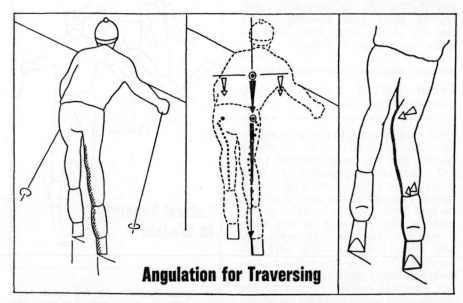

Angulation for Traversing

You will be angulating effectively on a steep, icy slope when you feel the inside of your ankle pressing firmly against the inside of your boot top and when you feel the weight of the mass of your body balancing on the head of the femur of your support leg.

on a steep, frozen slope : the inward push of your knee and the balanced support on your downhill hip.

But be careful! Do not exaggerate the movement and forget what your foot is doing. If you can edge your ski without angulating, great! With angulation, then, you will be able to hold on steeper slopes more easily than other skiers, even on slopes where others cannot hold at all. Do not make the mistake of tipping your trunk laterally so that the line of your shoulders and head tips downhill as is advocated by some national ski schools. Your trunk is not a rigid block. Your head and the back of your neck, which contain your precious reflex centers for balance, must remain free in a normal position.

You will notice that when you angulate, your trunk will pivot slightly downhill. This is normal and results from human anatomy. However, this is not a good reason for exaggerating the movement or for not continuing to look in your direction of travel.

How to hold during turns

I intend this section for those of you who are using speed to help you turn (see page 56). Learning to use speed in turns requires that you learn to resist centrifugal force, which pushes you laterally. When the snow is very hard, the same problems found in traversing arise in holding. You already know that you must balance mainly on your outside ski. In order to make this ski hold more effectively, do exactly the same thing as you do on your downhill ski in a traverse. Weight the inside edge of your outside foot and, thus, the inside edge of the outside ski. Push your knee inward in order to increase the ski-snow angle, and displace your trunk in order to balance on your outside hip and on the inside edge of your outside ski. *In one word, angulate.*

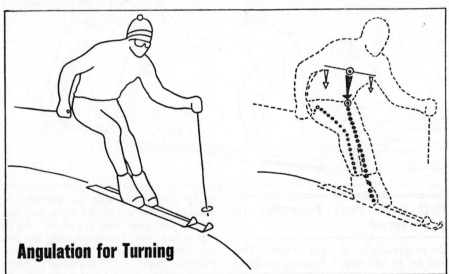

Angulation for Turning

Making skis hold during turns on ice poses the same problem as making them hold while traversing. In addition, the skier must lean in to counteract the centrifugal force resulting from the turn.

INTERMEDIATE SKIERS, LEARN TO USE A NARROW STANCE

If you have followed my suggestions, you are now skiing with a more or less wide stance because such a stance offers three advantages. For the beginner, it allows an easy parallel ski instruction method, and for those who must use the stem, it allows an easy passage from stem to parallel skiing. For good skiers the wide stance remains indispensable in certain circumstances and particularly in competition where even the greatest champions use it constantly. This does not mean that the wide stance is a universal panacea. In some cases, for elegance, economy of movement, or even effectiveness in some kinds of snow, one must know how to use a narrow stance, and now is the time for you to try it.

downhill ski. You can even lift it off the snow, or at least lift the tail off, in order to feel the balance on your downhill ski and in order to hold a narrow stance more correctly later on. Avoid the bad narrow stance which results from distributing your weight over both feet and which decreases your balance considerably.

Pull your feet together a little during turns

However, do not pull them together at the beginning of the turn. You have already noticed that it is better to spread your feet a little at this instant. On the other hand, immed-

Controlling the Arcs of Turns While in a Narrow Stance

Wide Stance

into Narrow Stance

Pull your feet together in a traverse

Do so especially on hard snows. This will be all the easier because on hard snows your weight is almost totally on your downhill ski. As your uphill ski affects your balance very little, you can easily leave it close to your

iately afterward, that is, during the control of the arc of the turn, you can try to pull your skis together. As in traversing, you balance mainly on one ski, the outside ski. It is then easy to pull the other in. But careful! Here again, when narrowing your stance, do not make the mistake of weighting both skis equally or, yet more serious, that of weighting mainly your inside ski.

This section is intended especially for the strong and dynamic skiers who turn anywhere, but too brutally, not smoothly enough. The opportunities for sideslipping are so frequent for the less dynamic that they must be becoming "virtuosos" of sideslipping.

Do sideslip garlands through braquage

We have seen how to start a sideslip through *braquage*. Now you can try little by little to steer, then to sideslip in a narrower stance, to hold a higher position, and to pivot into the beginning of the sideslip more smoothly. When you have a long favorable traverse at your disposal, you can sideslip for five or ten yards, traverse again, sideslip, etc..., gradually shortening your sideslips. You will soon be doing the exercise called a sideslip garland, due to the track it leaves in the snow. In sideslipping as in the garlands be very careful to pivot only your legs and skis. Your head and

trunk must continue to face your direction of travel. If your trunk does turn with your skis, you are making one or probably both of the following mistakes :
You are watching your ski tips instead of looking in your direction of travel, and/ or you are not putting enough weight on the tails of your skis to control the sideslip. If this is the case, your skis sideslip badly. They tend to climb uphill. Try to feel as if the weight of your calcaneus (your heel bone) were controling the sideslip, and your legs will immediately feel freer under your upper body.

Once you have learned to do garlands with your feet fairly close together, you will have reached another important technical stage. In effect, from this moment on you will no longer steer because *braquage* requires a wide stance. You will begin to use a more subtle movement called *vissage* which is explained in the chapter entitled "Technical and Pedagogical Analysis".

Quick Sideslip Garlands in a Narrow Stance

IN MOGULS TURN WITH DOWN MOTION

Bumps, called "moguls", resulting from the repeated passage of skiers in the same place, are tending to spread all over most ski areas. In many of these areas they are scraped down mechanically, but when they are there, you must learn to cope with them.

Easy moguls

Easy moguls can be a pleasure for the intermediate skier who knows how to ski them. Be one who knows how. Pick out a mogul, and approach it with moderate speed. At the instant you reach the top of the bump weight the ski which will become your outside ski and pivot your corresponding leg. You will start into a long turn. Your inside ski will follow without difficulty because while you weight your outside ski, you unweight the other ski which then pivots into the turn all by itself. Maybe you even lift your inside ski for a fraction of a second when you start to pivot the other ski.

Higher moguls on steeper slopes

In higher moguls you must do exactly the same as above at the top of the bump, but you must check beforehand. In any field of moguls there are small

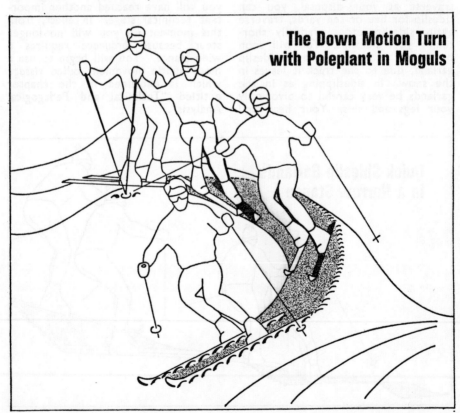

The Down Motion Turn with Poleplant in Moguls

flat sections where it is possible to check after having turned on a crest. You should learn to check very quickly on these flat sections in order to reach the top of the next moguls at a very slow speed. You then use your downhill pole plant for support and plunge into the turn by pivoting your outside ski as we have already seen. You can also accentuate your down motion in order to make your skis hold better on the steeper slope.

How do you check before the turn? You check with either a quick downhill stem if you are a stem specialist or with a lateral thrust of your downhill ski if you ski with a wide stance. Otherwise, if you have learned to ski parallel from the beginning, steer both skis uphill, that is, pivot them in the direction opposite to the coming turn.

You should never try to slow down with a stem check while turning! This is an error under any circumstances, but it is even more serious here because your outside ski, pivoting most easily at the beginning of the turn, would pivot crosswise to your direction of travel and catch or jam as soon as you started down the steep portion of the bump. This mistake always results in

the very serious habit, discussed on page 52, of stiffening the outside leg.

In moguls discover anticipation

You have already understood that your skis pivot more easily from the top of a bump and that the bump can also help your legs to move into the turn more easily. However, your body also follows your skis, and you have realized, perhaps, that your primary problem is not making your skis turn, but the fact that your body follows them around the turn. Watch some excellent skiers make short radius turns through the moguls. They do not have this problem. In fact, their upper bodies remain facing constantly down the fall-line, and only their legs move. Why don't you do the same thing? At the same time as you check, turn your shoulders downhill, and plant your downhill pole while your trunk remains facing downhill. When your skis pivot, they will first move into their normal position under your trunk, then continue to pivot. Your upper body ends up in another position of anticipation before the coming turn.

The Position of Anticipation before the Turn

INTERMEDIATE SKIERS, START RACING

Intermediate skiers start racing ? Perhaps not if you are particularly cautious or if you are getting on in years. However, do not hesitate if you feel that you are in good shape physically. You can not imagine how much the few moments devoted to a race can help you to improve. You must, of course, find a race for your level of ability, not a downhill, nor a slalom to begin with, but an easy giant slalom, a NASTAR for example (see page 181) or a simple race organized by a ski club for its members.

How to « make it through » a giant slalom

Just use what you have already learned. Keep a cool head, and judge the situation clearly. Do not let yourself get out of control. Check before the turns if they are going to be difficult. Above all, do not try to slow down in the turns. Spread your feet and, if you start to lose your balance, lower your stance. *Do not improvise !* You are not yet ready to use your agressiveness, your rapid reflexes, or your athletic ability for the acrobatics that could win you the race, if you were not to fall in the third gate... Just as in tennis where you must know how to play before you can hit the ball hard, in skiing you must master your technique before attacking a giant slalom.

A tactical suggestion therefore : Race within the limits of your technique. The simple fact that you must adapt it to material obstacles (slalom poles and ruts) will make you improve considerably.

TRY POWDER SNOW

I would not suggest that you hunt for powder yet, but if eight to twelve inches of fresh snow falls over the whole ski area, do not stay in the lodge. If the powder is light and if you dare to use your accustomed speed, you will be surprised by the fact that you don't encounter any particular difficulties. If you do not dare to use your accustomed speed or if the snow is not light enough, use the sliding stem which I suggested to beginners on page 26. From a traverse, stem your uphill ski and let yourself be pulled into the fall-line. Remain in the fall-line a little longer than normal, and then pivot both skis very gradually in order to finish the turn.

INTERMEDIATE SKIERS CORRECT YOUR BAD HABITS

This chapter is intended for the great mass of skiers who are no longer beginners but who cannot pretend to be good skiers yet. A good skier is one capable of skiing any slope as easily as if he were driving a car. This is not your case. You do have problems, and I think I can help you solve

them. I have noticed that most skiers stop improving due to one of a small number of key errors.

Find your problem in the following pages and give the suggestions for solving it a try. There are nine chances out of ten that you too will become a good skier.

DO YOU FEEL WITH YOUR FEET ?

You have already been told about your arms, your trunk, or your legs which may be too straight, or your skis which may be edged too much or not enough, but has anyone mentioned your feet ? Has anyone told you to feel your weight distributed over the full length of your feet when you are schussing, and that in a traverse on a steep, frozen hill, most of your weight should be placed on the inside edge of your downhill foot ? If you have simply been told to push your knee inward or perhaps to angulate, you may have pushed your knee or hip inward without your ski holding any better. In this case you have never been "tuned in" to your feet. The feelings perceived by your feet are not going to your brain. Motor commands are being transmitted to your legs, hips, and arms but never to your feet, which are your most important motor elements. How has this elementary fact been neglected ? By pretentiousness, by incorrect analysis, by confidence in some sacrosanct principles which were developed who knows where, who knows when ? Worry about feet when we want to train a skier to "fly" ? This is like language teachers teaching literature and not lowering themselves to teach the language itself as it is spoken ! With thirty years of coaching experience behind me, twenty of them in skiing, I have noticed that simple common sense is the most difficult characteristic to find in all but the truly great coaches.

Why, for example, tell a person to push his knees uphill in order to turn his skis uphill, even if you have demonstrated previously that, seated on a table with your legs swinging you can pivot your feet through a lateral thrust of your knees ? It can be demonstrated just as easily that seated with your feet on the ground, you can move your knees laterally without causing your feet to pivot! Your knees can even be displaced while your feet pivot in the opposite direction. Why not just say, "pivot your feet uphill", pointing out that at the same time the knees will also move uphill ?

I would like to convince you of the importance of concentrating your attention on your feet the next time you ski. If you try to minimize all other movements, I am sure that your balance and effectiveness will improve. If you still stem some, try to feel the friction, the braking action, and the support of your edges. By trying to slide more slowly and more smoothly in your stem turns, you will end up using the stem technique which I have recommended.

If you are already skiing parallel, by concentrating on your feet you will be able to decrease the amplitude and the brutality of the movements you use to start a turn or to start wedeling. By trying to develop a smooth *glissement* you will develop a wide, or at least semi-wide stance, even if you have learned previously to ski with your feet close together. Your improvement will become much more rapid.

On foggy or stormy days you will notice that you are having much less trouble than before. Your feet will have become sensitive antennae. They will read and anticipate the relief of the terrain, and they will send to your brain for the appropriate reactions.

INTERMEDIATE SKIERS, CORRECT YOUR BAD HABITS

Are you too rough ?

This is generally the case with the robust skier whose improvement depends on his physical strength. Physical strength, if it is not combined with a great sensitivity and with good balance, can be a disadvantage. There is, in fact, one absolute principle in skiing : The skier should not fight the snow, he should work with it. I will explain. One of your skis is flat on the snow during a straight run and leaves a track in the snow. You push it laterally in order to start a turn. The ski catches on its outside edge, but you are strong enough to overcome the resistance, and the ski pivots. If the snow were not soft and if the edge caught, the resistance would be greater. As a result, you would have to force more, the ski would refuse to pivot. You would probably lose your balance and fall. Your fall would be due to "catching an edge". If you were not as strong, at the instant the edge started to catch, you might have tipped the ski slightly, and even on harder snow the edge would not have caught. You might be using your strength in a similar manner in order to sideslip without flattening your skis. This is possible if you exaggerate the pivoting of your skis. However, it is dangerous if you run into a rut, a pile of fresh snow, or an unpacked area. You would have to overcome a considerably greater resistance which could at any instant cause you to fall. At any rate, in order to resist, you would have to stiffen your legs, and thus disturb your balancing reactions. In conclusion, do not depend on your physical strength too much. Keep it in reserve, and try to ski with flexibility, smoothly, caressing instead of brutalizing the snow.

Are you too gentle ?

Being too gentle is also fairly common and not always characteristic of only weak skiers. Are you one of those skiers who loses all ability to react because the feeling of sliding inhibits him ? If so you could be in for trouble for many reasons. You may be using a poor body position, generally sitting back, but sometimes sitting slightly too far forward. Either position would interfere with your ability to react. Try to feel your weight distributed over the full length of your feet when you are straight running, not predominantly on your heels or toes. Perhaps due to your morphology, you bend too far forward at the waist (see page 184) and thus run the risk of catching an edge and of not being able to react. Maybe you lack agressiveness. You have not understood that skiing like most other sports requires more or less violent muscular action. In any case you must learn to react. Emphasize all the dynamic exercises that I have suggested : *braquages,* rudimentary wedeln, checks, platforms before turns, and unweighting. You can also try linked hops (similar to the hops use in skipping rope) while making straight runs on a flat slope. Your skis should leave the snow at each hop. Through this exercise you will discover if you are on your heels ("sitting back") or your toes ("too far forward").

Are you afraid of steep slopes ?

Are you afraid of falling down the hill ? Do your skis hold badly and tend to slip out from under you? This is probably true because the fear of a steep hill can make the skier lean uphill and balance on his uphill ski. Under these conditions his skis do not hold very well. You must learn to make the inside edge of your downhill ski bite into the snow so that you can gain confidence and avoid the bad reaction of leaning into the hill (see pages 62 and 63). This is the great advantage in learning technique. You will be better armed, thus gaining confidence, and your improvement will be more rapid. Because you know how to hold in a traverse, you will dare to sideslip, as the problem of sideslipping on a steep slope is in stopping, not in starting the manoeuvre. You will also dare to turn because the problem is the same. Turns on a steep slope will not be more difficult as long as you know how to check properly immediately before and afterwards. Tackle steep slopes when the snow is soft. This will help you overcome your fear.

big, too soft, broken, or which play in your bindings,...). Ask an instructor, a ski shop repairman, or an experienced friend to check over your equipment. You may also have morphological problems which disturb your edge set (bowed legs, flat feet, knock knees,...). There are several ways of canting your boots to overcome these problems (see page 183). Try them.

Are you afraid of badly packed slopes?

Everyone is afraid of badly packed runs and correctly so. However, if you panic in this kind of snow that is

Are you afraid of ice?

This fear is similar to the fear of steep slopes. The problem is to make your skis hold. The remedy is the same as above. Learn how to make your downhill ski bite (knee push, angulation, see page 62), learn how to check effectively with your edges, and ski as much as possible on steeper and steeper icy slopes in order to overcome your fear once and for all. However, it is possible that your fear results from faulty equipment (unsharpened or worn out edges, convex base or railed edges, skis which are too flexible or too stiff for your weight, boots which are too

Uphill lean = An Error

another thing. In this case, you undoubtedly make technical mistakes which ruin your effectiveness. There are many possibilities. *Maybe you are too rough ?* We just studied your case. You should try to become smoother and more flexible by trying to become more sensitive to what happens under your skis. Maybe on the other hand you are too gentle, and you do not use enough force to make your skis turn in this resistant snow. We have also studied your case. Be more dynamic. Discover more powerful movements like *braquage*. Perhaps you are stemming too wide and placing your ski at too great an angle to your direction of travel. The ski then catches in the unpacked snow or encounters resistances which make your stem similar to a snowplow, and because your speed is too great for snowplow turns, you get into trouble. *In badly packed snows you must maintain glissement throughout your turns.* Here again, more than in any other case, learn to check before or after but not during your turns.

Are you afraid of moguls ?

I am referring to the moderate bumps on intermediate slopes. Not only should you not be afraid of them, but you should appreciate these bumps because they make turning easier as long as you know how to use them. I have already made a few suggestions in this regard on page 66. There are also mistakes which should not be made when turning in bumps, for example, trying to remain continuously in the narrow depressions which separate the bumps. Checking then becomes impossible, and it is difficult

to initiate turns. However, nothing is easier than checking on the uphill side of a mogul. As for initiating turns, it is childishly simple if you do so on the top of a bump, your skis then pivot under your feet without encountering the slightest resistance. A stem check turn is also difficult in moguls. As I have repeated many times before, I do not believe in any turn which involves a check during the turn itself. Here, however, such turns can even be very dangerous. If you make this mistake, you will feel your outside leg stiffen immediately. In moguls more than anywhere else you must not resist with your outside leg. Slow down by sideslipping on this leg while carrying most of your weight on it and bending it more if you have trouble staying in balance.

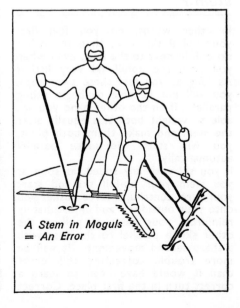

*A Stem in Moguls
= An Error*

The worst stem errors

The worst mistake you can make in a stem, a mistake that will halt your improvement completely, is to stiffen your outside leg. I will not return to this error which I discussed at length on page 52.

The second worst mistake is to throw your seat in the direction of the on-coming turn at the same time that you stem your uphill ski. Besides making you stiffen your outside leg, it can also cause the outside edge of your outside ski to catch and give you a hard spill. This error is very difficult to correct. You must learn a stem that depends only on the feelings you perceive under your feet and only on leg movements. Return to pages 26, 56, and 58.

Do you do the « two-step » stem ?

In other words, do you feel first your uphill ski stem, then the other ski pull in next to the first, even when you stem the uphill ski very little ? As long as you feel these two steps, you will not be able to begin skiing parallel. If on the other hand you are able to weight both skis equally after the stem and make them both pivot, you will start widestance parallel automatically.

If you ski with any speed, as soon as you stem your up-hill ski and start your turn, centrifugal force pushes you onto your outside ski and unfortunately reinforces your habit of pulling the other ski in parallel to the first with a sharp second movement. It will be more trouble correcting this error than it would have been to learn a correct turn in the first place. Correct

it just the same, preferably with slow turns preceded by a stem check.

Speed helps in moving on to widestance parallel

As long as you do not do the "two-step" stem, speed can help you learn widestance parallel through *braquage*. Return to page 56.

Constantly facing downhill leads to parallel skiing

Making stem turns down the fall-line is another way of learning parallel skiing. Little by little you will open a smaller stem, and you will be able to start your turns, even while in a fairly wide stance, simply by making the inside edge of your outside ski bite by pushing your knee inward (see page 37). Be careful, though, once the turn has begun. Do not pull the inside ski next to the other ski immediately, as you would then develop the rhythm of the "two-step" stem habit which you must avoid, and you would not be able to stop stemming. Instead, just pivot your inside ski or let it pivot by itself into a parallel position relative to the other ski. Do not try to pull the skis together. Only the wide stance can make you lose the habit of stemming.

Wedeln also leads to parallel skiing

If you still stem just a little, you must be having trouble with wedeln. Go

The "Two Step" Stem Turn, A Habit Difficult to Break

In the " two-step " stem there is, one, a stemming of the uphill ski, two, a pulling of the second ski in parallel to the first. In the stem which I suggest there is a stemming of the uphill ski, then an equal weighting of both skis followed by a pivoting effort on both skis. The essential technical element is the equal weighting before the pivoting effort. This detail permits a direct transition to parallel skiing while the skier is almost unaware of the change.

back to the instruction for wedeln (page 38). You will correct your mistake more easily if you learn a mechanism which does not depend on a stem.

Throwing the Hip to the Outside while Stemming is an Error

I am thinking of *braquage* in particular. Being an intermediate, you cannot expect to wedel as flexibly, harmoniously, and effectively as a good skier. You should simply be able to link successive widestance, semi-wide stance or stem turns together on a flat slope while facing down the fall-line and *with the wedeln rhythm*. If you cannot do this, you must certainly have a bad habit to correct.

You are not dynamic enough to wedel

No matter what technique you use for making turns, if you want to pass from a simple succession of linked turns to wedeln, you must gradually accelerate the speed of your movements until you feel that you have learned the wedeln rhythm.

Make a considerable effort to increase the speed and incisiveness of the initiation of your turns. Then be careful not to turn too far out of the fall-line. Instead, develop speed and sharpness in the movements of your skis, not agitated, but precise movements. If you make no other mistake than to move too slowly, you will eventually learn. Otherwise, you must find an appropriate remedy for your bad habit.

A turning technique incompatible with wedeln

Nine times out of ten, the intermediate skier who cannot wedel is the one who "rotates". This habit is a result of the rotation techniques formerly practiced by many ski schools and of the light christy circular projection developed later. Even though these techniques have been abandoned by most schools, rotation of the upper body persists, and even regenerates

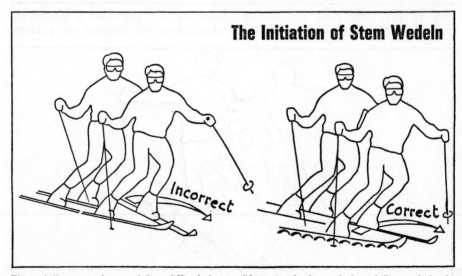

The Initiation of Stem Wedeln

Incorrect

Correct

The uphill stem makes wedeling difficult by modifying its rhythm. A downhill stem helps by facilitating unweighting, lateral thrust, and the pole plant.

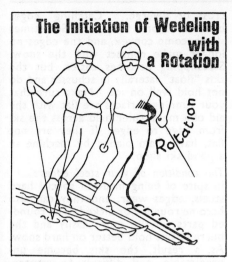

The Initiation of Wedeling with a Rotation

Rotation makes Wedeling more Difficult.

your downhill ski in order to establish a lateral support, the error is not very serious. On the contrary, this stem will help you to understand unweighting by down-up motion, and true lateral thrust. However, if you stem the ski on the side of the coming turn and pull in the other, (the "two-step"), you will never learn a real wedeln. You should change your stem (see pages 41 and 58) and improve your chances of learning to ski parallel.

Are you too rough or too dynamic ?

Wedeln is a dynamic but nevertheless smooth movement. There should be an incisive platform at the end of each turn, but the skis should flatten and sideslip between platforms. The rhythm is in two-four time : "One" (very dynamic), "Two" (*glissement*). If you shorten the second beat, you will not be able to do a real wedeln, but you will rebound from one side to the other of the fall-line in a manner which is neither elegant nor effective. Concentrate. You must discover the *glissement* phase, the flat ski, skidded phase. Perhaps your weight is too far forward on your toes. Put more weight on your heels, and maybe you will side-slip more easily between platforms. If on the other hand you shorten the first beat and slide too uniformly from one side to the other of the fall-line, be careful not to weight your heels excessively. It is impossible to react dynamically and precisely on skis unless you are in good balance.

itself due to the almost exclusive use of down-up motion. During the up motion, because he has not learned to use his legs, the pupil is tempted to throw his upper body laterally or, at least, to throw his outside hip into the turn. If this is your case, you will have a difficult time learning to wedel, and once you do learn, yours will be a poor type of wedeln. The inertia of your swinging upper body will result in a slowness and heaviness difficult to overcome. To learn to wedel correctly with your legs moving under your upper body which faces constantly down the fall-line, you must review the *braquage* exercises which lead directly to wedeln (page 36).

An incompatible stem turn rhythm

It is possible to wedel with a stem but not with just any stem. If you stem

If you have spent years as an intermediate skier and if you do not think you are making any of the mistakes already mentioned, there is another possibility to consider. Have you always been using the same pair of skis ? If so, have them checked over carefully.

The length and stiffness :
Camber is the gap which appears in a pair of skis, held running surface to running surface at the shovels and heels. Normal camber for shorter skis is between 5/8 and 1 1/8 inches and for longer skis (210 centimeters) between 3/4 and 7/8 of and inch. You should be able to flatten your skis running surface to running surface by clasping them between thumb and two forefingers in the middle. This manner of verification implies that the strength of your hand is proportionate to your overall strength. A ski should be stiffer for a heavier person, but the camber should not, as is commonly thought, be wider. Light or cautious skiers with a fear of speed should pick soft and lightly cambered skis. (In extreme cases the skis should clasp shut, running surface to running surface, between thumb and index finger.) By heating a ski to 85 to 105 degrees, it is possible to bend it and modify its stiffness and its amount of camber, but these corrections rarely last.

The flatness of the running surface :
Running surfaces wear, particularly on poorly covered runs, and frequently sink below the level of the edges through aging. The combination of unlike materials used in the construction of skis results in internal tensions which cause concavity to develop. Because the edges stick below the base, the skis sideslip poorly and tend to cross or diverge. "Catching" edges becomes more frequent. Sometimes skis become convex, and the edges no longer make contact with the snow. Sideslipping becomes easier, but the skis "float" laterally in schusses and do not hold well on ice. Make sure that your running surfaces are flat with the aid of a metal ruler held across the ski from edge to edge. If they are not flat, have tham planed by machine in a good ski shop.

The condition of your steel edges :
In spite of being made of special hard steels, edges wear, and they can also become rounded or nicked. The rounded parts sideslip more easily and the burred parts hold better on hard snow. As a result, the skis become unpredictable, and difficult to manage. You should have your edges sharpened at least once a year and more frequently, (many times a season) if you ski in areas with sparse snow.

Your skis can be faulty in many other ways : They can be warped or bent. They can be broken on the inside or delaminated. The relationship between the stiffness of tail and tip sections can be abnormal. Their shovels or heels could be hooked. The edges could stick beyond the plastic or vice-versa when the plastic is delaminating. The bindings could be mounted too far forward or back, or they might not hold your feet parallel to the axes of the skis. The axes of your feet might be held too far inside or outside the axes of your skis. You will not be able to judge all of this for yourself. Have your skis checked by a good skier or better yet, by a good benchman in a recommended ski shop.

GOOD SKIERS IMPROVE

What is a "good skier"? He is one of the many winter enthusiasts who skis as well as he walks. He is never stopped by a difficulty on a run, and he skis in powder. Occasionally he races.

He is a NASTAR medalist, sometimes a silver medalist. He could be classified as a "C" racer by his regional division of the United States Ski Association, or he could be a ski-touring enthusiast. Nevertheless, when a "very good skier" skis with a group of good skiers, the difference is obvious. The behavior of the very good skier's skis on the snow, the precision, the *glissement* through the arcs of his turns, his balance, the rapidity of his leg action through the moguls, his ease of movement, all serve to prove that the good skier has a lot to learn before he reaches the level of a very good skier.

The intermediate skier generally worries too much about the initiation of his turns and not enough about controlling the arc once a turn has started. However, once the skier is able to initiate a turn when and where he wants, the way he controls the arc of his turn determines how much at ease he will be, how well he will keep his balance, and how easily he will be able to ski in varying snow conditions.

Discover the pivot point of your skis

The engineers in charge of development for ski manufacturers are constantly improving the capability of skis to make smooth turns. The distribution of flexibility over the length of ski and the distribution of the torsional flexibility, the arcs describ-

Tight Garlands with Weight Distributed over the Full Length of your Feet

ed by its curved sides, the position of its narrowest point, all work together to give the ski a capability of pivoting in the snow around a precise pivot point. You must discover the location of this pivot point by improving your sensitivity to what is happening under your skis, and then you should use the pivot point to your advantage. This is the only way for you to develop the *glissement* in turns that is characteristic of the greatest skiers.

To discover the pivot point, do quick, flat ski sideslip garlands over well packed intermediate slopes. Hold your skis as close together as possible and avoid scissoring. Weight both, but mainly your downhill ski. If your balance is good enough, squeeze your knees together while you pivot your skis. The pivoting action will result partly from a pivoting action of both legs called *vissage*. (For explanation, see "Technical and Pedagogical Analysis", the last chapter of this book.) and partly from a subtle use of ski-snow friction. How the mechanism works does not matter much. The important thing is to feel the ease and precision with which you are now able to pivot your skis.

When turning, try to make narrow tracks

An elementary turn results from placing the skis more or less crosswise to the direction of travel during the initiation phase, and then making a long pivoted sideslip. Advanced turns require a less ample, more gradual initiation, and more attention to *glissement* during the control of the arc while the skis point as closely as possible to the direction in which they are traveling (not crosswise to it). Later on, I will try to help you improve the initiation of your turns. However, it

The Purchase of the Skis on a Steep, Icy Slope

Jean-Pierre Augert's position in the upper photo illustrates perfectly what a skier should do in order to make his skis hold on a steep, icy slope. He pushes his knee inward as much as possible and balances on his outside leg by leaning his upper body downhill (angulation). This photo is the third in the photo-montage and corresponds with the precise instant when the edges bite the most (the edgeset).

Gustavo THOENI in Slalom

This young Italian, who shared most of the victories of the first half of the 1970 season with Patrick Russel, was with Russel the most observed and most imitated of racers. His peculiar position is very different from that of the best slalom skiers five years ago. Note the often « seated » position, the sometimes very wide stance, the emphasized knee action (inward knee push for starting the turn, controlling the arc, and for establishing the platform for starting the next turn).

Controlling the Arc of the Turn with Weight Distributed over the Full Length of the Foot — Skis "Flat"

Carving with the Tails

Carving with the Tips

ON INTERMEDIATE SLOPES, LEARN TO CONTROL THE ARC OF YOUR TURNS

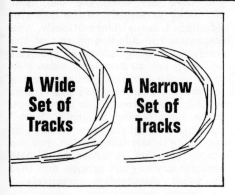

A very slight pivoting of the skis during the initiation of the turn and a close correspondence between their direction of travel and the arc of the turn result in a narrower, smoother set of tracks.

is imperative, regardless of the type of initiation you use, that you try right now to control the width of the

track your skis leave in the snow during turns. The closer your skis remain to facing the direction of travel, the narrower the tracks they will leave.

How do you leave narrow tracks? Try this exercise on intermediate slopes and at a moderate or slow speed at first. Try also to keep your skis as flat as possible on the snow. Once you have initiated a turn, follow the same suggestions as those I gave you for discovering and using the pivot point of your skis through sideslipping. Support yourself mainly on your outside ski, but put some weight on both skis. Scissor as little as possible. If possible, work with your knees squeezed together. Distribute your weight over the full length of your feet, and be sensitive to the slightest reactions of your skis. In one word, *guide* your skis through the arc of the turn using

The Start of a Flat Ski Turn

as much feel as possible. You will discover that there are many ways of maintaining the pivoting action of your skis by playing with ski-snow friction, but that there is only one way to make them pivot and conserve maximum *glissement* at the same time. *You should be neither forward nor back but exactly on the pivot point of your skis.* Your position should be perfectly normal, slightly flexed as usual and slightly angulated in order to avoid catching outside edges. Your trunk and arms should be relaxed because everything should happen in your legs. Be careful not to bend your ankles excessively so that you can avoid putting your weight too far forward. Be careful to avoid sitting too far back, as well.

If you have trouble leaving a narrow track, there are three possible explanations. Either you pivot your skis too much during the initiation phase of the turn,

you have developed the bad habit of leaning excessively to the inside of sideslipped turns (Unconsciously, you emphasize the sideslipping so that the resulting braking action of the skis will help you to remain in balance in spite of the fact that you are leaning too much. Lean less, and your tracks will become narrower.), or thirdly, you might be assuming a single, "sure" position throughout the turn. By remaining in this stiff position, you are unable to react in order to remain continuously in good balance, and thus to avoid sideslipping excessively.

Learn to carve your turns on the tails of your skis

What does "carved" turn mean ? It is time you learned to distinguish the two ways of controlling the arc of a turn : 1) with a flat ski, 2) by carving. You

The Start of a Turn Carved on the Tail of the Outside Ski

The Control of the Arc of a Turn through Carving with the Tail of the Outside Ski

are already familiar with the first kind which we just discussed. In the second kind the skis are no longer used for sideslipping but for cutting an almost unsideslipped curve with the steel edges. Carved turns require good quality skis. The use of carving by the best racers has only become common in the last dozen years. Pleasure skiers who know how to carve effectively in order to hold better on icy slopes or on hard snow, in slalom and in giant slalom, are rare. There are also two kinds of carved turns. The older, probably first promoted by Guy Perillat, is carved with forward lean, and the second kind, of which Patrick Russel was the first specialist, is carved with backward lean. The first depends on the bite of the forward two thirds of the inside edge of the ski, the second on the bite of the back two thirds of this edge.

You could be wondering why I have described a carved turn with forward lean and one with backward lean but not one with evenly distributed weight. It is simply because I can only describe what I have seen. It would seem possible to carve with the full length of a modern ski only at very high speeds, and I will discuss this possibility further in the chapter concerning downhill. For now, if you have become a good skier by following my suggestions, try to learn to carve with the tails of your skis.

How do you carve with the tails of your skis? Try first on an easy slope in long fairly high speed turns. Start off in a semi-wide or wide stance. Initiate your turns and try to weight the latter half of your outside ski. Do so by pushing your knee inward slightly and by feeling the pressure on your ski as much as possible under your heel bone (calcaneus). Also, feel the inside of your shin bone (tibia) press laterally against the inside of your boot top. However, do not overdo anything. Do not exaggerate your backward lean. Use your movements precisely enough to make the back half of the inside edge of your ski act like the rudder of a boat. This "rudder" will determine the arc which your outside ski will follow. As for your inside ski, it will follow along without your doing anything in particular and without difficulty.

You will be fascinated by the feeling of *glissement,* and the precision that this type of turn gives. You might even be too fascinated by it and feel tempted to carve all your turns while sitting back slightly. This would be an error because on steep slopes, especially at the instant your skis plunge into the fall-line, you would lose your balance backwards. You would also have trouble initiating a rapid series of turns, you would not unweight enough, nor would you properly emphasize the setting of your edges. You would ski very undynamically. Do not forget that in most of your turns you should remain in perfect balance over your skis, that is, exactly over their pivot point.

At higher speeds carve on your tips

In order to learn to carve with forward leverage, use an intermediate slope covered with hard snow. At a fairly high speed once you have initiated a turn try to weight the inside edge of your outside ski while leaning forward slightly. In order to do so, feel the pressure under your big toe on the inner sole of your boot and the thrust of your shin bone against the inside of

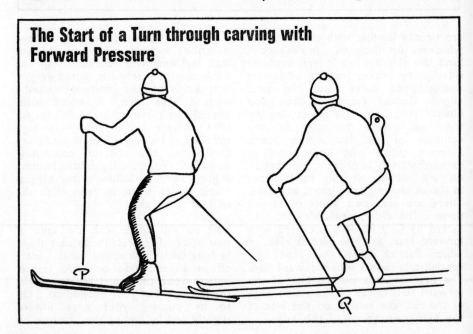

The Start of a Turn through carving with Forward Pressure

The Finish of a Turn with Forward Pressure

your boot top. You exert this pressure by pushing your outside knee forward and inward. Your upper body is balanced over your outside ski through a slightly more angulated position than normal. The edge under the forward part of your ski will bite, and you will feel as if your ski had been engaged in a smooth curved groove. Your ski has then become an actual tool for carving the hard snow. The radius of your turn will depend on your edgeset angle and on the amount of forward leverage you use. I have only mentioned your outside ski because it plays the major role. Carving on the inside ski is also possible, and if your legs are bowed, you will tend to do this. However, carving on the inside ski is a bad habit which I will discuss further in the chapter on "very good skiers". For now, concentrate all your effort on your outside ski, and if you do not feel in good balance, lift at least

the tail of your inside ski off the snow. You will thus feel the necessity of pushing your knee forward and inward and the need of angulating with your hips. "Carving on your tips" will then be very helpful to you, mainly for holding on ice. Though it is very effective on intermediate slopes at fairly high speeds, you will have to avoid this technique on steep slopes where it is not very secure, and on flat slopes where it slows your skis.

Making a habit of constantly carving on your tips would be a serious mistake. Your balance, your *glissement*, and your reaction time would all suffer. *Depending on the snow and slope conditions, you should control the arc of your turns either with a flat ski or by carving with your tails or your tips.*

Once you have become a virtuoso, you will be able to combine these three types of *glissement* in a single turn.

Check in 1/10th of a second with an edgeset

You have probably been surprised by the sight of good skiers, slalom skiers in particular, "hitting" their edges for a fraction of a second in order to slow down, sending a burst of snow into the air. You are now ready to learn the same movement; however, in order to really feel it, follow these steps.

Set your edges from a lateral sideslip. On a hard frozen, steep slope, sideslip laterally while facing the fall-line with your upper body, ready to plant your pole. Suddenly set your edges by pushing your knees inward (uphill) and increasing your angulation. At the same instant, plant your pole down the hill in order to stabilize your balance. Your sideslip will stop instantaneously. Sideslip again right

A Lateral Sideslip
into an Edgeset

down the fall-line, then hit your edges

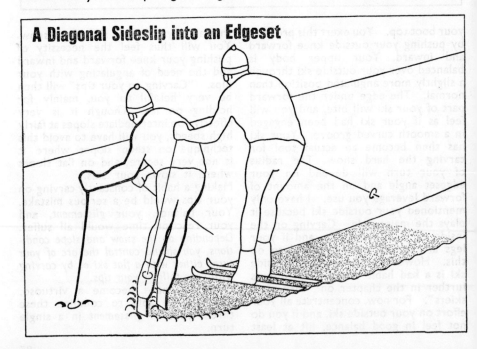

A Diagonal Sideslip into an Edgeset

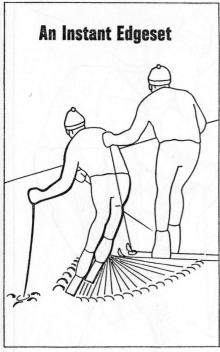

An Instant Edgeset

planting your outside pole. To do the exercise better try to weight primarily the tails of your skis as you begin pivoting. At the same time turn your upper body toward the fall-line in preparation for your pole plant. Try it first at a slow speed, and once you have understood the movement, start directly from a traverse. By a slight down motion and a predominant weighting of the tails, your skis will pivot while you prepare to plant your pole and hup! You set your edges. Start again and repeat this exercise hundreds of times until you have mastered "hitting your edges" which will permit you to stop completely, to check, or to feel a solid platform on the snow, all in a tenth of a second. This platform, by the way, will be useful for initiating some turns.

On steep slopes turn with rebound

and plant your pole. Repeat the exercise dozens of times. Little by little, through accentuating the inward push of your knees and flexing your legs slightly each time, you will feel your edgeset improve. Now, try the exercise from a traverse.

Set your edges from a traverse. Try it first from a diagonal sideslip. You will notice immediately that it is necessary to pivot your skis slightly. Pivoting here will not be any more difficult than at the beginning of the sideslip. You will also feel that the slight down motion you use for pivoting will prepare you for hitting your edges. You will set your edges in exactly the same way as you set them from the lateral sideslip, that is, by making them bite abruptly by pushing your knees inward, increasing your angulation, and

If you have learned, and only if you have learned to "hit your edges", will you learn rebound turns for steep slopes quickly.

How do you make a rebound turn? Start a slow traverse on a steep slope. Set your edges sharply (sideslip the tails, then hit your edges and plant your pole), but instead of stopping on the edgeset, rebound from the snow continuing to balance on your pole plant while pivoting your skis toward the fall-line. Through reading, this movement will seem very complicated. In fact, it is much easier than it seems because all the successive moves link together naturally. Because of the slight sideslip before your edgeset, your legs are "compressed" during the edgeset and they make you rebound just like a rubber ball once it has been compressed. A similar mechanism of

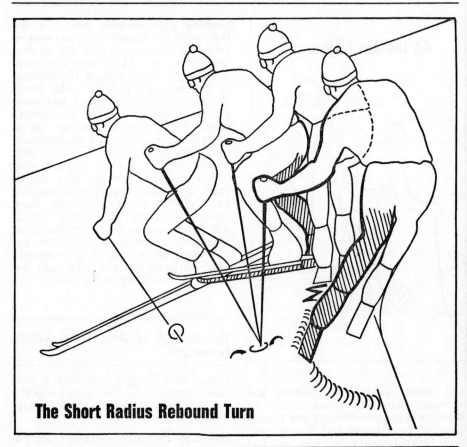

The Short Radius Rebound Turn

torsional compression results in the pivoting of the skis at the time of the rebound (see chapter on "Technical Analysis"). To convince yourself, do the following exercise which will prepare you for the rebound turn.

First improve your rebound garland

Rebound is a type of recoil, that is, an explosion, or a dynamic thrust. Start in a traverse on an intermediate or steep slope. Pivot into an edgeset,

The Rebound Garland

and plant your pole. Then, instead of stopping with the edgeset, rebound and traverse again. Use your pole plant during the edgeset in order to improve your balance. You will be surprised by the fact that during the rebound your skis will pivot downhill and come back into contact with the snow in a traverse which is often steeper than your initial traverse. The vertical rebound following the downward thrust of the edgeset, and the pivoting preceded by the uphill pivoting before the edgeset, are one and the same movement. They are the release phase of a wind up-release movement. Such movements are difficult to describe but easy to do once one has felt them because the nature of the wind-up determines that of the release. Do not try too hard to understand. Keep practising the exercise, and once you feel it work, you will avoid pivoting too far!

Wedel on steep slopes

On a steep slope set your edges

sharply, plant your pole, and make a very short radius turn while straightening your body as little as possible. As soon as you have passed the fall-line, slow down your sideslip and set your edges again when your skis are across the hill. Make a second rebound turn, etc...

The Seated Position in Check Wedeln

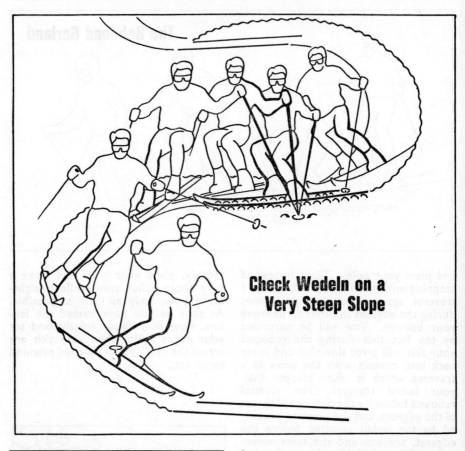

Check Wedeln on a Very Steep Slope

Verify your body position during your edgeset

Your trunk should be facing down the fall-line, your arms opened wide, and your pole planted down the hill. These are the conditions which during the rebound will cause your skis to pivot downhill enough (to at least a 45 degree angle) to allow you to start a turn without throwing your hips or stemming. Your upper body should be facing down the fall-line at each edgeset. In addition you must try to keep it constantly facing down the fall-line during your turns so that your wedeln results 100 % from the work of your legs underneath.

Check constantly with the tails of your skis

The error which could most easily prevent you from doing a good check wedeln is an insufficient weighting of the tails of your skis. Current ski design makes it necessary to use the support of the tails as much as possible

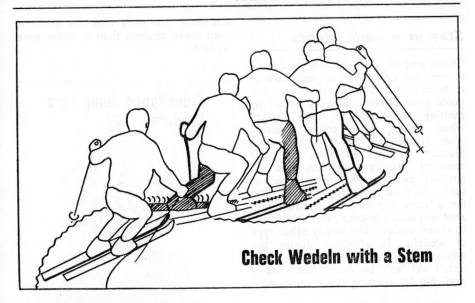

Check Wedeln with a Stem

in order to make the skis hold effectively when they are placed across the fall-line. Since you must prepare to make your skis hold during the second half of a turn, you should weight the tails as much as possible as soon as your skis come back into contact with the snow after the rebound. Because you are balancing on the tails, you will be able to allow your legs to pivot under your trunk during the turn without pulling your trunk into a rotation.

Do not straighten up during your rebound

You know and you have felt that following your edgeset your skis are unweighted and pivoted at the same time, and that both mechanisms are aspects of the same "release". But careful! If instead of remaining in a low body position, you straighten up during your rebound, your skis will

resist pivoting, and you will have to start the turn with some other movement (rotation or hip projection either of which would result in a turn impossible to control in wedeln rhythm). Also, be careful to avoid straightening up with an up motion after setting your edges. Remain constantly in a low, flexed position.

Lateral Thrust in Check Wedeln

WEDELN ON STEEP SLOPES

Stay in a wide stance

Check wedeln is much easier in a wide stance, not only because your balance is better, but also because you can make your outside ski hold better by pushing your outside knee inward when setting your edges. Because your outside ski holds better, your platform is more effective, and your rebound projects you up the hill farther, pushing your skis into the turn. In a wide stance you will also feel a lateral thrust (from one turn into another) which is even more important in check wedeln than in any other type of wedeln. In addition, during the edgeset on the downhill ski, your uphill ski will be more immediately available for starting the coming turn.

Check wedeln with a stem

Even the best skiers move through a slight stem position when they check wedel down a steep slope. What kind of a stem is it? Exactly the same as the downhill stem check which I suggested to the intermediate skier. Would you like to try it? At the instant you are going to set your edges, let the tail of your outside ski slip downhill a little farther, then set your platform mainly on your outside ski. As soon as the rebound begins, your uphill ski, which has remained free, pivots into the turn. It moves before the downhill ski and the stem position is thus accentuated, but the other ski catches up very quickly. You continue the turn by weighting both skis until your next edgeset which is accompanied by a slight downhill stem. In check wedeln with a stem, the lateral thrust which occurs at each edgeset and which throws the

skis from one turn into the other is even more obvious than in widestance wedeln.

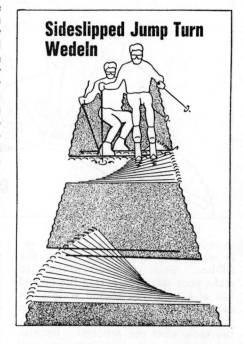

Sideslipped Jump Turn Wedeln

A preparatory step, sideslip jump wedeln

If you have trouble with check wedeln, I suggest you try its simplified form. Start on a steep slope from an exactly lateral sideslip right down the fall-line, trunk facing down the hill, downhill pole ready to plant. Set your edges sharply and rebound in place lifting your skis fairly high off the snow and pivoting them at least ninety degrees. Come back into contact with the snow weighting the tails of your skis, and start another exactly lateral sideslip immediately on this side. Repeat...

In Moguls Turn with Anticipation and «Reploiement»

As an intermediate skier you learned to use moguls for turning (page 67). Reaching the top of a mogul, trunk turned downhill (position of anticipation), you planted your downhill pole, pivoted your outside ski, and turned, sideslipping down the downhill side of the mogul. Now, however, you are going too fast when you reach the top of a bump for this technique to be effective. You can not make the same kind of turn that you use for smooth slopes either. You no longer have to unweight your skis to make them turn. On the contrary, the moguls tend to throw you into the air and your main problem is to stay in contact with the snow. You will now have to replace rebound or any up motion at the beginning of a turn with an inverse, folding movement called *reploiement*. You have just finished a turn in a field of moguls, and you are approaching a high, steep mogul with lots of speed. Standing in a relatively straight body position, head for the top of this mogul. A yard before reaching it, plant your downhill pole and flex, that is, bend your legs rapidly. Having reached the top of the bump in a low body position, pivot your outside ski into the fall-line, then,

extend your outside leg so that your ski will stay in contact with the snow. Balance on this ski. As you finish the turn on the downhill side of the mogul, you will straighten up and in good balance start traversing toward another. In this technique the bump is, in a way, "erased" by a retraction of the legs. Lurking ahead of you is the mistake of remaining in a low, flexed body position constantly. *Remember ! This folding of your body is not possible unless you straighten up beforehand.*

The pivoting effort of the outside ski is nothing more than the movement of *braquage* of the outside ski which I suggested very early to beginners, and which is valuable even to the best international ski racers.

As soon as you have understood *reploiement* you will no longer be "thrown" by moguls. You will be able to ski faster and with more security. In addition, you will have made a step toward learning *avalement* which many mistake for the simple folding movement described above. *Avalement* is really a technique for only the very advanced.

I have asked you to improve the control of the arc of your turns. I also hope

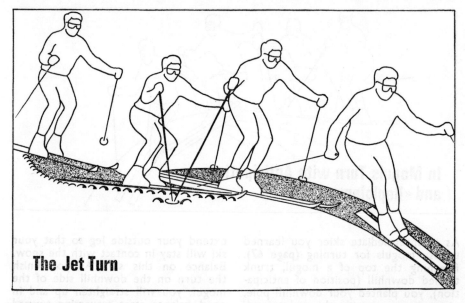

The Jet Turn

to have made you feel a real edgeset on steep slopes, not only a check edgeset, but an edgeset which is also a platform for starting a turn with rebound or for starting the short turns of wedeln. If you have learned how these two movements feel, you are ready to learn what is often called a pure christy, that is, a turn of perfect elegance and economy of movement which is effective in all kinds of snow. In other words, you can learn the instructor's "final form" parallel turn.

How do you make a jet-turn

To begin, start traversing on a well-packed intermediate slope. Pivot your skis uphill slightly by letting your tails sideslip, and prepare to plant your downhill pole. You will thus be able to stop sideslipping and support your-self with the pole plant during a single precise edgeset movement.

Set your edges much more softly than you would for a rebound turn, and remain in a higher body position. Flex your legs slightly as your edges begin to bite and as you plant your pole for balance. You will not feel a real rebound but a sort of upward thrust which you accentuate by extending your legs without, however, straightening them completely. You then feel your skis start gradually into the turn. This movement is called down-up motion. In sum, this is a slow-motion description of the mechanism which you felt while learning the rebound turn. You will tend to be a little too rough in your movements at first. After the edgeset your skis will lift off the snow and pivot too incisively into the turn. This mistake is not too serious. You will gradually learn to move with more sobriety, more economy. As for the rest of the turn, you can make it either on a flat ski or

TURN WITH PRECISION IN A NARROW STANCE, THE JET-TURN

by carving as you choose. I suggest, however, that you practise a large number of flat ski jet-turns, making sure that your tracks on the snow remain as narrow as possible. In this way you will acquire the "ski-snow" sensitivity common to all very advanced skiers.

The essentials for jet-turns

First, it is essential to start the sideslip by weighting the tails of your skis slightly. In this way it is easier for your skis and legs to remain pivoted uphill without affecting the position of your upper body which remains facing downhill. Next, it is necessary to be in the correct position in the platform-pole plant phase, that is, in a position of angulation and anticipation. (Anticipation in this case is a slight downhill pivoted position before the initiation of the turn.) Finally, after the up motion, even in a narrow stance, it is necessary to balance mainly on the outside ski of your turn and to angulate

slightly in order to avoid catching your outside edges at the initiation of the turn. In addition, you must no longer be sitting back slightly but you should balance over the full length of your skis in order to avoid sideslipping the tails excessively at the beginning of the arc of the turn. If you want to carve on the tips, you must move from the tails of your skis in the platform phase to the balls of your feet during your up motion.

The gliding jet-turn, skis glued to the snow

The jet-turn which we just described, in spite of being initiated by a very dynamic down-up motion, nevertheless involves a check. It is therefore a poor turn for the development of *glissement*, our constant goal. From now on you can move toward a much more effective turn which also involves a platform but almost no checking. (This turn is described as a preparation for the "S" turn with *avalement* in the

The Gliding Jet Turn

95

chapter entilted "Very Good Skiers" page 126.) Instead of sideslipping and pushing laterally on your edges by down-up motion from a traverse use a down-up motion to make your skis describe a smooth arc and, head back uphill. Then, during the following unweighting phase pivot your skis into the turn just as you would pivot them into a normal jet-turn. If you are able to do this movement, you will notice that your skis will not only check less, but also that they will tend to lift off the snow less during the initiation of the turn. They may even remain constantly in contact with the snow. This sliding jet-turn is more effective on ice because it is carved, more effective in powder because it facilitates backward lean at the beginning of the turn, and more effective in moguls as it facilitates *glissement* in the narrow grooves between the bumps.

Classic wedeln

Several types of wedeln exist since this type of skiing is characterized essentially by the rhythm of the turns which are linked together down the fall-line. From the first chapter on, I have suggested different forms of rudimentary wedeln, one with a wide stance, another with a stem, and I have just discussed check wedeln on steep slopes. There are types of wedeln performed only with the knees, others which involve inward lean, and still others which involve bouncing from mogul to mogul. Some are technically sound and have evolved from the wedeln called "classic". Others are unsound and add little to ski technique. This is why I think you should learn classic wedeln. In order to do so you should have already understood and felt how to set your edges, how to

make a jet-turn, and how to control the arc of your turns with a flat ski.

How to do classic wedeln

On an intermediate, or even on a flat slope start a jet-turn from a fairly steep traverse, that is, a traverse fairly close to the fall-line. In a fairly straight body position, while ready to plant your downhill pole, start a sideslip with the tails of your skis. Now make your edges bite by bending your legs slightly and plant your downhill pole while your trunk faces the fall-line. Profiting from the support of your edgeset, straighten up by extending your legs, and let your skis pivot downhill. Balance carefully on your skis so that they pivot smoothly, flat on the snow. Balance mainly on your outside ski. As soon as your skis have crossed the fall-line, check their pivoting action slightly, prepare to plant your pole, and begin another jet-turn. Your wedeln will be classic if these two phases are obvious: 1) platform phase (the expression "edgeset" gives the idea of a movement which in this case would be too brutal), and 2) pivoted flat ski sideslip phase. The first is quick and dynamic; it is the power phase. When the rhythm accelerates, the second phase becomes shorter and shorter, but must be present because the first phase can become extremely brief. At the limit of possible reaction time a truly expert skier can make two and a half turns per second in classic wedeln.

Other types of wedeln

Once you have learned classic wedeln, you can go on to other types: check

Anne-Marie Proell, one of the best young Austrian slalom specialists, demonstrates perfectly a Jet Turn with marked unweighting and carving with the outside ski.

Check Wedeln on a Steep Slope
by Patrick RUSSEL

Check wedeln on a very steep, icy slope is a valuable exercise for any skier, even the virtuoso. No other exercise develops so well the sense of balance on the skis, the speed in using the edges, the ability to check with the tails of the ski, the use of the legs while holding the trunk stable, and an effective use of the pole plant for stabilizing and for slowing down. Only check wedeln can help the imbalanced skier develop a balanced position with dynamic unweighting and lateral thrust. Check wedeln also helps the skier, who holds his feet too close together, to discover the advantages of the wide stance.

Rebound is a more dynamic down-up motion performed from a low body position. The relaxation movement which results in the compression of the skier's body is checked by the contractation of the extensors. The rebound results from this action which resembles the action of a compressed tennis ball. Using rebound effectively depends on the body position assumed during the down motion and especially on the pivoted position of the trunk in the direction of the fall-line (*vissage* or anticipation). This position results in the rapid pivoting of the skis once they are unweighted.

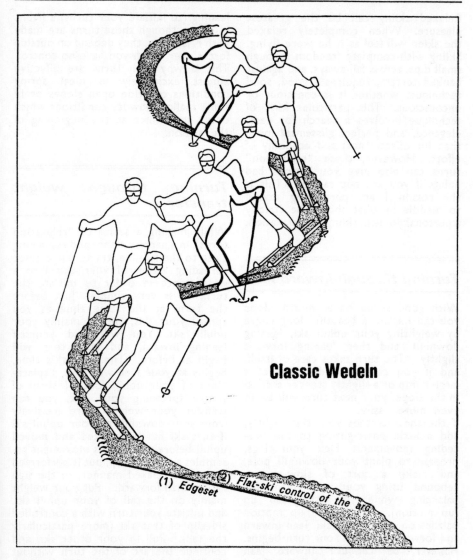

Classic Wedeln

(1) Edgeset   (2) Flat-ski control of the arc

wedeln, which we have already seen, wedeln in powder, and *avalement* wedeln which you will see later, wedeln carved on the tips, wedeln carved on the tails, *reploiement* wedeln in moguls, or wedeln by lateral thrust from one ski to the other. The essential element

in all of these forms will be the rhythm : 1) platform, 2) control of the arc of the turn, no matter how quick the turn. Therefore, neither a bounce from edgeset to edgeset nor a simple jump from outside ski to outside ski can be considered real wedeln.

GOOD SKIERS, LEARN RELAXATION TURNS

Relaxed skiing can be the greatest pleasure. When completely relaxed the skier will feel as if he were flying. Skiing with complete freedom through small dips, across fall-aways, and against banked terrain, requires a good, solid technique, whether it is conscious or unconscious. This particular kind of technique involves a search for ease, elegance, and perfect *glissement* more than for effectiveness and economy of effort. However, these "relaxation" turns can also give you serious bad habits if you are not careful. This is the reason I am permitting myself to meddle in what should be strictly a personal domain, skiing for relaxation.

Turning through inward lean

With good speed on a smooth slope you can initiate a beautiful long curve by weighting your uphill ski, leaning downhill, and then leaning forward slightly. The turn takes care of itself, and if you can take advantage of a large bump or a slightly steeper section in the slope, your next turn will begin even more easily.

If the snow catches your skis slightly, add a little unweighting to the preceding movement. Flex your legs, prepare to plant your downhill pole, and make a sort of slow-motion rebound using your pole plant for balancing while you straighten up (up motion). During the up motion balance on your uphill ski, lean inward and forward slightly. Your turn begins. *However, be careful !* Inward lean creates sideslipping which centrifugal lorce then accentuates. Too much fean results in too much sideslipping and in instability because any variation in the amount of friction caused by the sideslip will disturb your balance. Furthermore, you should not make

leaning (to initiate your turns) a habit. In effect, though these turns are made with relaxation, they depend on outside forces over which you have no control. This is why such turns are effective almost exclusively in ideal spring conditions on wide open slopes or in some shallow powder conditions which occur sometimes at the beginning of the season.

Turning through weight transfer

While making a series of "relaxation turns" in a narrow stance and remaining close to the fall-line, try to use a quick spreading action of your skis into a wide stance in order to initiate the turn. It is very simple. Just before the turn, at the same time as you spread your skis, weight mainly your uphill ski. You will find yourself leaning inward, and your turn will begin as before. The lean, this time, begins at your feet with the displacement of your uphill foot. Instead of simply spreading your feet, you can transfer your weight more incisively from your downhill to your uphill ski if that ski has been lifted and moved uphill beforehand. This movement resembles a skating step, but is performed in a more relaxed manner, to the side rather than forward. Put your weight mainly on the tail of your uphill ski, and initiate your turn with a controlled sideslip of that ski (more particularly the tail). Pull in your other ski, and continue the arc of the turn without sideslipping very much. Next, move your uphill ski uphill again, and start a new turn by weight transfer. *This turn has three advantages.* It is more effective on snows which catch your skis. The braking action of your skis is not as great as in a forward leverage

A "Relaxed" Turn through Simple Inward Lean

turn. (It will be useful in powder snows for this reason.) It causes you to use the support and *glissement* of the tails of your skis. (You almost sit back.) In addition the turn favors a prolonged support on your outside ski. This support counterbalances the unfortunate tendency, caused by simple inward lean, to weight your tips and inside ski.

through Down-Up Motion and Inward Lean

from a Wide Stance or a Lateral Step

It is becoming very fashionable to ski powder, and the increase in the number of powder skiers is a very satisfying sign of the improvement of the general level of ability of most skiers. It is also a sign of a greater appreciation of nature. For some, however, powder skiing is only a form of snobbism. One encounters an increasing number of skiers who are technically incapable of skiing deep snow but who insist on trying it, and thereby multiply their chances of injury. They have not understood that, like international competition, good powder skiing technique is a result of many long years of skiing. They have not realized that it is necessary to know how to ski well before trying to ski deep snow and, finally, that the search for powder snow can even lead to death. I am thinking about those young and not so young fools whose tracks move closer and closer to avalanche zones and sometimes stop there...

However, from time to time you will hear that there is unpacked snow on such and such a run. You will hear it from returning skiers proud to talk about their exploits, or you might see these skiers for yourself moving through the deep snow with ease. Don't miss the opportunity; make a run in the powder!

A Seated Position and Narrow Stance for Powder

In powder, keep your skis flat, hold them together, and sit back

The condition of your skis will make a great difference. Over-cambered or stiff skis, or skis with an imbalance between tip and tail sections will make powder skiing difficult for you.

As for your general body position in powder, you should :

1) *ski with your feet together.* If you hold a wide or semi-wide stance, your skis will tend to cross or diverge because of the inconsistency of the snow. However, if you hold them together, they will be easier to control.

2) *sit down with a straight back.* If the powder is not deep, you will be able to pull your tips up where you can see them. Thus, you will gain confidence and make your turns more easily. If the snow is deep and the full length of your skis remains completely covered, weighting the tails will force the tips upward in an oblique position (similar to the position of hydroplanes or waterskis) which allows your skis to plane in this largely fluid element.

3) *hold your skis flat during turns.* Their sides will then cut through the snow whereas if there is an edgeset angle, the skis must push snow laterally. The snow then compresses under the

A Turn with Hip Projection

pressure and makes lateral movements of the skis more difficult.

In powder, long radius turns with hip projection

This down-up motion turn requires that you sit back and that you throw your outside hip. Start in a traverse, in a balanced but slightly seated position and with your feet together. To prepare for the turn, weight your tails by flexing your legs, and get ready to plant your downhill pole by pivoting your trunk downhill. Your tips move up to the surface of the snow. Immediately after your down motion, plant your downhill pole and straighten up slowly, gradually accelerating the up motion so that your skis will not sink. At the same time as you begin straight-

ening up, throw your hip to the outside, and your unweighted, practically flat skis (either at the surface of the snow or parallel to that surface underneath it) will begin to turn. You then start to weight your skis (mainly the tails) as gradually as possible. During the turn you should feel as if you were sitting down in a chair.

For difficult snow, the two phase, short radius turn

The preceding turn is only possible in light powder whereas the two phase short turn is possible in heavy or even rotten snow. The principle is simple. Jump from the traverse to the fall-line, then after building up momentum and balance in a straight run of a yard or two continue the

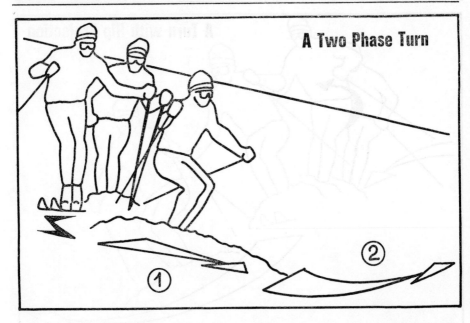

A Two Phase Turn

①
②

turn. You must prepare your jump to the fall-line in exactly the same way as you did the preceding turn but more dynamically. Flexed into a seated position, pole ready to be planted, trunk facing downhill, you plant your pole and straighten up. Your skis then pull up out of the snow as they pivot to the fall-line. Absorb your landing carefully by flexing your legs into a seated position and weighting your tails. Let your skis run a yard or two down the fall-line, and in good balance pivot on the tails of your skis in order to continue the turn to a traverse.

In powder, wedel with hip projection

If you wedel well, it will certainly be easier for you to wedel in powder than it would be for you to make long

radius turns. There is a simple explanation. In the second half of your turns the snow is compressed under your skis and makes the rest of the turn difficult. In wedeln, this second half of the turn is very short, and in this case the compressed snow serves as a beneficial support for starting the next turn.

This form of wedeln resembles classic wedeln very closely. In order to adapt it to powder : 1) Increase your backward lean by flexing your legs during the platform phase. 2) During the following up motion, as you balance on your planted pole, throw your hip to the outside of the turn. Your skis will start into the turn while remaining flat, that is, parallel to the surface of the snow and will cut through it laterally. 3) Weight your skis gradually, mainly the tails, by taking a seated position. When you feel the snow compress under your tails, start another up motion, etc...

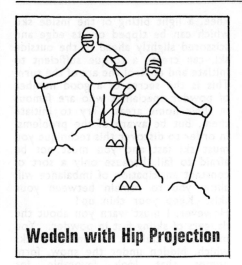

Wedeln with Hip Projection

In very difficult snows, learn to stem

There is nothing dishonorable about turning with a stem in snows saturated with water. Sometimes stem specialists show up even virtuoso skiers who have avoided this important movement, because the stem in heavy snow is not easy. I can only repeat the suggestions I have already given so abundantly to beginners. The suggestions will simply be more difficult to follow because heavy snow will not let you get away with the slightest error. To turn downhill, stem your uphill ski. Weight both skis by holding your seat exactly between both of them. Adjust the edgeset angle of both skis in order to control your speed while you plunge toward the fall-line. *Let your skis run down the fall-line for an instant* and then weight your outside ski slightly so that you "complete" the turn. Do not try to pull your inside ski over to your outside ski immediately. Pivot the ski

until both are parallel, then pull them together.

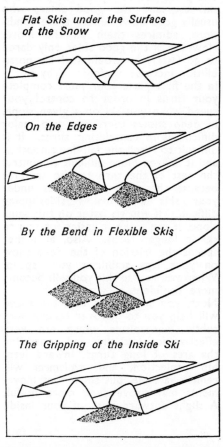

Flat Skis under the Surface of the Snow

On the Edges

By the Bend in Flexible Skis

The Gripping of the Inside Ski

During turns made in powder snow, flat skis cut laterally through the snow and encounter little resistance. Edged, they compress the snow laterally and turning them is more difficult except if they are very flexible. Flexible skis bend in an arc similar to the arc of the turn. Deep powder specialists also use their inside ski by pushing their inside knee to the inside of the turn. The gripping of the inside ski results in the turn.

GOOD SKIERS, TRY POWDER

Speed can be of precious assistance

The great powder specialists generally ski fast, and the good skier, who usually goes slowly under these conditions, admires them all the more. However, if the good skier only dared to go faster, he would feel his possibilities increase tenfold. Why ?

In the first place your must complete your turns in order to control your speed when you ski on a given slope. In deep snows there are two major difficulties in completing turns. It is difficult to reach the fall-line smoothly, and it is even more difficult to control the rest of the turn to the traverse because the snow compresses under your skis and makes sideslipping difficult. If you go faster on this same slope, it can make it easier for you to ski in longer turns. Also, at higher speeds the friction of the deep snow on your legs stabilizes your speed. When you realize this you will become more confident.

Next, you will notice that the speed will help you to discover certain very subtle mechanisms which are very effective for initiating and controling the arcs of long turns. Inward lean, hip projection, and *avalement* will remain valuable, but slight foot movements may prove even more useful. A slight outward push of your inside knee, a light biting of the inside ski, which can be tipped on its edge and scissored slightly ahead of the outside ski, can create a torque sufficient to initiate and control the arc of the turn. This is the secret of a good number of powder specialists who are famous in their home areas. Try to initiate them, but be aware of the problems. In order to discover this technique you must ski fast and you must not be afraid to fall, because only a sort of constant anticipation of imbalance will allow you to remain between your skis. Keep your chin up !

However, I must warn you about the dangers of skiing fast in powder. You must be careful not to run into rocks which, hidden under the snow, form humps that look favorable for starting turns. You should also watch out for drifts which form overnight on some ridges and which could give way underneath you, burying you under several feet of snow. A treacherous funnel shaped hole can form in a matter of hours, and hide a huge boulder underneath. You must also be alert for unmarked avalanche areas or areas closed by the ski patrol. Several powder fans are killed each year in these areas. Do not get carried away with the excitement caused by beautiful powder snow and a bright sunny day. Remember that this beautiful snow can increase the dangers of the mountains.

GOOD SKIERS CORRECT YOUR BAD HABITS

Any good skier capable of skiing on any slope in almost any condition has trouble in some cases. Maybe you have trouble on ice, in powder, in the increasingly monstrous moguls, or in slalom or giant slalom courses. If so, chances are that you are making a mistake, maybe a very slight one which can be corrected. Maybe too you have

acquired a bad habit which disturbs your balance, or your elegance or effectiveness, and which you have been unable to discover and correct. Would you like to try once more ? In our club we have had so much experience developing racers from good skiers that I am sure the following suggestions will be very valuable. In some cases they may also be completely new to you.

When you ski with other good skiers of about your same level, do you feel that you cannot do some of the things they do because your balance is poor ? You would feel this way particularly in uneven or unpacked snow and on difficult terrain. Perhaps it is true that your balance is not as good. Just as some people can high jump six feet while others barely make three, some people have better balance than others. However, my experience indicates that limited balance results more often than not from certain technical mistakes which can be corrected.

Balance depends on sensitive feet

I emphasized very strongly the fundamental role of the feet (in the chapter "Intermediate Skiers, Correct Your Bad Habits", page 70) first in perceiving the pressures exerted underneath them, and more precisely, under any single part of the sole of your ski boot. Next, there are the pressures which vary in strength, and which you exert with your feet on different parts of the soles of your boots, or with your ankles against the tops of your boots. Many good skiers have never thought about this sensitivity even though they attach a great deal of importance to their trunk, arm, and hip movements. For a few years now much more has been said about the action of the legs in skiing, but not enough has been said about the role of the feet. Try to develop a conscious sensitivity in them and you will immediately enrich the thousands of balancing reflexes which are transmitted to and from your feet.

A very serious mistake, watching your skis while skiing

This mistake is very common and almost never corrected. It is, by the way, very difficult to correct. To do so takes a long time. However, you should make the effort. Not only will you be able to ski better, but you will better enjoy your beautiful snow covered surroundings by observing the terrain around you. Only under these conditions will your sense of sight be able to play its important role in helping you to stay in balance. If your field of vision is restricted to a pair of zigzagging tips and a couple of square yards of snow, you will miss certain points of reference, certain landmarks, which are indispensable in maintaining your balance. To correct the mistake, fix your eyes on a single point about one or two hundred yards down the slope and make short turns or wedel without losing sight of that point. At first your gaze will flicker back and forth constantly from the point to your skis, but persevere and you will soon succeed. Another remedy

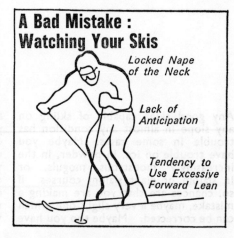

**A Bad Mistake :
Watching Your Skis**

Locked Nape of the Neck

Lack of Anticipation

Tendency to Use Excessive Forward Lean

which could act as an intermediary exercise consists in following about ten yards behind a friend and watching him constantly. Try it. You will feel much more freedom and you will be much more at ease. Your skis will no longer be instruments attached to your feet which you must force around. They will become simple extensions of your feet. Only then will you be able to discover the effective balance of a truly good skier.

Is your body position correct ?

It is very possible that like thirty per cent of all intermediates and good skiers you have adopted a poor body position. All of your movements, grafted onto this position, take on a questionable form and become much less effective. The two most serious of the common body position problems are sitting back or leaning forward constantly. We will discuss these further along. Let's take a look at the more benign errors which might still disturb your balance.

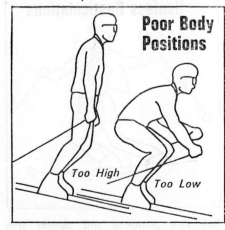

Poor Body Positions

Too High

Too Low

Too straight a body position, especially if it is used by a tall, thin skier, is

very poor at higher speeds. First, because the position is unstable and second because the play of unflexed joints is very unfavorable for recovering one's balance. This position impedes the incisive, rapid reactions characteristic of good skiers and prevents good balance.

Too low and too stiff a position is just as bad. In order to remain in a low, flexed position, a skier must contract his muscles. If he is an athlete in perfect condition, there will be no problem. Otherwise, his muscles will stiffen because of their excessive contraction, and they will prevent the small readjustments in muscle tension which form the basis of good balance.

Stiffness

Broken at the Waist

Risk of Forward Falls

"*Breaking at the waist*" will not allow good balance. Most often, breaking at the waist occurs simultaneously with an insufficiently flexed leg position, or with stiff legs. On smooth slopes this presents no problems, but in bumps or in short turns, if the skier's trunk starts to swing forward, it will tend to unbalance him. It could cause dangerous forward falls. If this is your problem, you will be able to overcome it in only an indirect manner. Try to flex your legs a little more, and try to keep them more flexible. Absorb bumps and the compression phase of turns by simply bending your legs. Also, check to see if your pelvis is properly "placed" (see following pages). Another very effective method of remedying the problem is to hold your hands chest high without ever letting them fall. Holding them this way will stabilize your trunk.

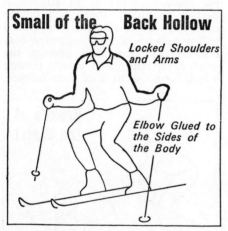

Small of the Back Hollow

Locked Shoulders and Arms

Elbow Glued to the Sides of the Body

A hollow or stiff lower back can also cause trouble. This is difficult to see in others, let alone in oneself. Too upright a position and a certain rigidity in the trunk, shoulders thrown back too far, elbows and hands held too close to the plane of the upper body, chest thrown out too far, all point to this position error. The problem could be morphological, but even if this is the fase, it should be corrected. Otherwise, during turns your trunk will move as a solid unit accompanied systematically by your shoulders, both arms, and sometimes even your head. More often than not, you will be unable to plant your pole correctly. Not only is your balance disturbed, but your technique is falsified. The correction of this error is difficult, and it takes a

long time. Ski with your hands as far forward as possible and pull in your chest, thus curving your spinal column. This is the only way you will be able to relax your back and disengage your shoulders and arms from your body.

Do you control your arm movements ? Do you plant your poles ?

Have you acquired the habit of letting your arms go any which way, or have you exaggerated movements which, performed with more moderation, might be correct ? If so, you will have a lot of trouble correcting the problem because nothing is more difficult than eliminating a useless movement which has become a conditioned reflex. As human organisms have a very poor ability to "erase" habits, you will have to substitute certain somewhat artificial positions or certain effective movements, for your poor positions and unnecessary movements.

Useless Gesticulations

Bad arm positions and useless arm gesticulations are most often associated with incorrect trunk movements or

Elbows Sticking Out

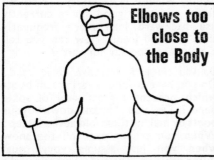

Elbows too close to the Body

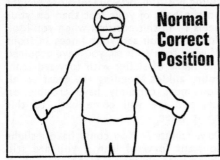

Normal Correct Position

time to make a poleplant is characteristic of the skiers who sit back too far. An arm which plunges downward is characteristic of the skier who leans to the inside of his turns excessively. Rounded arms held wide are usually associated with the excessive hip movements of some skiers.

Exaggerated Movements

positions. Arm locked too far back, elbows glued to the body or placed behind the back, as well as crossed arms, occur most often in skiers whose backs are hollow, or flat and stiffened. High elbows and rounded arms, which stiffen the shoulders and the nape of the neck, are found most often in the skier who rolls his seat forward and who uses rotation in order to initiate and control the arcs of his turns. An arm thrown high and then lowered in

We have noticed at the University of Grenoble Ski School that the chances of a pupil exaggerating any arm movement taught him are so great that we have not taught any arm movements at all for several years. Experience has proven that a correct positioning of the arms from the very first session on skis is the sole effective means of obtaining the sobriety in shoulders and arms which is absolutely indispensable to good poleplants and good balance. The poleplant at the beginning of the turn is often dispensed with altogether or performed incorrectly, either too late or too early, by skiers who use too much arm movement or too many poleplants per turn. If this is your case, you must realize that you cannot correct the problem without making an effort to plant your pole systematically at the right time and in the right place during your edgeset, counter-turn, or simple platform at the beginning of a turn (see preceding chapter). If in spite of planting correctly, you continue to gesticulate, force yourself to position your pole an instant before planting it. In tight turns or wedeln, you can position one pole as soon as the other loses contact with the snow.

Are you too far forward on your skis ?

This mistake is very common among those who have learned to ski in ski schools influenced until recently by the teaching methods called "French" or "Austrian" Technique. The desire to make clients, even beginners, ski with their feet together, and the orientation of their instruction toward a "pretty" turn, never proven effective through competition, resulted in the use of forward lean as the predominant mechanism for initiating sideslips and turns. This, to me, seems radically

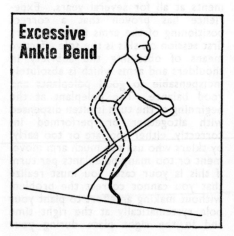

Excessive Ankle Bend

unnatural. For the beginner, every sideslip and every turn involves a control of speed and as a result requires sitting back slightly. Until recently it could have been thought that forward lean was one of the basic elements of the technique of good skiers and racers. I am now convinced that it is not. Beginners improve more quickly if they are taught nothing about forward lean. Intermediate and good skiers learn to use forward lean very rapidly when it is necessary. Virtuoso skiers and very good skiers currently use backward lean more frequently than forward lean. How can you tell if you lean too far forward ?

Do you ski with excessive ankle bend ? Do you have trouble wearing stiff boots which prevent a great deal of ankle bend ? Do you "break down" your boots by making them fold at the instep ? When you ski, or even off the snow when you just assume your usual skiing position, do you feel more weight on the balls of your feet than on your heels ? In this position when you look down, do you see your knees in front of your toes ? If so, you have acquired the habit of skiing with forward lean, your ankles bending a great deal. You must certainly have trouble on ice, and we will come back to this point later.

Do you rotate ? You could have a slight constant forward lean if you are still skiing with ski school techniques which overemphasized rotation or circular projection. These two ways of starting turns with momentum almost always require forward lean, and most ski school clients adopted it definitively. If this is your case, you will have to correct your forward lean and your technique for turning at the same time. Discover independent leg action, the wider stance, edgeset, and wedeln, and you will correct all of your bad habits simultaneously.

Rotation and Excessive Forward Lean

position easily when standing up by pulling your stomach in and pushing your pubis forward. Your seat moves down and forward. Now push it back and upward. Your pelvis tips in the opposite direction into a position which is also incorrect and which I will discuss soon. If you tend to push your seat forward, you will probably push your knees forward each time you flex your legs. You will then bend your ankles excessively, and end up leaning on your ski tips. The remedy ? Balance your pelvis by trying to stick your seat out constantly as you ski. If you are not too well endowed in this area, your friends will notice a definite improvement in your form. Notice that most racers, boys and girls, are particularly well shaped in the rear.

Do you ski with your seat pushed forward ? Here is a case of a morphological problem which becomes more apparent than usual in skiing. Having your seat pushed forward means that the top of your pelvis is tipped backward on the heads of your femurs (the thigh bones). You can feel this

Do you ski with your seat sticking out ?

This problem is not very serious right now if it is not accompanied by a stiffening in the lower back which we have already discussed. If your morphology has led you to ski in this position, you may have noticed that your ability to make your edges hold is not very good. On the one hand you must push your downhill knee inward a great deal in order to traverse on steep and icy slopes. On the other hand you cannot set your edges very dynamically. This position could also help to cause backaches if you ski very much. How do you correct this mistake ? Push your seat forward consciously and constantly while you ski, especially when you want to make your edges bite. By persevering you may be able to change your conditioned reflexes and to correct this mistake when you ski.

Pelvis Tipped Backward Seat Pressed Forward

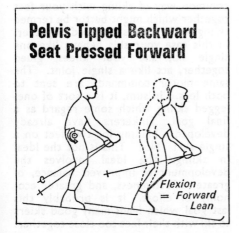

Flexion = Forward Lean

Pelvis Tipped Forward Seat Stuck Out

Edges
Hold
Poorly

to another the way he does, it would be logical that *braquage,* carving on the tails of the ski, and *avalement* would develop a generation of skiers who would sit back too much. This is already an established fact at the University of Grenoble where certain escapees from our C and D level courses (where they have learned enough to get along) come back into view sitting back in a wide stance in some fun race. These skiers normally hold too wide a stance. They are often too brutal, and they almost always lack vertical movement. They seem stiff and are slow to react.

Do you sit back excessively ?

I would be surprised if you did because most skiers, other than a few poor imitators of the champions, do not overuse this position. That could change in the next few years if this book is as successful as our preceding works... Man passing from one exaggeration

Excessive Backward Lean

Trunk Back

Seated

Do you ski with your feet too close together ?

There is a correct way to ski with your feet together. It is that of the virtuoso who has perfect feel and who succeeds, even in a narrow stance, in retaining a certain autonomy of each leg, in weighting mainly the outside ski, and in working from one foot to the other without it being noticed from the outside. And then there is the more common way of skiing with your feet together which might better be termed skiing with your skis glued together. In this case your skis behave like one single ski, and your knees, glued together, act like a single joint. The same motor commands are sent to both legs. In sum, it is a sort of one-legged skiing which some regard as a final goal. Tinkerers have already developed a binding for two feet on a single ski! No! This is not the ideal in skiing. The ideal involves the development of improved balance, of greater effectiveness, and greater economy of effort. It is probably this last goal which leads many good skiers to ski with their feet too close together.

Reploiement in Moguls

The photomontage at the beginning of this book shows Patrick Russel skiing through enormous bumps in Val d'Isère using *avalement*. *Avalement* is a technique for very good skiers. At lower speeds I suggest that intermediate skiers use *reploiement* as Patrick Russel does here. The legs begin to flex a yard before the top of the mogul; the pole is planted, and the trunk is in a position of anticipation.

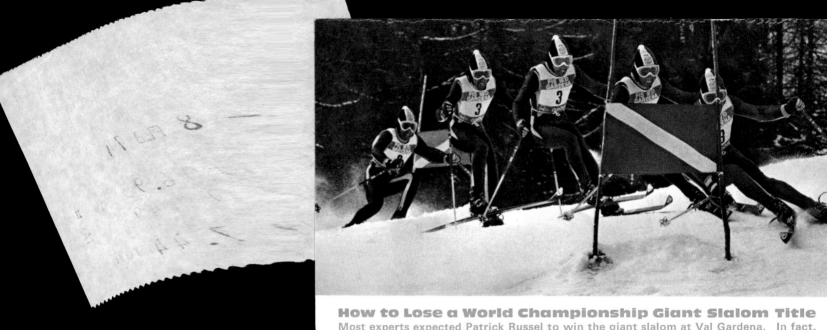

How to Lose a World Championship Giant Slalom Title

Most experts expected Patrick Russel to win the giant slalom at Val Gardena. In fact, he had the best time at the end of four-fifths of the course. He tried to cut too close to a difficult gate, leaned inside excessively, and fell. One of the primary difficulties in racing is judging the limit. In order to win a series of events, a skier should dominate his competitors by a wide margin and race while conserving a margin for error.

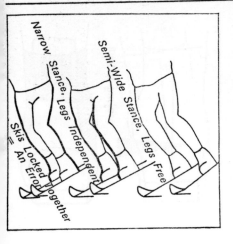

Narrow Stance. Legs Independent

Semi-Wide Stance. Legs Free

Skis Locked Together = An Error

It is true that two skis held together are effected less by divergent forces than skis which are farther apart. It therefore requires less effort to control them. This is why I will ask you to try constantly to develop independent leg action rather than to spread your feet apart. In order to feel this independence at first, however, you must spread your feet a little while making regular turns and jet-turns, or when wedeln on intermediate to very steep slopes. Once you have felt independent leg action, you will retain it when skiing in a narrow stance.

Do you balance on your outside ski ?

Good balance in a turn depends on the use of the outside ski just as good balance in a traverse depends on the use of the downhill ski. The work from outside ski to outside ski is indispensable to effective skiing. Patrick Russel, asked by a journalist for the most important hint he could give, answered without hesitation, "to work constantly from outside ski to outside ski". Surprisingly, this hint is not given much attention. For twenty years the emphasis has been on a narrow stance, and at the same time on the development of a similar action in both feet which resulted in the equal weighting of both skis. Only certain unpacked snows justify this last technique. Everywhere else, it makes no sense at all and decreases your balance and effectiveness very seriously. If you have this bad habit, you will have to make a big effort to overcome it. You should repeat "outside ski, outside ski..." to yourself constantly, whether you are making long or short radius turns. By spreading your skis apart slightly you will correct the error more easily. You can also lift your inside ski clear off the snow, not only during its initiation but also through your turn and right into the traverse. This movement will be much easier if you are trying to carve (see page 82). When you must make a particular movement with your outside leg, you will do so much more easily.

Could you be putting too much weight on your inside ski ? This mistake is even worse than the habit of continuously weighting both skis equally and is nothing more than an exaggeration of this fault. It is most common among skiers who have bowed legs and have not compensated for the problem by canting their boots (see page 183). In carved turns these skiers have less difficulty holding with their inside ski than with their outside ski. In flat ski turns they tend to catch the outside edge of their outside ski, and they try to avoid this problem by predominantly weighting their inside ski. If this is your case, cant your boots and follow carefully the suggestions given in the preceding paragraph.

Do you have good equipment ?

Having paid a great deal for it is not enough to insure that your equipment is good. It should also be the correct equipment for you as an individual, and it must be kept in good shape.

Let's look your skis over first. Are they the right length for you ? Shortskis are specially designed for adult skiers. Do not buy a normal ski in a shorter length, as manufacturers design skis for given sizes of people. A regular ski, which is too short for your height and weight, will be too soft, and your weight will not be distributed properly over the ski but remain centered under your foot. Too long a ski will generally be too stiff, and not enough of your weight will be centered under your foot. In both cases you will have trouble holding on ice. Your skis can also have defects which would prevent them from holding well. Some of these are : 1) a concave or a delaminated base sticking above the level of the edges, 2) edges which stick out above the level of the base, or which are nicked and burred due to the skis knocking together while in a narrow stance, 3) camber which is excessive or too stiff, 4) too little camber, 5) a poor distribution of flexibility over the full length of the ski, 6) torsional warping, 7) unsharpened or badly sharpened edges. Check your skis over yourself, then consult a ski specialist. At any rate, after fifteen or twenty days of skiing do not hesitate to give your skis to a specialist in a good ski shop equipped with a special sanding machine for ski bottoms and edges. After the sanding, your skis will perform like new.

Are your boots stiff enough ? I should say, are they still stiff enough because

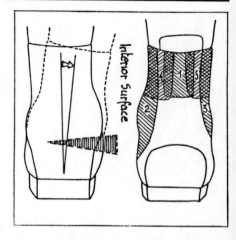

The triangle on the left boot indicates a fold. An inward movement of the leg bends the boot and makes a poor edgeset. The cross-hatching on the right boot indicates the zones which transmit leg movements to the ski. 1 transmits forward thrusts, 2 the inward thrusts which make the inside edge bite, and 3 the outward thrusts which make the outside edge bite. Zone 4 transmits the forward and inward thrusts made during a turn carved with forward pressure. 5 transmits the backward and inward thrusts for carving on the tails. The upper part of the back of the boot is also used by very good skiers for pushing on the tail of the ski.

the main problem with boots is the fact that they "break down" and lose stiffness. Plastic boots, however, seem to stay in good shape longer. This is important because, as most good skiers will tell you, good stiff boots are more important than good skis. In addition, your boots should be properly canted so that your weight is distributed properly on the ski and so that you can exert pressure properly on the tops of your boots (see page 184). Only then will you be able to make your skis hold on ice.

Is there any "play" in your bindings? If the sole of your boot is not held firmly by your toe and heel pieces, if you can move it up and down or to the side even one sixteenth of an inch, you will have trouble holding on ice. You will tend to "chatter" more, that is, your skis will vibrate sideways, catching and releasing at the end of your turns. Have your bindings adjusted properly or replace them if they are worn out or badly designed.

Maybe your body position is poor

A constant, slightly forward position causes difficulty in holding on ice. If you ski with your ankles bent a great deal, if you feel your weight predominantly on the balls of your feet, you will have trouble holding. I have analysed your problem and made suggestions for its correction on page 109.
All of the body position problems presented in the preceding chapter can give you trouble when you are trying to hold on ice. I have already discussed these problems which can limit your balance and effectiveness, but you might not be aware of them except in icy conditions where you have trouble. Maybe your body position is too straight or too low or stiff. Perhaps you break at the waist excessively and keep your legs too stiff. Perhaps you watch your skis and therefore angulate insufficiently. Maybe you are not sensitive enough with your feet when you set your edges. Perhaps you sit too far back because you are trying to ski with a modern style. I have already discussed all of these cases in the preceding chapter. Try to determine which cases apply to you and follow the suggestions I have made.

Three essential points for holding on ice

You must hold eighty per cent with your downhill ski while traversing and eighty per cent with your outside ski while turning. We will therefore be concerned here only with your corresponding foot. 1) *Your foot:* You edge your ski with pressure from your foot and shin bone against the inside of your boot. 2) *Your knee:* Without pushing your knee inward slightly you

The Edgeset

cannot exert any pressure against the inside of your boot with your shin bone. 3) *Your hip:* Without angulation, that is, without the outward displacement of your trunk in order to place the weight of your upper body on the head of your femur (thigh bone), there would not be enough inclination in your leg to cause your edge to bite. Also, the "hinge", used for the transmission of your weight to the femur, would be too soft.
The essential element in making your skis hold is the feeling of your total weight being supported on the head of your femur. Have you felt it?

You have trouble « Holding » on ice

Excessive scissoring is also a common error which makes it difficult to hold on ice. It is often due to a morphological problem. In this case the skier scissors a great deal in order to lock his outside knee behind his uphill knee. If this is your problem, a correction through canting is guaranteed (see page 183). Maybe you scissor excessively in order to start your turns. This case is more serious. Learn to initiate turns with other mechanisms. Make jet-turns and especially rebound turns, and eliminate your scissoring not by pulling your inside ski back but by pushing your outside foot forward.

Do you lack independent leg action ?

In spite of the fact that you are a good skier, you notice that you lack the ease with which your friends can work from one foot to the other in order to get out of trouble when their skis cross, sideslip too much, or catch in crusty snow. You feel very stable as long as everything is going well, but you lack the ability to react instantaneously like a slalom skier who can recover under almost any conditions. There could be many reasons for your trouble. Perhaps you ski with your feet close together too much of the time, or perhaps you hold them too close together. Maybe you have adopted a constantly forward body position. You could also be weighting both skis equally all the time instead of weighting mainly your outside ski in turns, your downhill ski in traverses. I have

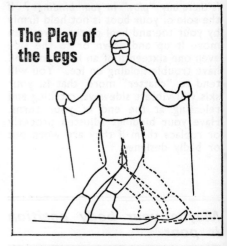

The Play of the Legs

The skier's legs should be able to move freely under his trunk which remains stable. Braquage with one leg or both, lateral thrusts, and rebound pivoting, which I suggested to beginners and intermediates, teach these skiers to use their legs without excessive movements of the trunk. Rotation and circular projection do not lead to free leg action.

already examined these problems and suggested remedies (page 112) because they not only prevent independent leg action, but also limit your balance and general ease of movement. Another error which causes a lack of independent leg action is the too frequent use of rotation or circular projection. You will find a more detailed study of this error which causes difficulty, particularly in wedeln, further along.

Do you have trouble wedeln ?

As a good skier you should by definition wedel easily. It is possible, however, that in spite of being perfectly at ease in turns or on difficult slopes in difficult snow conditions, you have trouble wedeling even on easy slopes. You must not forget that twenty years ago nobody wedeled and that the book, *Ski Technique Moderne,* which appeared in 1956 and which Jean Vuarnet and I wrote together, was the first book ever to mention wedeln. It has only been roughly ten years since wedeln first became widely practised, and this relatively recent appearance is due to a very simple fact. The techniques for turning used in the past and almost always based on rotation did not lead to wedeln. The more recent techniques which we call "modern" lead to it automatically. It is, therefore, normal that you should have trouble with wedeln if you are an older skier or if you have always skied with an older friend who learned to ski with rotation. It would also be normal if you have tried to imitate a virtuoso of the past. In rotation techniques and even in the more recent light christy, the upper body, thrown into the turn, pulls the skier's legs, then his skis into the turn. The mental picture already established is very different from that of wedeln which is characterized by the movement of the skier's legs under his upper body which remains practically immobile. The feelings experienced by the skier and the mechanisms he uses are entirely different. There is no simple suggestion for the "rotator" who wants to learn to wedel. If this is your case, I can only suggest that you learn all the exercises that I proposed for intermediate and good skiers. You should learn sideslip garlands (with backward leverage) in particular. This exercise will make you aware of the possibility of pivoting your legs under your upper body (page 65), of setting your edges (page 86), of turning with rebound and from a platform in jet-turns. In discovering this new world of technique, you will discover wedeln.

If you do not rotate, not even a little bit, in order to initiate your turns and if you still have difficulty wedeling maybe you have only those relatively benign bad habits which have already been described and which limit your independent leg action. I am thinking of skis being held too close together, of too much forward lean, of poor pelvis position, of stiffness, or even of that stupid error of watching your skis. Do not underestimate the seriousness of these mistakes, and if you want to wedel easily, follow the suggestions which have already been given for ridding yourself of these problems.

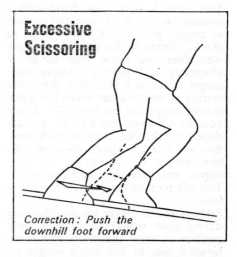

Excessive Scissoring

Correction: Push the
downhill foot forward

Excessive scissoring, skis together while the outside foot falls behind, is an error, especially if the flexion of the trailing ankle is excessive. The skier's balance is not good nor is he able to make his edges hold. His skis " chatter " easily on steep, icy slopes. It is very difficult to correct this bad habit. Above all, do not try to push your forward foot back. You should push your trailing foot forward in order to balance properly and in order to avoid " chattering ".

DO YOU HAVE TROUBLE IN MOGULS ?

It is understandable if you have trouble with the monstrous bumps which form on very steep, very busy slopes, especially if the snow is hard or icy. My suggestions will help you some but not enough to give you the aerial ease of the virtuoso skier in these conditions. My suggestions, then, will concern steep slopes and "normal" moguls but not the steep walls covered with bumps from six to nine feet high found in some areas today.

Do you have trouble checking ?

You know how to slow down with a sideslip, but in the tormented terrain of moguls you do not know where to check. Yours is the case of any skier who does not know how to check effectively and quickly. Above each mogul there is a favorable short flat section where you can make the quick checks suggested on page 87. Learn how to do them on a steep, smooth slope first, then use them in the bumps. You will learn to check whenever you like, ending up in balance on your edges, stabilized by your poleplant. You will then be ready to turn without fear.

Perhaps you also have trouble checking during your turns. If so, your body position is poor (generally too much forward lean or too much weight on the inside ski) or your choice of where to start your turn is bad. You should initiate your turn on the exact top of the mogul in order to be able to slow down immediately by sideslipping on its downhill side. You should use mainly your outside leg in checking. If the downhill side of the bump is too steep, you will just have to check in a fraction of a second on the next flat section.

Are you indecisive ?

This is explained in part if you are by nature not very aggressive, but you probably have technical problems as well. If you sometimes traverse across a whole field of moguls without making up your mind where to turn, you must be using too slow a movement in initiating your turns. If, for example, you ski with your arms dangling at your sides and if you must lift your hand, push your shoulder forward and flex your legs before planting your pole in order to launch your turn, your problem is obvious. Try to start with your trunk already turned toward the fall-line and your pole ready to plant. You will improve immediately. However, it would be better if you learned to make turns with counter turns, or jet-turns, or platform turns. A yard before the top of a favorable mogul, at the same time as you control your speed, you can balance on your outside foot and your poleplant, and your skis will pivot rapidly into the turn. In addition, these types of turns will be very helpful elsewhere, for example on steep, icy slopes where you probably run into trouble also.

Are you thrown into the air ?

You do not dare ski very fast because once you reach a certain speed, you feel yourself catapulted into the air. Would you be a down-up motion specialist ? At slow speeds a handsome up motion will bring you just to the top of a bump and result in a very elegant pivoting of your skis, but at higher speeds the mogul turns into a

A Mistake

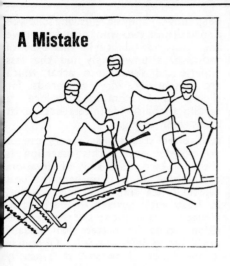

front of your upper body without causing you to lose your balance, especially if your arms are spread wide and if you use your pole plant at the beginning of the turn for balancing. You should not remain constantly in a flexed position, rather you should straighten up through the hollows and fold up over the moguls. As a result, your center of gravity and your head will not be disturbed so much by all of the variations in the terrain. By folding and unfolding your body, you almost "erase" the bumps. This implies, of course, that you know how to turn your skis at the same time as you fold. If you do not learn this movement instinctively, refer to page 66.

Perhaps you are also thrown around by the bumps because you ski with a stiff outside leg. It may be practically imperceptible on smooth slopes but it is easily detected in the moguls. In this case, make a real effort to feel your outside knee bend during each turn. "Sit down on the tail of your outside ski" as I overheard one wise old instructor explain. And remember that nine times out of ten a stiff outside leg means there is too little weight on the outside ski.

jump and your up motion throws you into the air. There is only one remedy. You must replace your up motion with a rapid down motion which is called *reploiement.* A down motion is used over the top of a mogul at slow speeds and before the top of the mogul at higher speeds. Follow the directions for intermediate skiers first (page 66), then those for good skiers (page 98). Later, you will be able to move toward learning *avalement,* that extraordinary movement responsible for the superiority of virtuoso skiers in bumps.

Are you thrown around?

If you have the habit of skiing in a very straight body position, you are probably thrown around by the bumps, and are subjecting your spinal column to dangerous vertical shocks. Assume, therefore, a more flexed, and especially a more seated position. The shocks will then throw your knees up in

Is deep snow a specialty ?

Many of those I refer to as good skiers are not good deep snow skiers. I use the term "deep" in referring to snow where your skis can no longer come into contact with the underlying base of hard snow. The fact is, a depth of four to eight inches of very light snow over a hard base presents no difficulty at all. It even makes skiing easier by providing an unaccustomed softness, as long as the skier is aggressive enough and takes advantage of the friction exerted by the snow against his boots and lower legs. This is not always the case. Some good skiers are frightened by this kind of snow, which should be a dream for them. If you are frightened, here is a cure. Join a large group of enthusiastic powder skiers who share more or less your same level of technique otherwise, and on a bright sunny day take off with the others on one of those wide open slopes where it is difficult to judge either the degree of the slope or your rate of speed. You will realize that this kind of snow poses no particular problem. No matter what technique you use, you will adapt to the conditions. The only thing you will have to accept will be to ski closer to the fall-line in order to overcome the added friction.

Real deep snow is not as easy. It is so difficult in fact that only excellent skiers can ski it easily. These excellent skiers might look like just any other good skiers on packed slopes, and they might make you think that you could do just as well as they do in deep snow, however, this would be an illusion. They have a long backlog of experience that you lack completely. After hundreds of miles and thousands of turns in a multitude of different snow conditions, they have acquired a perfect knowledge of the element, and a ski sense especially adapted to it. No one could teach you either. A similar effort in training would have turned such skiers into very good racers. In order to imitate them you will have to practise ! It is a curious fact that though good skiers will admit that because they lack race training they are not very good racers, they dislike admitting that they are poor deep snow skiers. This is why it is a fairly common occurrence to come upon a few less experienced powder skiers lost on a run in difficult

deep snow. They have usually followed a specialist or two who, proud to prove their superior ability in this type of snow, have unwittingly led the less experienced skiers into areas which are potentially very dangerous for them. As I mentioned before, a certain snobbism definitely does exist in powder skiing.

It is often stated that racers cannot ski powder well. This assertion is absurd. According to my observation, competitive skiing is perhaps the best vehicle for learning to ski deep powder, at least with current modern techniques. This is not to say that competition would be better than actually practising in deep powder. Of course it would not. However, it is usually possible to train more often than it is to practise in deep powder. Most of the time, it is less dangerous. In opposing deep snow skiing to competitive skiing, the most frequent argument is the fact that good powder skiers are often poor racers. This fact simply means that the development of deep snow technique does not include the development of certain elements essential to racing, however the inverse is not necessarily true.

The mistakes which make deep powder skiing difficult

Do you have good skis for powder ?
It is very difficult to ski in deep snow with overcambered skis or with skis that are too stiff. (Holding them base to base, you should be able to squeeze your skis together easily between your thumb and two fingers.) Shovels which lack enough surface area or which are not long enough also make powder skiing difficult as do many other elements, for example, poor distribu-

tion of flexibility between tip and tail sections, a transversally concave base, or a center groove which is too deep or too sharp. Your skis might also be too thick. It is not necessary, however, that your skis be particularly soft. Very soft skis lead to the use of a special technique and also tend to impair the balance of a skier of average talent.

Do you ski with excessive forward lean? If so, it would be normal for your skis to submarine at the beginning of your turn. You must learn a technique of turning which will allow you to sit back. Perhaps you should follow the suggestions given in the preceding chapters for intermediate and good skiers.

Do you work from one foot to the other? If so, you are naturally dynamic. You may have learned to ski from reading our earlier books, and you overcome your troubles by working from outside ski to outside ski. This will not work in deep snow. You must learn to hold your feet and knees together and to ski somewhat as if you were on a single ski.

Do you initiate your turns too brutally? In deep snow the initiation phase of your turns must be smooth and gradual. Your tracks should be perfectly regular and as narrow as possible. Try to make your movements gradually, almost in slow motion.

Do you generally ski with a straight body position? You will have to change. Simply by flexing your legs and assuming a more seated position you will improve your balance and gain greater ease. Maybe you also feel your outside leg stiffen. This is probably one of your old bad habits that reappears whenever you have trouble. Here, more than anywhere else, try to bend your outside leg. Sit down during your

turn, and absorb the pressures which you exert on your skis after unweighting.

Are you afraid of skiing close to the fall-line? In this case you make turning more difficult than it should be. Choose flatter slopes, and to begin with do not turn out of the fall-line very far. Do you know that it is easier to wedel in deep snow than to make long radius turns?

Do you have trouble "completing" turns when you wedel? This case is very common. You must learn to unweight more, to absorb more effectively after unweighting, to prolong the flexing phase of your outside leg, and to hold your outside ski flatter so that the snow is not compressed underneath. You must do all of this while in balance on the tails of your skis, particularly on the outside ski.

Are you able to stem in difficult snow? It would not be surprising if you have trouble because the stem in difficult deep snow is not an elementary movement. It requires a particular ski sensitivity developed through long experience. I will give you only one suggestion. Stem your skis and balance on both of them in the traverse before starting your turn. Let the slope pull you into the fall-line and only then finish your turn on your outside ski. It is curious that what seems to be the most effective stem turn in deep and difficult snows should be exactly the same as the first stem I suggested for beginners (see page 26). Because you are only a "good" skier you may have just as much trouble with slalom and giant slalom as you had with deep snow. Just the same, you should be able to run an easy slalom or an intermediate giant slalom without any particular trouble. To be precise, a bronze or possibly a silver medal in NASTAR should be within your reach. If this is not the case, let's look at some of the possible problems and some of the cures.

Do you have trouble with slalom ?

Do you make a few gates and then find yourself thrown out of the course ? Yours is a very common case, that of the good skier who can ski anywhere but who is not in complete control of his skis. In general, it is the relief of the run or the nature of the snow which is determining where your turns start and end, or whether they have a long or short radius. This sort of haphazard way of skiing is okay, although it can be dangerous, but it is simply not adaptable to slalom. If you want to learn to run slalom, you must learn to check instantaneously with an edgeset (page 86), to make a jet-turn (page 94), and to wedel in the "classic" manner with edgesets (page 96). Thus, you will learn to make your skis hold, and you will learn to control them through a slalom.

Especially on steep slopes you sideslip excessively and displace your skis across the fall-line too much. You probably have these problems because of the reasons stated above, and the same suggestions will be helpful. Perhaps you have some more distinct bad habits. Maybe you start your turns by throwing your trunk or your hips. Your pivoting momentum is then too great, and you have trouble controling it during the turn. Your skis, as a result, pivot across the fall-line. You then start an even more powerful rotation, and you sideslip even more. I have already discussed how this habit can prevent you from wedeling well. You will have to correct yourself through free skiing by learning a true wedeln in which only your legs move under your upper body (see page 96).

Do you hop too much ? There are three possible explanations. You might be holding your feet too close together. Your body position could be constantly too far forward. Perhaps your weight is distributed on both feet, or maybe you are having trouble because of all three problems. Widen your stance slightly and work more from outside foot to outside foot.

Are you slow in easy turns over flat sections of the slope ? This is not at all surprising because this is one of the major difficulties in slalom. In thinking of slalom we always think about turns, but rarely about *glissement*, that is, the technique for controlling the arcs of your turns. Even good slalom skiers lose precious seconds in the relatively easy, long, flat sections and flat turns usually found at the end of a slalom. Depending on the condition of the snow, soft or hard, use a flat ski and pivot on the pivot point of your skis, carve with your tails p. 181, or if the slope is slightly steeper and it is your habit, carve on your tips (see page 84).

Are "flushes" too fast for you ? If you have never practised them, it is perfectly normal that you should have trouble because their rhythm is much faster that a normal or even a very tight wedeln. Borrow ten or fifteen slalom poles. Plant them at twelve foot intervals on an intermediate slope, and practise your wedeln around the poles. Do not use just any wedeln. Use "classic" wedeln with your legs and emphasize the two phases : 1) quick phase, edgeset and poleplant ; 2) smooth phase, pivoted sideslip, etc. The faster you go, the shorter the second phase becomes.

You do not have time to plant your pole. Something is wrong with your technique. In the first place, are you holding your arms correctly with your hands placed constantly in front of you ready to plant your poles? Placing your hands correctly, force yourself to set your edges incisively and plant your pole about four to six feet before each pole. As soon as you begin the next turn, prepare to plant your other pole.

Are you afraid of ruts? Do you slam into the bottom of the ruts and lose your balance? You must be throwing your whole body into the turn (rotation, circular projection, or hip projection) instead of pivoting your skis. A good way to avoid slamming is to lead each turn with your future outside ski while you are still in balance on the outside ski of the turn you are finishing. Your outside ski will then come into contact with the rut in advance, and you can balance on it as you initiate the coming turn.

Do you have trouble with giant slalom?

At first sight, giant slalom seems easier than slalom. It actually is in many cases, but in top international competition it requires as much technical finesse as slalom. At your level, the main problem is the speed at which you must make your turns.

Do you feel that you are going too fast? This is a very subjective judgment, and you might feel out of control because you are having trouble checking. Try to get used to the speed dictated by the particular course, and be aware that it will soon reach a ceiling and not

increase any more. You will discover that it is often easier and less dangerous to let your skis run than to check. If, however, you must slow down, never check during or at the end of the turn, but in the traverses or immediately before the turn. You will thus have a more solid support for starting your next turn.

Do you sideslip excessively between gates? You probably have the same bad habits as those mentioned above for slalom. Perhaps also, you have trouble making your skis hold on hard snow and ice. I studied your case very thoroughly on page 115. Make your outside ski hold by concentrating all your effort on your position of angulation and on the three fundamental support points which have already been discussed. If you only sideslip excessively in giant slalom, perhaps you just make your turns in the wrong place. You should initiate them several yards before the inside pole of the gate and several yards above it. At the end of the turn you should start a new traverse as soon as possible in order to position yourself well above the next gate.

Are you afraid of ruts? The problem is similar to that posed in slalom but more severe because of the greater speed. Essential to skiing comfortably in a rutted giant slalom is using the outside of the ruts and not trying to ski close to the poles. The ruts establish the course you should follow, not the gates. You must turn against the outside of the rut, starting where it begins and following it to its end. Your position should be flexed low, and rather seated. Your arms should be opened wide, positioned like those of a tightrope walker, in your field of vision, and ready to plant your poles for balance. Try it. It is like a toboggan run and lots of fun.

ARE YOU AFRAID OF SPEED ?

You feel that you are a good skier, but you feel limited by your fear of speed. This is possible, but let me encourage you. Many skiers, especially the young ladies who become good skiers, are too satisfied with what they are doing. They cannot understand why they should make an effort to do better or to go faster. You have a very different attitude, and that is important because, as in any human activity, when one does not improve, one regresses. The complacent skier will go slower and slower through the years. Using less and less speed, he will eventually choose shorter and shorter skis until his skis are only as tall as himself, or even shorter. He then has less stability and will go slower yet until he quits skiing altogether.

How can you overcome your fear of speed ?
First, there are psychological means. Ski with friends whom you enjoy and who ski a little faster than you do. Let your skis run when the slope is ideal, the snow is perfect, and when

you feel yourself in a state of euphora. Maybe after a good lunch and good wine as long as a drunk skier test is not in use on the slopes...

There are also technical means. Maybe you are afraid of speed because your body position limits your stability. That would be perfectly normal. Perhaps you do not know how to use your feet, or you ski standing too straight, broken at the waist, too far forward, or with your feet too close together. I have already suggested possible remedies for these problems (pages 106-113). The most serious mistake for you is probably holding your feet too close together. It is very elegant to do so but very poor for good stability at higher speeds. On wide, intermediate slopes try to spread your feet eight inches apart while straight running. Feel your legs work independently and you will create the natural balancing reflexes necessary for gaining sufficient confidence for faster skiing.

VERY GOOD SKIERS IMPROVE

This chapter is intended only for very good skiers and classified racers. I can understand that those of my readers who belong to the great mass of good skiers, and who enjoy looking through these pages, will eventually start reading this section enthusiastically. However, I must stress the point that only a skier already capable of doing all the manoeuvres recommended for good skiers in the preceding chapter will be able to truly profit from reading this. I would also like to include an aside for excellent skiers, for the virtuosos who have never had trouble with ski technique and who, blessed by the Gods, seem to have been born with skis on their feet. These skiers might think that I am wasting a lot of energy for nothing in analysing movements which they have discovered themselves by imitation. I also intend this chapter for them, because the confirmed champions of any well evolved sport master its technical problems consciously. Any competitive skier can learn precious lessons through a clearer vision of the true nature of skiing movements. I have worked personally with two great champions who confirmed my opinion : Jean Vuarnet, Olympic downhill champion with whom I developed the "egg", and Patrick Russel, two-time World Cup slalom champion who helped me perfect *avalement*.

The "S" Turn with «Avalement»

The technical element which has revolutionized high level skiing in the last few years is *avalement*. I observed the first movements of this element in Jean-Claude Killy while he was only a "hopeful" on the French National Team. I thought then that *avalement* would open the way to considerable technical progress, and I took the risk of training several young racers with a technique mainly involving this movement. Since the experiment proved conclusive in 1966, we included many pages about *avalement* in the chapter on competition in *How to Ski the New French Way*. Many of the illustrations were photomontages of Patrick Russel, then a young, unknown, high school racer from the city. Today, *avalement* is known world-wide and the name I gave to it has been universally accepted because of the publication of our last book in nine languages. However, all over the world even mediocre skiers have wanted to use *avalement*. Some of them saw only the seated position of the movement, and they now ski while constantly sitting back, leaning continuously against the back of their boot tops! Others were struck by some of the very low, flexed positions of the champions. They did not notice that these positions lasted only fractions of seconds, and now they ski in a constant crouch appearing as if they had no legs. Yet others remembered only the forward thrust of the feet. These skiers now hold their legs glued together and initiate their turns only by thrusting their feet downhill. They only avoid falling on their rear because

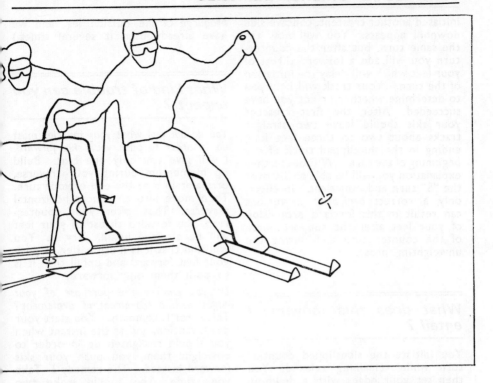

of their slow speed and the solid support of their pole plant.

The observation of these inevitable excesses brought me to propose a common turn, classic in its sobriety and appealing due to its elegance, a turn which would include *avalement* without the risk of causing excesses to develop. It is a sort of "instructor's final form" turn incorporating this last born element of competitive skiing, *avalement*.

How to make an « S » turn

You know how to make jet turns, or in simpler terms, a turn with a dynamic counter-turn. I use the word "dynamic" in order to stress the fact that this counter-turn is incisive enough to

result in a springboard effect which launches the skier into the turn. The track left in the snow by such a turn is characteristic : the sideslip of the counter-turn leaves a crescent, concave side uphill, and as soon as the turn is

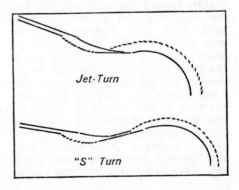

Jet-Turn

"S" Turn

initiated another crescent, concave side downhill appears. You will now try the same turn, but after the counter-turn you will add a forward thrust of your feet which will delay the initiation of the turn. Your track will help you to determine whether or not you have succeeded. After the first crescent your skis should leave two straight tracks about two to three feet long ending in the sideslipped track of the beginning of the turn. Without further explanation you will be able to discover the "S" turn and *avalement*. In effect, only a correct *avalement* movement can result in this forward propulsion of your feet after the support phase of the counter turn and during the unweighting phase.

What does this movement entail ?

You initiate the sideslipped counter-turn while remaining relaxed. You then set your edges with a down-up motion and plant your pole. Instead of pivoting your unweighted skis into the turn immediately, you push them in the direction of their tips with the use of your legs and your abdominal muscles. Soon you will feel your weight come back onto the skis, slightly toward the tails, and you will feel your skis start pivoting into the turn. You then balance on your outside ski. You can accentuate its pivoting, and you control the arc of the turn either with flat skis or by carving on the tails (see page 82). I will explain why your skis pivot into the turn at the end of the book (in the "Analysis" chapter). If you would like to increase their pivoting, the process is simple. After pushing your skis forward, pivot with your outside leg. (We call this pivoting effort

braquage of the outside leg, and we have already used it several times.)

What kind of trouble can you expect ?

You do not feel what your muscles must do in order to push your skis forward. I will give you only one hint. Build up momentum during your traverse, or maintain it at the end of your turn. Then move into an almost horizontal traverse. Thus, after your counter-turn, the forward thrust of your feet will be directed uphill. Try it. You will find that it is much easier to push your feet forward and uphill than it is to push them only forward.

Do you confuse the purchase of your edges with a movement of avalement? This error is common. You start your down motion, and at the instant when you should straighten up in order to unweight them, you push your skis forward instead. The remedy ? Take your time. You should make two movements successively : 1) Unweight by down-up motion, and 2) push your feet forward and uphill with a movement of *avalement*. If you combine both phases, you will no longer unweight your skis, and you will have trouble regaining your balance once you have pushed your feet forward. Your upper body will remain "back", supported by your planted pole. If you separate the two phases, on the other hand, the forward thrust of your feet resulting from the work of your legs and your *abdominal muscles* will pull your upper body forward. You can then regain balance over your skis during the initiation of the next turn. *Avalement is a sort of "jacknife" movement.* A jacknife is a gymnastic movement made during a jump and during which the performer's abdo-

Down-Up Initiation
of a Slalom Turn

The two classic modes of initiating a slalom turn are demonstrated by Patrick Russel, photographed during the last World Championships. This proves the necessity for a slalom specialist to use a great variety of technical tools in order to adapt to the snow conditions, the terrain, the radius of the turn, the speed, his own physical strength, etc. It should be noticed, however, that Patrick performs a down-up motion slightly different from that used ten years ago. He sits back a little more not because of a backward movement of his trunk, but because of a slight forward thrust of his feet. This thrust is in itself a form of *avalement*. (See the gliding jet-turn presented in the following pages).

Initiation through Avalement

Short radius " S " Turns

Patrick Russel demonstrates the turn which I have named the « S » Turn and which can be used as a preparatory exercise for *avalement*. In slalom *avalement* is performed without a preceding platform because the skier is constantly compressed on his skis by centrifugal force. The same is not true in free skiing. In order to establish the compression, which must precede *avalement*, it is enough to turn the skis uphill from an almost horizontal traverse before initiating the turn. There are successively : 1) a more or less sideslipped counter turn into an edgeset, 2) a traction resulting in a forward thrust of the skis through a use of the stomach muscles, and 3) a pivoting effort, *braquage* of the outside leg which starts the turn. Anticipation at the instant of the platform and a pole plant are enough to initiate the pivoting of the skis.

The Gliding Jet-Turn

This is an improvement of the jet-turn and a first step toward *avalement* and the « S » turn. There is a counter-turn as in the jet-turn, but there is no sharp lateral movement of the skis into the turn (a movement which results in the edge change after the skis are lifted more or less from the surface of the snow). The un-weighted skis are pushed forward, their edges change, and they start into the turn gradually while remaining in contact with the snow. A discrete *avalement* has already appeared.

The Five Errors in the "S" Turn

1) The skier approaches in too low a body position.   2) He does not use a down-up motion or even a rebound in order to establish a platform.   3) He makes no uphill counter-turn. 4) He pushes his feet forward while letting his upper body fall backward instead of using an avalement, *jacknife, movement.   5) He balances on and grips with his inside ski because he did not use a* braquage *of his outside ski after having pushed it forward.*

minal muscles pull his legs forward and upward while pulling his trunk forward and downward.   The down-up motion preceding the *avalement* makes the jacknife easier.   The down-up motion serves as a muscular preparation for *avalement* just as down motion does for up motion.

Do you lose your balance backwards and to the inside of the turn? There could be many reasons.   Perhaps you are overexaggerating your *avalement*. Maybe you are making the error just mentioned above.   Perhaps you are trying to weight both skis, or your inside ski, instead of weighting only your outside ski.   It is also possible that you lose your balance backwards at the instant you start your up motion.   Actually the down-up motion of your counter-turn should project your upper body forward slightly. Only afterwards should you project

your feet in the direction your skis are moving.   In this way, regaining your balance over your accelerating feet will be made easier.

The carved « S » turn

The mechanism is exactly the same as that of the sideslipped turn we have

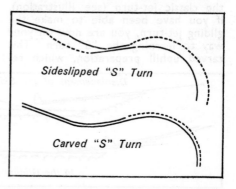

Sideslipped "S" Turn

Carved "S" Turn

just seen, however, instead of side-slipping in the counter-turn, your skis make a slight carved uphill turn before being thrust forward. In order to carve the uphill counter-turn, try to set your edges, starting directly from your traverse without sideslipping beforehand. At the same time as you make your down-up motion and plant your pole, put pressure on the uphill edges of your skis by increasing their edgeset angle through an uphill thrust of the knees, and through angulation. Your skis will flex and carve an uphill arc in the snow. Next push your skis forward, and start a carved arc, weighting the heel of your outside ski which you have simultaneously edged slightly. The carved "S" turn is more difficult than the sideslipped "S" turn, but more elegant, more effective, and much closer to the round turns of the greatest slalom and giant slalom champions.

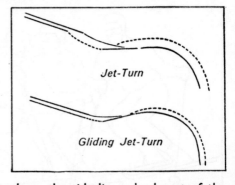

Jet-Turn

Gliding Jet-Turn

The gliding jet-turn prepares you for the « S » turn

We have seen on page 94 that in the classic jet turn, that is a turn with a dynamic counter-turn, less friction could result if the counter-turn were carved. This jet-turn is then called a "gliding jet-turn", and the track it leaves on the snow differentiates it from the classic jet-turn (see illustration). If you have been able to make the gliding jet-turn, you are now on your way to learning the "S" turn. This carved uphill preparation, which re-

places the sideslip and edgeset of the classic jet-turn, cannot be made without a slight forward thrust of the skier's feet in the final phase of the platform resulting from down-up motion. This very brief forward thrust of the feet does not necessarily cause the skier to sit back, because he often initiates the movement from a position of slight forward lean. The down-up motion which results in the carved platform is made while the skier's feet move from a position slightly behind, to a position slightly in front of his body. The sort of swinging movement of the skis under the skier's body reminds one of the movement of a reclining armchair. The skis are then automatically flattened on the snow and then tipped onto their inside edges. They can remain in constant contact with the snow and immediately initiate an arc, either remaining flat or edged for carving on the tails.

You will see that your effectiveness in powder as well as on ice or in moguls will increase.

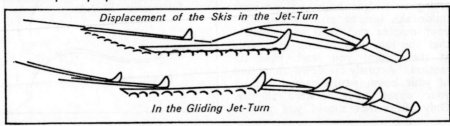

Displacement of the Skis in the Jet-Turn

In the Gliding Jet-Turn

Avalement *in check wedeln*

Begin to use *avalement* in your check wedeln. Your check wedeln will

become more effective, and you will feel how carving with your edges through *avalement* can be substituted for an edgeset which slows your skis considerably on a steep slope. Start

Wedeln with «Avalement» or "S" Wedeln

a normal check wedeln (see page 90) : edgeset with your skis almost horizontal to the fall line, downhill pole plant, trunk facing downhill — rebound into a folded (flexed) body position, skis pivoting under your body — *weighting of your skis* (especially the tails of your skis) *and sideslip,* describing a very tight turn, trunk continuing to face down-hill. At the precise instant when you would use a powerful edgeset to end this sideslip introduce *avalement.* You simply begin your edgeset with a pole plant in good balance over your skis, but instead of thrusting downward powerfully with your skis in order to make them bite, you push them forward

with a very dynamic *avalement.* Your skis carve a short uphill curve. They will then lose contact with the snow and begin pivoting rapidly while suspended, just as in the rebound phase of normal check wedeln. You will then weight your skis again, especially your outside ski. You will make another very tight sideslipped turn and repeat the same movements. The first advantage of *avalement* in this wedeln is the fact that you are able to make your skis hold on a very steep slope without brutalizing the snow. The second advantage is the fact that you are able to make much tighter turns with much less sideslipping than in classic wedeln. As a result you

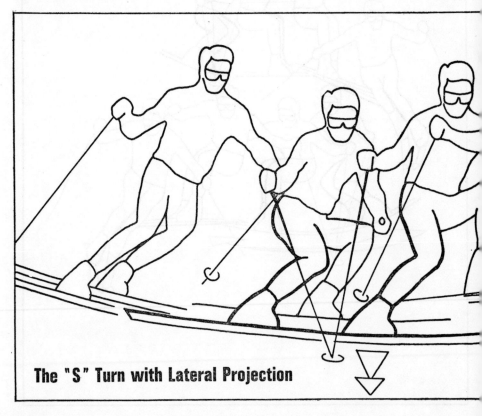

The "S" Turn with Lateral Projection

become more elegant and more adaptable to racing type turns.

Two secrets for check wedeln with avalement

The first is not a secret to you if you have been able to make handsome "S" turns. You must wait until your skis are almost horizontal to the fallline, that is across the hill, in order to make your platform and *avalement* movement. Your skis, then, projected forward, curve back uphill, or at least you should feel as if they do.
The second secret is to begin setting

your edges before making your *avalement* movement. Start by simply shortening the end of your edgeset a little, then shorten it more and more, but do not cut it out completely. A certain downward reaction is indispensable to the necessary unweighting. Only in slalom, where you resist considerable centrifugal force during each turn will it be possible to replace this platform completely with *avalement*. In free skiing if you did not use this downward reaction to unweight, you would have to exaggerate your *avalement* movement, or you would have to force your unweighted skis to pivot, slowing them down considerably.

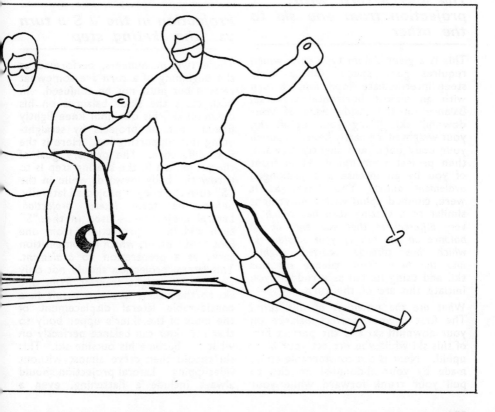

WORK LATERALLY FROM ONE FOOT TO THE OTHER

The observation of international competition, especially through television, has convinced all good skiers of the utility for racers of lateral projections from one ski to the other both at the beginning and at the end of turns. The observation of these same racers free skiing in difficult terrain has proven to me that these projections often help them, and permit them to get out of many difficult situations. Why should you be deprived of this weapon ? In addition, if you ski competitively, it will be a great advantage for you to adopt and improve movements which you will be able to use when racing.

outside ski prepares to initiate the turn. Finally there is the perfect control of the amount of pivoting of your outside ski at the end of your *avalement* movement, so that the turn begins without slowing your skis (too much pivoting) or without loss of balance backwards (not enough pivoting).

This turn adapts perfectly to intermediate moguls. Look for a favorable place to start your turn, for example a round bump about one or two yards above the track of your traverse. Four or five yards before the mogul, project so that your uphill ski initiates its curve at the top of the mogul.

The « S » turn with projection from one ski to the other

This is a giant slalom type turn which requires good speed. On a fairly steep intermediate slope, finish a turn with an almost horizontal traverse. Balance on the inside edge of your downhill ski, lifting your uphill ski, your weighted leg partly flexed. Launch your body uphill and slightly forward, then project your uphill ski in front of you by an intense and prolonged *avalement* effort. You have, as it were, climbed uphill with a movement similar to a skating step *but which is very different in that you end up in balance on the tail of your outside ski which has already started slightly into the turn.* You balance on this ski, and using its tail as a rudder, you initiate the arc of the turn.

What are the essentials of this turn ? The first is your perfect balance on your downhill ski and the perfect bite of this ski while you project your body uphill. Next is the considerable effort made by your abdominal muscles to pull your trunk forward while your

Projection in the « S » turn vs. the skating step

These two movements, performed at the beginning of a turn are somewhat related but must not be confused. In both cases the skier balances on his downhill ski, his downhill knee lightly flexed, then he projects by straightening this supporting leg. Here is the first difference. The primary goal of the projection in the skating step is to throw the body forward, while in the "S" turn the body is projected laterally, hence the term *lateral projection*. Lateral projection is used in the "S" turn and in all projections from one foot to the other, which in competition serve as a preparation to *avalement*. This lateral projection should not only permit the weight transfer from one ski to the other, but also result in a considerable lateral displacement of the mass of the skier's upper body so that the skier can balance perfectly on what has become his outside ski. This ski should then carve almost without sideslipping. Lateral projection should always include a flattening, even a

The "S" Turn with Lateral Projection through Moguls

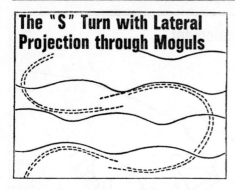

This turn necessitates a relatively flat or intermediate slope and large bumps or small smooth bumps.
Before initiating this turn, you should make a practically horizontal traverse between the bumps.

changing to the inside edge, of the uphill ski through an early inward movement of the uphill knee. In the traditional skating step, the edge change of the uphill ski is generally made later.
The second difference : After a skating step the skier's upper body remains forward relative to his skis. The skier adjusts his balance either by plunging into the next turn or by using a double pole plant and pulling himself through it. In the projection of an "S" turn the forward thrust of the outside foot, which links to the projection of the upper body, results in the skier sitting back relative to this foot. Another important difference which often makes it impossible for a skier accustomed to the skating step to make effective "S" turns : after the projection onto his uphill ski during an "S" turn, the skier should not weight the ski and straighten up while the turn begins. Many good skiers and even some of the great international racers straighten up at the beginning of the turn and do not realize that the straightening movement slows them down considerably at the beginning of the turn.

You know how to turn through moguls with reploiement

You will be able to learn *avalement* most easily in moguls, but you will also have a great tendency to learn a false *avalement*. First, it is essential before trying *avalement* to have learned to make turns with *reploiement* (page 93). These turns have a double advantage. They accustom you to the very ample flexion and extension movements which you will also find in *avalement*. They also allow you to remain in good balance on your skis, that is neither forward nor too far back. This feeling for balanced support will be indispensable in turning effectively with *avalement*.

How to turn in the moguls with avalement

First of all, you should be skiing with good speed, as this turn is very dynamic and impossible to do at slow speeds. At the end of a normal turn start a horizontal traverse. Pick out a fairly high mogul slightly above your line of traverse. Just before reaching the slope of this bump, in a straight body position, make a very long counter turn and a down-up motion with pole plant. Then through *avalement,* project your skis forward and uphill against the side of the mogul so that their upward climb ends at the exact top of the bump. Next, weight your

At High Speeds in Bumps : « Avalement »

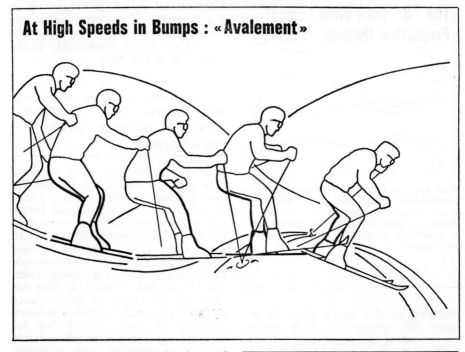

skis, especially your outside ski, and the arc of your turn will begin. When a mogul is very sharp, emphasize the pivoting of your outside ski by pushing your outside knee inward in order to balance on the edge of this ski at the beginning of the turn. During the turn you straighten up gradually and are thus able to maintain good pressure on your skis. In addition you will end up in a favorable position at the end of the turn for initiating another *avalement* turn.

At *higher speeds* you may feel yourself thrown into the air by the mogul. This is not important. Unfold your body while in the air and prepare for the contact of your skis, either on the other side of the same bump or against the side of another. Flex in order to absorb your landing, and continue.

Avalement *on difficult, bumpy slopes*

The technique of such turns is related to that of wedeln with *avalement* already described. You should take advantage of the flat spots which are located between moguls in order to establish a vertical support on your skis in a fairly straight body position before starting your *avalement* in approaching the crest of a mogul. You cross this crest in a very low, flexed position. Then you unfold while your skis slide on the downhill side of the mogul, or come back into contact with the bottom of the small troughs which separate the moguls. You reach another flat section in a straight body position and again establish a vertical support on your skis while planting your

136

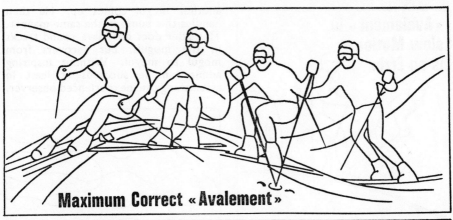

Maximum Correct «Avalement»

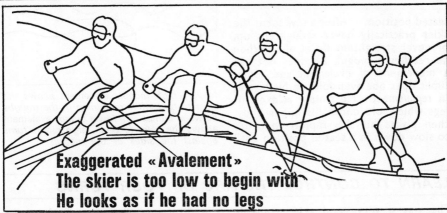

Exaggerated «Avalement»
The skier is too low to begin with
He looks as if he had no legs

downhill pole. Another *avalement*, etc... When the moguls are very sharp on very steep slopes, it is often impossible to check on the downhill side of the mogul which is too steep. *Avalement* turns then allow the best skiers to thread easily through the narrow troughs which wind between the moguls.

False avalement *in moguls*

There are two types of false *avalement*. *At slow speeds* some skiers reach the top of a bump, plant their pole, and push their skis, pivoting them into the fall line. Because of the support of their planted pole, they do not fall over backwards, but regain their balance a second later as their skis sideslip down the bump. These turns, which are easily performed with skis held tight together, are fairly elegant but do not lead anywhere, unless to creating the habit of sitting back constantly. This position of sitting back serves to prevent desirable reactions on the part of these skiers on their skis (unweighting, edgesets, pivoted rebounding, etc...).

At high speeds false *avalement* is nothing other than *reploiement* (described on page 93) to which is added a constant

PLAY IN THE MOGULS IN AVALEMENT

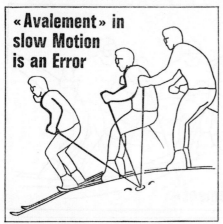

« Avalement » in slow Motion is an Error

another mogul comes up. He then handles this bump in the same manner. This skier does not leave round tracks in the moguls, but recovers from mogul to mogul. Without inspiring admiration he succeeds at least in astonishing the inexperienced observer.

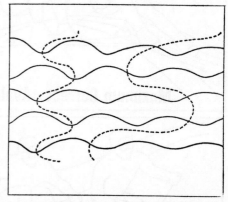

seated position.   After a few turns the skier practically never straightens up, or never straightens up at all.   When he reaches a mogul, he does not use a movement of *avalement* and sometimes does not even fold up his legs as in *reploiement*. He simply relaxes his legs which fold under his upper body, then pivots his skis rapidly in order to slow down in a seated position until

In very high moguls avalement *allows the skier to turn while remaining in the troughs between bumps. In lower bumps* avalement *allows the skier to bank large radius turns against the sides of the moguls.*

LEARN TO CONTROL THE ARC OF YOUR TURNS

The way a very good skier controls the arcs of his turns characterizes him at least as much as the way he starts his turns.   In fact the type of initiation chosen for a turn is largely determined by the desire to control its arc in a particular manner : flat ski, or carved on both skis, or only on the outside ski, in a balanced position over the full length of the skis, sitting back, or leaning forward.

Why attach so much importance to the control of the arcs of your turns ? Because this control is the basic problem of skiing. To like to ski means to enjoy sliding, and slowing down or checking is not sliding. When

the direction of your skis does not correspond closely to the direction of the arcs of your turns ; when the skis are always crosswise to this direction or to the direction of your traverses, they do not slide perfectly, they slow down and your pleasure in skiing can no longer be as intense. To ski the same run with check turns, or with long radius, complete turns with *glissement* does not give the same feelings, of that you can be sure. A student who did not have much money once made the remark that for the same price he could ski twice the distance in this second manner ! If you do not feel it important to ski one particular way or another as long as you are able to take advantage of the beautiful surroundings and of the pleasure of loosening stiff muscles, you should not be reading this chapter which is exclusively reserved for those who have already become very good skiers and who want to improve even more.

The three phases of the arc of a turn

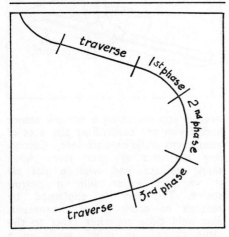

Three parts of a turn can be distinguished, that is, if the turn is complete enough : The first third, which follows the initiation and which approaches the fall-line, the second third, the fall-line phase, and the third phase which we call the completion of the turn. Your skis are not subjected to the same forces during these three phases : 1) In the first third, centrifugal force, which pushes you to the outside of the turn, is in part neutralized by the resultant of gravity which pulls you downhill, thus toward the inside of the turn... Due to this fact, you do not have much difficulty holding, and there is little risk of sideslipping or slowing down, except if your

initiation was too powerful and your skis ended up crosswise to your trajectory. 2) In the second third of the turn, obviously you must resist centrifugal force, but you also feel a considerable forward acceleration which helps to hold your skis in the arc. This acceleration is due to two causes. First, because of the fact that the slope followed by your skis, fairly flat in the beginning (in the traverse) increases until the fall-line. Next, because the resultant of gravity, which pulls you downhill, is exerted in a direction close to that of your displacement. 3) In the third phase of the turn this is no longer true as the resultant of gravity which pulls you downhill adds its effect to that of centrifugal force in increasing your sideslip. The braking effect of this sideslip is even greater because your skis move from a maximum slope (the fall-line) to a lesser slope (your traverse). This explains the greater difficulty in controlling the last third of the arcs of your turns without sideslipping. You will notice this difficulty especially when the snow conditions are difficult (ice, powder, among others) and when you must shorten the radius of a turn as you complete it. It is quite obvious

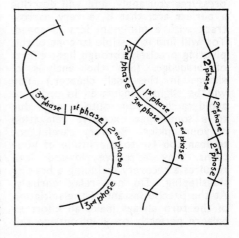

that for turns which do not leave the fall-line very much, the first and the third phases practically disappear and the problems posed by such turns are essentially those posed by the second phase of a completed turn.

Do you like to ski « relaxed »?

In this case use a "flat" ski as often as possible especially in soft snows, on flat or intermediate slopes, and in turns which are not entirely completed. Ski in a straighter, a "higher" body position than usual, and avoid any superfluous effort. The running surface of your skis should be almost flat on the snow, and it is essential to remain in a perfectly balanced position. Only in this manner will you be able to take maximum advantage of what we have called the pivot point of your skis (see page 80). Because of their form and because of the distribution of flexibility both frontally and torsionally, your skis will pivot by themselves as a reaction to the slightest pressures you apply, and will describe a perfect arc, that is, a very narrow track with a minimum loss of speed. You will find it possible to control this pivoting precisely through light efforts of *braquage*. (See the analysis of *vissage* in the final chapter.) You will be slightly angulated in order to avoid catching your outside edge due to a sometimes excessive relaxation of your ankles. Be very careful not to lean too far to the inside of your turns. Any excessive inward lean requires a recovery including a braking sideslipping. Do not relax entirely. At the precise instant of the initiation of the turn always make an effort to balance perfectly on your outside ski,

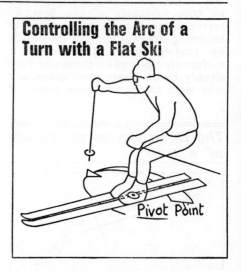

Controlling the Arc of a Turn with a Flat Ski

Pivot Point

even if you are using a narrow stance and if you are controlling the arcs of your turns while on both feet. *Controlling the arcs of your turns when skiing relaxed and with a flat ski is in fact easier with a narrow stance.* This fact is explained by reasons of economy of movement. Skis held close together react to the same changes in relief, while in a wider stance each ski reacts to different changes in relief and necessitates an assymetrical motor action for the control of the arc of the turn. The control of their pivoting throughout the arc is also easier muscularly when they are held together (*vissage*).

Control the first third of the arcs of your turns with « flat » skis

The first third of many, even very tight, turns can often be controlled with flat skis. In a preceding analysis I explained that the forces exerted on your skis in this part of the turn are not very great and do not correspond with a great deal of work of your skis on the snow (except in the case of extremely tight turns in which centrifugal force is considerable from the very initiation). On fast, slippery snow the pivoting of flat skis in the first third of the turn often results in less slowing than would a setting of the edges. Sometimes this advantage extends even through the fall-line, but almost never further. In snow conditions in which the edges sink in and cause the ski to slow down considerably (some snows saturated with water for example), it is an advantage to finish a turn with a flat ski sideslip rather than by carving.

On soft snow and in long turns use a « flat » ski

When you want a maximum *glissement* in very long turns, on intermediate or flat slopes, you should always try to feel if it would be advantageous to use a flat ski and accept some sideslipping, or to carve slightly with your edges

in order to avoid sideslipping. In the second case your edges sink in farther, accumulating and compressing more snow, thus performing more work and causing your skis to slow down. You must therefore opt for the method which slows your skis the least. It is often necessary to time several tries in the same giant slalom course while using alternate techniques in order to determine which is better adapted at a given instant to a given course. The rarely equal ability of a racer in each technique must also be considered. With less gifted skiers the wrong choice results in a visible loss of speed. In fact, even in ideal fast, soft snow conditions it would seem that a flat ski control can be improved by a slight carving of the tail. At the end of the turns weighting the inside edge of the outside tail in a fairly wide stance would seem to improve the *glissement* and to prepare the start of the next turn through a weight transfer very effectively. This movement becomes even more effective in competition once the course starts to become rutted at the end of the turns.

CARVING WITH FORWARD PRESSURE

When to carve with forward leverage

I explained on page 84 how a carved turn with forward pressure can be performed and how the carving of the forward half of your skis pulls them into the turn as if they were placed in a curved groove. I also pointed out that this carving with forward pressure on hard snow, even if it results in better *glissement* most of the time, could slow your skis if it were excessive. It could also result in instability in the

last third of a turn. *Carving with forward pressure is especially valuable in the middle of a turn.* When your skis approach fall-line during a turn on hard snow, the speed of their *glissement* tends to increase. If you have been in a perfectly balanced position, you will not feel as much pressure under the forward part of your skis. We will see farther along that a weighting of the edges of the tails of your skis could also solve your problem, but we are going to imagine the case of carving with forward pressure. Your skis are flat; you are angulating slightly, and you have weight-

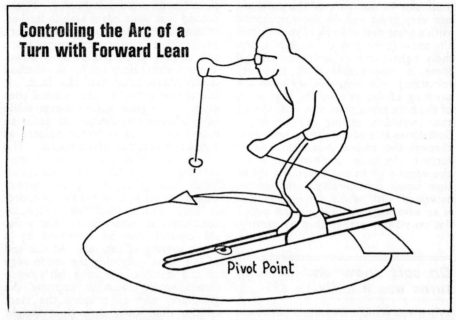

Controlling the Arc of a Turn with Forward Lean

Pivot Point

ed both skis almost equally. Weight your outside ski more. Push your corresponding knee forward and inward, and increase your angulation. You feel your ski begin to carve. Hold your ski on its edge forcefully while it begins to turn. Even increase your edgeset angle if necessary, but be careful to avoid increasing your forward lean at the end of your turn, especially if the turn is very tight. On the contrary, decrease your forward lean in order to come back into balance over your skis in the traverse at the end of your turn.

If you are making long radius turns down a fairly steep slope, carving with forward pressure can be very useful. Doing so will make your skis hold well and give you a feeling of security due in part to the braking action of your skis through the gripping of your edges. However, this is only true if the slope is not steep enough to cause your

speed to increase drastically. If you are obligated to tighten your turns because your speed increases continuously, you will no longer be able to

Carving on One Ski with Forward Pressure

Carving on Both Skis
with Forward Pressure

content yourself with this mode of controlling the arcs of your turns.

Carving with your inside ski, cramponnage

This type of carving entails forward pressure not on the outside ski but on the inside ski of the turn. Generally, this type of carving is started in the last third of the turn : The skier weights his inside ski by emphasizing the forward pressure on this ski. The outside ski then turns less than the inside ski. The skier next picks up his outside ski and pulls it in parallel to the other. If a second turn is to be linked immediately to the first, the skier continues to weight his inside ski, which has become the uphill ski, and initiates the next turn while continuing to weight this ski. Anatomically speaking, the skier can establish better purchase on the edge of his inside ski during a turn than on his outside ski. We will not discuss the reasons for this fact here. The

fact is even more obvious if the skiers legs are slightly bowed (cowboy type) or if they bow when he flexes his legs. This morphological characteristic decreases the edgeset angle of the outside ski and increases that of the inside ski. This point having been brought to your attention, you will notice that many skiers turning on hard snow push their inside knee laterally and thus spread their knees while their skis remain together. You can be sure that these skiers carve or hold, perhaps even without being aware of it, with their inside ski, sometimes successfully, but more often not.

The efficiency of this type of carving is questionable. We were the first to mention it in 1963 in our book, *Savoir Skier*. The French specialist of this type of carving at that time was François Bonlieu who was to become Olympic giant slalom champion the following year. Is this the reason why *"cramponnage du ski amont"* became so popular among competitive skiers ? I do not know, but I am certain that the importance of this movement was

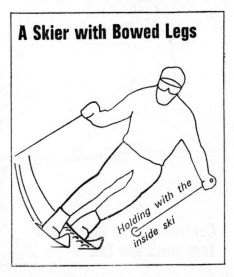

A Skier with Bowed Legs

Holding with the inside ski

exaggerated and that many young skiers deformed their techniques by using it too methodically, and too early in the turn. The spreading of the tips of the skis resulting from the biting of the inside ski at the end of the turn should not be confused with leads to the somewhat similar action of the skis associated with a skating step or with a lateral projection.

What are the advantages and disadvantages of this type of carving?

On some extremely hard snows where it is difficult to make skis hold, some skiers sideslip less at the end of their turns with this type of carving. This advantage has become less evident in the last few years among the very good racers. The quality of skis has improved so much that the great international racers practically never have difficulty holding on ice. The three essential disadvantages of this type of carving for races are in my opinion : 1) a slowing of *glissement* probably due to less finesse in the reaction of the foot which is weighted

on its outer side ; 2) the impossibility, if the racer must make a second turn immediately, to transfer his weight dynamically from one foot to the other (a very simple act if he were on his outside ski) ; 3) holding with the inside ski on a very steep hill comports the possibility of hitting the outside edge of one's ski boot against the snow causing the ski edge to lose contact with the snow. For pleasure skiers this type of carving presents other well known problems. It gives the skier the habit of leaning to the inside of his turn in order to weight his inside ski.

This inward lean, if increased beyond a useful angle, results automatically in a sideslip. In addition, balance on this inside ski is delicate and necessitates an incisive forward motion during the weight transfer from one ski to the other. The forward transfer is easy on intermediate slopes with good snow conditions but psychologically difficult when snow conditions or the slope become difficult. Finally, finish-

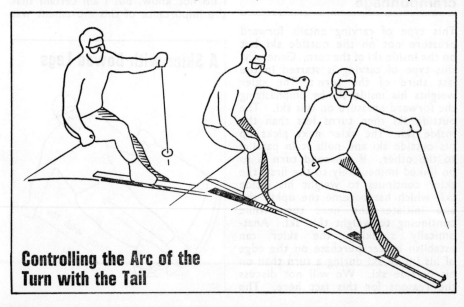

Controlling the Arc of the Turn with the Tail

ing the turn on the inside ski leads to a traverse with the uphill ski weighted. Weighting the uphill ski, though sometimes valuable, leads most of the time to a loss of balance.

The start of an arc carved on the tail

This manner of controlling the arc of a turn is recent. It appeared and developed at the same time as *avalement*. It even imposed a certain evolution in ski design (see following paragraph). At the present time it appears to be the most effective type of carving in competition when it is used by champions like Patrick Russel and Gustavo Thoeni. I started teaching you this type of controlling the arcs of your turns on page 82; now I am going to try to make you learn to feel how and when you should use it. We have already seen that in the first third of a turn, unless the initiation of the turn was too brutal, the skis do not tend to slide to the outside. This is why the start of an arc is often made with flat skis. However, when you must make a very tight turn on a fairly steep slope, especially in competition, it may be to your advantage to tighten the first third of your turn in order to avoid having to tighten the rest of the turn during which it is more difficult to make your skis hold. To tighten the first third, as soon as you have initiated the turn, weight the tail of your outside ski and push your

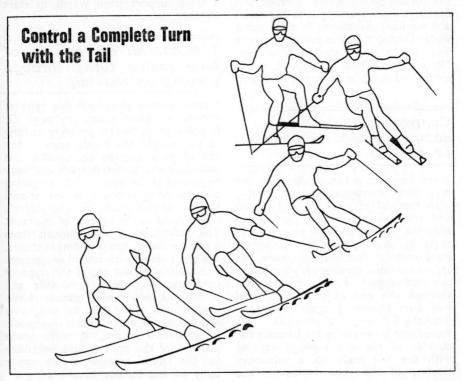

Control a Complete Turn with the Tail

corresponding knee inward. Balance toward the outside of your turn. This balancing to the outside of the turn as soon as your turn begins is essential in allowing the tail of your ski to control the arc of the turn as the rudder controls the turn of a boat. The essential problem which you will have to resolve in order to start your turn by carving with the tail of your ski, will be to feel how much you should pivot your ski at the initiation of your turn. Not pivoted enough, it will accelerate out from under you when you begin to weight it again. Pivoted too far, your ski will slip sideways and slow down. Pivoted correctly, your ski will accelerate into a carved arc. This exact pivoting results from an inward movement of the corresponding knee. I called this *braquage* when teaching it to beginners and we have mentioned it many times since. During this first part of the turn your inside ski is absolutely useless. Many international champion racers even hold it up as a matter of habit.

Controlling the arc of a completed turn with the tail of the ski

If you have started controlling the arc of a fairly complete turn by carving with the tail of your ski and if you find this type of carving particularly effective, you can increase your edgeset angle by pushing your corresponding knee inward. Flex your legs more, and try to continue carving on your tail in the second part of the arc, and even through the end of your turn until you start traversing again in balance over the full length of your ski. This movement is very effective because the control of the arc through carving with the tail leads to a minimum slowing of the skis. However, not

everyone is capable of doing it. First, because it is very athletic, it very often requires a low, flexed and angulated position. Next, it does not permit a constant control of speed as does carving with forward pressure. It seems to be more a technique for attacking. The superiority of carving with the tail is obvious in bumps and on irregular terrain. While in carving with forward pressure the skier feels all of the changes in terrain and snow and the skis are slowed down noticeably as the tips hit obstacles, in carving with his tail the skier remains more stable and his *glissement* is superior. If you carve in this manner, it will be essential that you come back into balance over your skis at the end of the turn, otherwise you will not have a solid support from which to start another turn.

The control of the arc of long radius turns through carving on the tail

I have already proposed this type of carving to good skiers on page 82. It poses no particular problem as long as you weight the inside edge of the tail of your outside ski totally, and balance on it perfectly from the very beginning of the turn. This weighting and balancing requires an intentional lateral displacement of the skier's upper body to the outside of the turn. The movement is very difficult from a narrow stance, easier in a wide stance, and even easier with lateral projection. The control of the arc of this type of turn also requires a semi-wide and sometimes even a wide stance, as the inward push of the knee for weighting and edging the outside ski is impossible in a narrow stance. A wide-spread position of the arms is also necessary for the lateral transfer of the upper body to the outside of the turn.

VERY GOOD SKIERS START RACING

You will not have to learn a particular technique of turning for slalom, giant slalom, or downhill. In reading this book, you have already understood, and perhaps felt, the mechanisms of all the types of initiations and all the manners of controlling the arcs of turns currently used by the great champions of skiing. You can practise all of these mechanisms while free-skiing. This is the source of strength of the collegiate and other racers who are able to spend relatively little time skiing (and even less training) but are still able to compete with those professionals, the racers of most national ski teams. I will simply specify which technique to adopt according to the snow and course and depending on whether your goal is to ski as fast as possible or to ski with security.

I would also like to state that the technical ability of a true racer includes a considerable variety of movements. Only this wealth of reflexes will allow an optimum adaptation of the individual racer's strength under any circums-

tances to the difficulties of a given course. It would therefore be impossible to impose a standard reaction on all of my readers for a given situation. However, I could not content myself with presenting all of the possible techniques for a given situation without giving my preferences. An inescapable technical evolution is currently taking place and is resulting in a 1% improvement in the times in international competition and even more at national and regional levels. I must therefore orient my readers toward an evolution favorable to their techniques. This is why I emphasize the new movements. I know that I risk orienting my readers too exclusively in this direction, possibly causing them to abandon other movements which sometimes remain superior under certain circumstances. I am aware of this obstacle, but I do not know of any solution for it other than to point out the danger of an excessively exclusive technical orientation, and to have faith in their common sense.

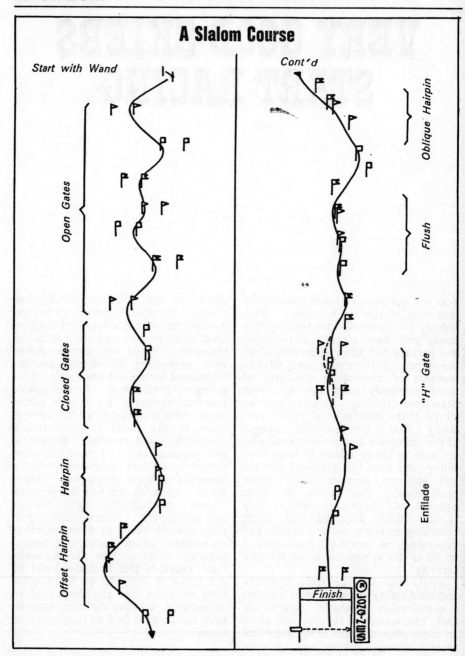

A Slalom Course

Start with Wand

Open Gates

Closed Gates

Hairpin

Offset Hairpin

Cont'd

Oblique Hairpin

Flush

"H" Gate

Enfilade

Finish

Enfilades

A succession of gates set in such a way that the turns required are not very round, that is not "complete" turns, is called an *enfilade*.

On soft snows try to initiate almost imperceptible arcs around these gates and get as close to the inside poles as possible. If the *enfilade* is tight, balance over the full length of your skis which you hold flat and together. If the rhythm of the gates is quick, you can turn simply by moving your knees. If not, it may well be better to use a semi-wide stance and to carve your turns slightly with the tail of your outside ski. The weight transfer from one ski to another will be enough to initiate your turns.

In rutted courses balance as much as possible on your outside ski which you bank against each rut. In addition, weight mainly the tail of the ski, and at the end of a turn, project laterally in order to put your new outside ski into contact with the bank of the next turn. In general, do not try to ski too close to the poles. From time to time, when a pole is leaning to the inside of the turn, for example, take the shortest line; however, do not hesitate to move back into the ruts again right away.

On hard snows and relatively flat slopes ski as close as possible to the poles, and carve your turns either in a balanced position or with tail pressure. Never carve with your tips in these conditions or you will slow down considerably.

On hard snows and intermediate slopes, enfilades pose a delicate tactical problem. Should you go as close as possible to the poles at the risk of

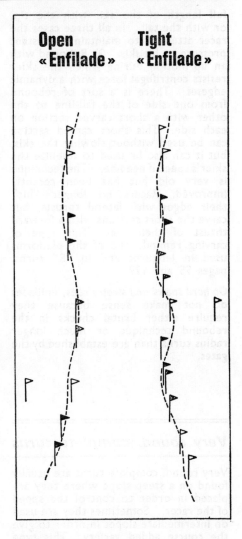

Open « Enfilade »   Tight « Enfilade »

gaining too much speed and side-slipping, or should you make your turns rounder and stay away from the poles at the risk of taking a longer line ? Technically, there are two fairly different ways of taking these *enfilades* which constitute the major part of most slaloms : 1) Carving with the full length of the ski, with the tip, or with the tail. In all three cases the racer attempts to maintain a constant pressure on his skis. 2) Rebound with an up motion during which the skier resists centrifugal force with a dynamic edgeset. There is a sort of rebound from one side of the fall-line to the other with a short carved section on each side. This short carved section can be used without slowing the skis, but it can also be used to stabilize the skier's speed if need be. The technique is very old but has been recently improved. Racers no longer "hit" their edges with lateral thrusts, but carve the short sections with a forward thrust of their feet. This type of carving reminds one of the platforms used in jet-turns and in "S" turns, pages 95 and 129.

On hard snows and steep slopes, enfilades do not make sense because they require either brutal checks in the rebound technique or much longer radius turns than are established by the gates.

Very round, complete turns

Very round, complete turns are usually found on a steep slope where they are placed in order to control the speed of the racer. Sometimes they are used on intermediate slopes in order to give the course added variety. This type of turn requires maximum technique and some slalom specialists, who have become great because of natural athletic ability, have trouble with them. The best technique at present would seem to be *avalement* preceded by lateral projection from one ski to the other.

Normal turns

I consider any turn which is not in an *enfilade* or which is not very round a normal turn. At present, there are generally three ways of making this type of turn :

With pure avalement. Having resisted centrifugal force in the second half of your turn, you initiate a carved *avalement* movement as soon as your skis start into the short traverse between turns. During this *avalement* you transfer your weight from mainly on your outside ski to mainly on your uphill ski. You will thus avoid "hitting" your edges, which is the traditional way of launching the following turn and which always slows your skis. Your carved , *avalement* movement starts the next turn.
You can also finish the preceding turn in perfect balance on your outside ski and project laterally onto your other ski which you have displaced uphill and which starts into the next turn as a result of *avalement*.

With up motion and vissage. While finishing a turn, you are holding with your edges in a very angulated and anticipated position. To the compression of your legs which results you can link a kind of up motion in the direction of the coming turn. Your upper body is projected in the direction of the turn (not in a rotation, which would be an error). During the resulting unweighting, your skis move into the turn. You weight your skis again while angulating in order to make your edges carve, and you gradually flex your legs through the completion of the turn. You then start another. This type of turn is generally performed by skiers who use a narrow stance and a slightly forward body position. It

Flushes

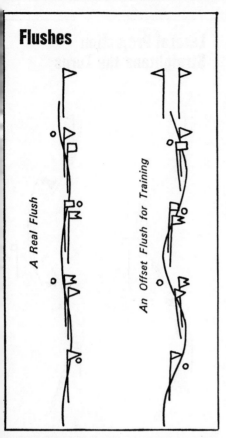

A Real Flush

An Offset Flush for Training

Running flushes requires almost no turning. When the course is not too rutted and the poles have been pushed out slightly by racers there is practically no turning at all. This is why it is advisable to set offset flushes for training. The starting point must be well defined with two poles. Flush practice is excellent to increase quickness of movement and slalom rhythm and in particular to develop pole planting at the right time and at the right place (notice pole plant marks on the sketch).

leads directly to what was called the rebound technique in *enfilades.*

With up motion and avalement. This turn begins as does the turn above, but an *avalement* is performed at the end of the up motion and allows the skier to balance over the full length of his skis or slightly on the tails. This type of turn is used most often by skiers moving from the rebound technique to the more recent *avalement* technique. It allows, little by little, the substitution of carving with the tails for carving with the tips which, as we have seen, can often slow your skis.

Very rutted turns

Very rutted turns require *avalement* or at least *reploiement.* Their difficulty resides mainly in the sort of bump which forms between two ruts. The bump acts as a lip of a jump at the beginning of the turn and, if the skier has unweighted, he is thrown into the oncoming rut, or at least has trouble starting the next turn early enough. What should you do ? In spite of the fact that your body is compressed against the outside of the rut at the end of the turn, you should reach the end of the turn in a partially extended position, and a yard before the bump absorb with an *avalement* movement. Your skis, unweighted and thrust forward, come back into contact with the snow at the top of the bump and immediately start into the next turn. At the same time as you make your *avalement* movement, you transfer your weight from your downhill ski to the other, initiating the next turn. This technique corresponds exactly with that described for *avalement* through moguls (page 135).

Checking

Brutal checking does exist in slalom, and it is very different from traditional checking through a sideslip, an edgeset, or a combination of both. It is obviously not a good idea to check by pivoting your skis completely out of the fall-line because you would then have to pivot them all the way back. A quick check is generally made between two turns on the outside ski, which is pushed laterally into a sharp edgeset. This ski may remain parallel to the other while the stance of the skier becomes wider, or its tail might stem downhill slightly. This check, which can be brutal and very effective, also serves as a platform for the launching of the next turn.

Gradual, controlled checking is also possible in any turn either by simply increasing the sideslip or by over edging and causing an increase in ski-snow friction without modifying the arc of the turn.

Accelerating

In modern slaloms which are becoming faster each year, it has become next to impossible to accelerate by forward projection and a double pole plant, a technique still effective only ten years ago. When a skier is said to be accelerating today, he is actually eliminating any checking action of his skis, or controlling his turn so that his skis accelerate more effectively. The lateral projections from one leg to the other, which have already been discussed a great deal, do not in fact result in an

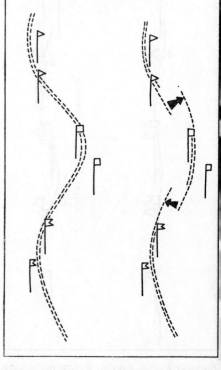

Lateral Projection Straightens the Turns

acceleration, that is, in an increase in speed. Rather they are the means of avoiding a certain slow phase in the turn. They allow the skier to place himself and his skis in a better position at the beginning of the turn. They also balance the skier instantaneously on the outside ski of the oncoming turn and, finally, allow the skier to shorten the radius of his turns noticeably.

The pole plant

Due to the ever increasing speeds in modern slalom, pushing with the poles hardly ever results in acceleration. However, the pole plant still has two important functions :

1) *It facilitates lateral balance.* At any instant you might have to recover your lateral balance. If your arms are properly positioned, that is, wide spread, poles pointed toward the snow, you can support yourself with a pole plant in one-twentieth of a second. This implies that you do not plant your poles uselessly so that you are ready to plant them when necessary. In addition, useless pole plants tend to tighten the muscles of your shoulders or your back.

2) *It helps in lateral projection and in avalement.* In order for a pole plant to be effective in helping you work from one foot to the other, or in giving you a solid support for *avalement*, your pole must be pointed forward. The pole plant should not be brief, nor should it be directed obliquely backward. You should not only feel a shock but a veritable exchange of forces between your pole and your shoulder. While the leg work of a modern slalom specialist is astonishingly rapid, his arm work is surprisingly economical and effective.

The start with a wand

If perfectly performed, a start through a wand activating electric timing can result in a gain of five to six one-hundredths of a second. Badly performed, it can result in as great a loss. The total difference can therefore add up to a good tenth of a second. Before discussing the technique of a good start, two important rules should be mentioned : 1) The racer's skis must not be supported from behind. Thus, any forward projection through leg action is impossible. 2) The racer's poles must be planted before the count of "five" and remain planted until "go". Thus, any movement of the trunk is somewhat restricted. The best technique would seem to be a downward fall of the skier's upper body started before his legs hit the wand, combined with a maximum traction of his arms at the end of the fall. Thus, both the force of the fall and the traction with the arms join to provide a force parallel to the slope which the skier is about to reach. Depending on the steepness of the slope in front of the starting platform, you will be able to judge how far behind the wand you should place your knees or shins and how far in front of the wand your poles should be planted. In any case be sure that your ski pole baskets are supported solidly so that they will not sink when you push off.

It has been said that Jean-Claude Killy gained several one-hundredths of a second by jumping before reaching the wand. This gain would seem theoretically plausible even if one excludes the fact that any forward projection would be impossible. It is in fact possible to hit the wand after a jump with one's ankles and not one's shins. The gain, in this case from four to eight inches, would be one or two one-hundredths of a second. In addition, the forward tipping of the upper body during the suspension phase could produce an increase in the downward force of the fall of the upper body. Combined with the force of the traction of the arms, it could increase the initial acceleration. However, during repeated timed experiments we have not been able to

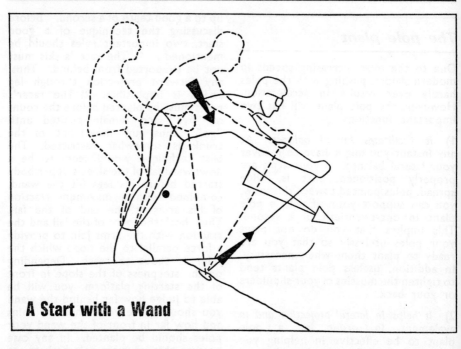

A Start with a Wand

establish that this complicated manoeuvre was more effective than the
traditional method described above.

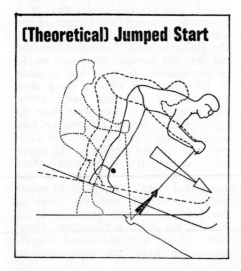

(Theoretical) Jumped Start

The finish

When photo-electric cells were first
used at the finishes of ski races, the
racers threw their upper bodies, arms,
and poles forward in order to cut the
beam and stop the clocks. This practice
resulted in many forward falls. The
photo-electric cells were soon adjusted
so that a swinging ski pole had no
effect on them. Only some part of
the racer's body will trip the stop
watches now. With the return to
popularity of seated positions in the
last few years, the racers have discovered another means of cutting the beam
at the finish line a few hundreths of a
second earlier. They project their
feet and knees forward, upper body
completely unbalanced over backward,
sometimes even sitting on the tails of

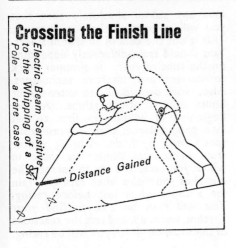

Crossing the Finish Line

Electric Beam Sensitive to the Whipping of a Ski Pole - a rare case

Distance Gained

depends, of course, on your speed and the distance to be covered, that is the distance without gates which separates you from the finish line. Sometimes skating accelerates the skier. Often it slows him down and sometimes causes him to fall. One fact seems certain : It is almost always better to make one or two strong skating steps rather than several quick ones. At Val Gardena, Patrick Russel made one more skating step than his direct adversaries, thus travelling a few extra inches, crossing the finish line at a less favorable spot, and losing... a world championship title.

their skis. These positions are dangerous because at the end of a race the competitors are tired and they tend to relax completely after crossing the finish line. Some serious accidents have already occurred. I think that a means of making these movements ineffective will soon be found. It would be enough, for example, to adjust the beam to a height above the racers' knees. Before deciding to lie down on the tails of your skis when crossing the finish line, find out how high the beam is adjusted. Otherwise, you might miss it altogether.

Judge the favorable angle for crossing the finish line. According to the F.I.S. rule the last gate of a slalom should be parallel to the finish line and should direct the racer into the axis of the finish. Nevertheless, in some slaloms like that of the F.I.S. World Championships in Val Gardena, which will be mentioned again below, it is preferable to cut the finish line on one side rather than on the other. It is sometimes possible to gain several hundredths of a second in this manner.

Should you skate at the finish ? This

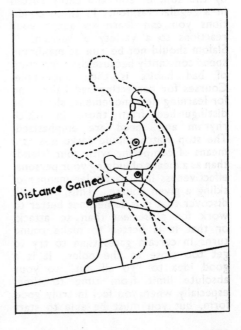

Distance Gained

How to train for slalom

I will be very brief concerning this subject because you could not hope to train alone effectively for slalom. Besides, this book is not a treatise intended for coaches.

It is enough to say that one trains for slalom by skiing thousands of gates in all types of conditions and terrain. Aware of the problems in slalom, you can work on all types of slalom turns while free skiing. This fact is very important for racers from the city who, unlike certain champions from ski areas, cannot allow themselves to ski with two different techniques, one for pleasure, another for competition.

Slalom should be worked on intensively and exclusively during a full day, or during a given period of time. Summer is the ideal time as the snow is consistent, either frozen, slightly softened by the sun, or soft and easily rutted in a regular fashion. In these conditions you can learn to adapt your reactions to a variety of terrain.

Slalom should not be run at maximum speed constantly because the correction of bad habits is then impossible. Courses for correcting bad habits and for learning new movements should be distinguished from those in which rhythm and speed are emphasized. The stop watch should serve less as a means of competing with your friends than as a means of judging your personal effectiveness in a particular manner of skiing a given course. Thus, you will discover that it is sometimes better to work for *glissement* than to attack, or that it is better to make round turns in certain gates than to try to get too close to the poles. It is a good idea to "go all out" to your absolute limit from time to time, especially when you feel in truly good form, but you must be able to start into any slalom absolutely sure that you will make it all the way through. This is not the case of all slalom skiers. You should train differently depending on the time of year. In summer work to correct and improve techniques. Also, work occasionally to extend your limits in acrobatic rhythms. At the beginning of winter try first to get into good balance, then increase your speed little by little. During winter train in courses similar to those in which you race, and try to correct the mistakes you make when racing. Train for a short while just before racing. You will thus be able to find your rhythm, warm up, and test the reactions of the snow on which you will be racing.

In races your tactics will determine your results

You should have a perfect knowledge of the course. It is less a question of knowing all the gates by heart than of judging their degree of difficulty and the speed at which you personally will be able to handle the various parts of the course. You should know the difficult passages well enough to recognize when you are about to reach them and well enough to know what you are going to do to make it through. You should also recognize the easier passages in which you will be able to get close to the poles in order to go faster. Ideally you should have the ability to run the slalom in your head just before the start, and to feel all the movements you will have to make in your muscles, but you will not be able to do so until you have had long years of experience.

It is important to observe the competitors who race before you. Unless you are just beginning to race and the observation of your adversaries inhibits you, watch racers that you know well on the parts of the course you can see. If necessary, move down the slope in order to be able to see better. You will thus be able to see if you have judged the possible speeds and the relative difficulty of the different combinations correctly.

Learn to change your technique and tactics while racing. Frequently racers repeat the same mistakes during the full length of the course. They hold too hard with their edges or attack too much or too little. This problem results from a maximum concentration before the race on a single, pre-determined manner of reacting. This type of concentration is necessary in racing, but it should not blind you. Make an effort to analyze what you are doing after five, ten, or fifteen gates, and, if necessary, change your technique or tactics. When you are a champion, you will adapt perfectly to each part of the course while at the same time retaining all of your concentration and aggressiveness. This ability results from experience. It permits racers over thirty years old to compete with the best slalom specialists. In order to gain this

ability, try to analyze your behavior in each part of the course after every race.

The problem of the second run occurs every time you race. It proves how much the psychological factor affects the racer's performance. Having made a good first run, he would be stupid to take too many risks and to chance falling. Having made a poor first run (or having been disqualified), he does not have anything to lose in the second and logically makes an all out effort. The results of a race can thus be drastically affected. Racers who are too cautious after having placed well in the first run are annihilated ; others, completely liberated, make surprising runs compared to even the best of the first run. Therefore, the importance of judging the possible speeds for different parts of a course is obvious. Having judged the maximum speed of a course, the racer should know how to ski it while adding 5/10 or 1, 2, 3, 4 seconds to the fastest time. These figures apply to different levels of skiers : the tenths of a second to the champions and the seconds for class B or class C racers.

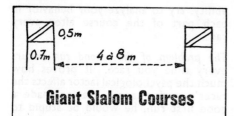

Giant Slalom Courses

The F.I.S. rule requires a minimum of 30 gates for a giant slalom and a minimum vertical drop of 250 meters for two runs or 400 meters for one for men. This rule requires 30 gates and a 300 meter vertical drop for women.
The gates are alternately red and blue. The distance between two gates must be at least five meters. The two poles holding the flag should be planted so that the flag is perpendicular to the direction of the race. In closed gates, oblique gates, or hairpins, the flags can be rolled on the poles so that they are only 30 cm wide in order to avoid hiding the rest of the course from the racer.

Giant slalom was born long after downhill and slalom. Considered a minor event at first, it was gradually acknowledged on an international level and became very popular in regional and national competition. It was recognized that the high speed turns required by giant slalom were at least as complex as the shorter radius turns in slalom. In addition, the rational use of the terrain through a perfect adaptation of the course to the run relates giant slalom to downhill, gives a "natural" character to the event and contributes a great deal to its interest.

Giant slalom is undoubtedly the *event which requires the best physical condition.* It often lasts twice as long as a slalom. Compared to downhill, for a similar

duration it generally does not contain "easy" sections which would permit the racer to recover partially. Giant slalom requires an intense action all of the time, a fact often unknown to the spectator. It is exhausting for the racer.

This physical condition aspect should not overshadow the importance of *technical finesse* in a good performance. During the last twenty years great champions whose successes were attributed to their superior physical conditioning have been overtaken by younger racers with "newer" techniques who were far from their maximum physical maturity. I mentioned "technical finesse" and not virtuosity, rapid reactions, or acrobatic talent, words which I might have used in discussing slalom. Most important is the perfect adaptation of the skier's movements to the terrain, the condition of the snow, and to the radius of the turn. This adaptation denotes continuous concentration, perfect judgment, the greatest possible sensitivity, a large technical "vocabulary", and the maximum precision in execution.

The essential technical problem posed by giant slalom is the control of the arc of the turns. This problem has already been discussed a great deal both in the section for intermediate skiers and in that for good skiers (page 81 and page 138). In the past, too much emphasis has been put on the initiation of turns and not enough importance given to what happens afterwards. If you would like to overcome this mistake, a very good way would be to train and race giant slalom. If you were to concentrate on improving your *glissement* during turns, you would realize very rapidly that the initiations you use depend essentially on the manner in which you plan to control the arc of the turn or on the manner in which you have controlled the arc of the preceding turn. Your passage from one turn to another would become a search for the most efficient movement for connecting the *glissement* of one turn to that of the next. Racers usually judge the *glissement*, the lack of deceleration in their adversaries turns, by observing the amount of snow thrown into the air by their skis. This is an effective manner of observing the amount of friction.

It is often said of a racer who does not kick up much snow that he "rides a flat ski". This expression should not always be taken literally because it is difficult to understand how a skier would make his skis hold on steep slopes, in spite of considerable centrifugal force, while keeping his skis flat on the snow. To ride a flat ski is in fact to avoid any unnecessary edgesets, any excessive edgesets, or any tight turns which would result in sideslipping on the edges. It is to ski smoothly, that is, to ski well.

Initiate turns without slowing your skis

Do not start easy giant slalom turns with an ineffective, slowing initiation just because the movement is pretty! Any counter-turn, edgeset, or weight transfer which could disturb your *glissement* should be avoided. Of course, you should use the support on the snow which does not slow your skis but which allows you to accelerate as we will see below.

In discussing "relaxed" turns for free skiing (see page 98), I mentioned how little movement is necessary for initiating a turn. A simple inward lean or even a weighting of one ski is enough.

This fact is often true of giant slalom turns as well. Starting the turn is then no longer the principal objective. More important becomes gaining optimum support from the skis (more particularly from the outside ski) for better *glissement* from the very beginning of the turn. A very gradual and smooth initiation including forward lean, was advocated for a long time. Skis were then fairly stiff, especially in the forward section, and a strong unweighting was used in order to reweight the skis as gradually as possible afterwards. The next body position used in giant slalom distributed the skier's weight more equally over the full length of the ski, and the forward half of giant slalom skis was made more flexible. Little by little racers have started using tail pressure (especially on the outside ski) in initiating turns. I have already discussed at length the initiation and control of the arcs of turns with a body position in which the skier sits back slightly (see pages 82 and 145). Perhaps you have already discovered by yourself the means of initiating your turns in this manner with maximum economy. If this is not the case, read the following suggestions.

When initiating an easy giant slalom turn, in a semi-wide or wide stance, start a very controlled forward thrust of your outside foot, combined with a very gradual edge change and total weighting of that ski. You will thus initiate the arc of a very "relaxed" turn with tail pressure. This movement is related to *avalement* in that you must use your abdominal muscles to control the work of the outside ski which starts the turn. The movement is, however, very gradual and not dynamic. This type of initiation requires a wide or semi-wide stance, or, at least a slight spreading of your skis at the instant when you transfer your weight from your downhill ski to your uphill ski, which becomes the outside ski of the turn. The sober quality of this movement makes it almost imperceptible. However, by watching the beginning of easy giant slalom turns made by the greatest champions you will notice its effectiveness.

This type of smooth initiation in turns on flat or intermediate slopes in more or less rutted courses (as long as your speed is great enough not to require movements to increase your speed) will allow you to improve considerably in giant slalom.

The shape of the arcs of turns

Because of the amount of confusion concerning this subject, I will discuss a certain amount of theory, here in regard to the shape of the arcs of turns. Theoretically, in finishing a turn at a given point there are a hundred different ways to shape the arc of the following turn in order to make the next gate, and to reach another given point in order to continue the rest of the course. The shortest line would consist of two straight lines connected by a "square" turn, which is obviously impossible. The longest line would be the continuous arc of a circle. Between these two extremes there is room for straight traverses of varying lengths with circular arcs of varying radii. It should be noted first that contrary to popular belief making round instead of "square" turns increases the distance traveled by the skier only a fairly small amount, 2 to 5 % for average turns. On the other hand, the relative loss of speed during turns under a critically short radius is considerable. It is, therefore,

absurd to try to aim at the poles and make your turns as short as possible! One should not attempt to shorten a turn unless he is certain that to do so will not cause his skis to decelerate. This would seem to be the first fundamental principle.

To attack turns from too high a position relative to the gate is a mistake often made in attempting to avoid the more basic mistake of falling too low at the end of the turn. In the first place, your desire to remain high makes you use a flatter and thus slower traverse than you would use otherwise. Next, if you must make a very round complete turn, starting the turn too high will often obligate you to turn twice in the same turn (see first illustration) or to turn at a long distance from the pole (see second illustration). The first is the more serious mistake because if you must increase the pivoting of your skis in the second half of your turn, you multiply the risk of sideslipping excessively.

The terrain often determines the shape of a turn. The possibility of a bank or the side of a large bump as a comfortable support, or the desire to avoid the risk of sideslipping on a fall-away slope or a patch of ice, can be the most important consideration in determining the shape of your turn.

When the course has been worn out by a large number of racers, it is more difficult to determine the best arc for a turn. Icy gates which might cause an unexpected sideslip at the end of the turn demand a longer radius arc. The ripples left in the turns by chattering skis require the same remedy. The "bathtubs", veritable holes with sharp edges all around, which appear in courses packed only on the surface are very dangerous. If you cannot avoid them, try to ski through them as directly as possible without side-

" S " wedeln with Avalement

This type of wedeln is performed on a steep slope and resembles check wedeln. As this series of photos illustrates, this technique allows the skier to make very tight turns. Its advantages are threefold : 1) It allows the skier to shorten the time normally spent braking in such a series of turns. The skis are pulled forward and cut the snow, thus carving instead of sideslipping. 2) Because of the preceding fact, turns can be made much more complete. 3) Rebound is reduced and the skis can remain in contact with the snow. « S » wedeln is the best exercise for very short complete slalom turns.

Two Different Techniques for
an Intermediate Length Racing Turn

Above, Patrick Russel makes a turn with the aid of an extreme *avalement* justified by the terrain. Below, he uses a classic down-up motion. Both of these turns are effective in slalom and giant slalom, but the first is used more often. It results in a better *glissement* at the completion of the turn, a better grip with the outside ski during the initiation of the turn, and a greater control of the arc of the turn with the ourside ski.

A Large Radius " S " Turn

Eric Stahl, a young scholastic racer at the time this picture was taken, three time winner of French National Junior Championships, performs a large radius « S » turn. The turn is used here as training in preparation for giant slalom. Racers, who do not train full time and who want to compete with those who train and race exclusively, must be able to practice techniques for competition while free skiing. Examples of such techniques are check wedeln, « S » turns, and « S » wedeln.

The " S " Turn with Lateral Projection

Avalement in a narrow stance, with an identical action of both legs, was found to be slower than an *avalement* combined with a lateral thrust and projection of the inside ski. Above, Er Stahl performs this movement while free skiing. Below, Ala Penz uses it in giant slalom. The three phases of the movemen are : 1) balancing on the outside ski, 2) projection of the insid ski in an exactly lateral plane, and 3) balancing on the uphill s which is immediately thrust forward and pivoted into the comir turn through *avalement*.

The acceleration at the end of the turn

In the photomontage below, Alain Penz finishes a turn while in balance on his outside ski and projects to his uphill ski in order to accelerate. Above, Jean-Noël Augert finishes the same turn by carving on his inside ski. From the very first photo he weights and remains on his inside ski. In my opinion, the second case is rarely superior to the first. In general it is more risky and results in inferior *glissement*. In the past, racers used the skating and double pole plant for accelerating. Today, giant slalom speeds are too great for these techniques to remain effective.

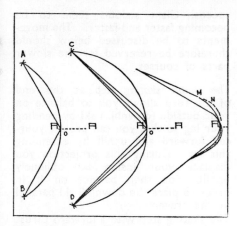

The Shape of Turns

It is difficult to visualize the different lines followed by a racer who turns very round and one who uses a " square " turn. This diagram should help. In order to move from A to B via O, the roundest line is a third of a circle while the most square would be the angle AOB. This first line measuring 40.8 meters, the second would measure 30 meters. The difference is very slight and a turn following angle AOB would lead to a considerable braking action of the skis. In the COD line the arc is 2/3 of a circle and the respective distances would be 61.2 meters and 55.2 meters. There are intermediate lines which include two traverses and the arc of a circle. It is the possibility of describing a certain arc of a circle with a minimum braking action of the skis which determines the most favorable line.

A turn initiated too high or too early will require tightening the arc while turning. This will result automatically in a sideslip and a braking action of the skis. It will sometimes make you slide low. (See figure 3, the clear line into a sideslip sketch). From this excessively high line you could have started an even arc by starting the turn later (N instead of M). It is obvious that the darkest line is the best. It is the shortest and includes two steeper traverses. However, the shorter the radius of the turn, the better the technique required for avoiding excessive sideslipping and braking action.

slipping. If you run into them sideways, you will fall. The more or less regular banks resulting from the rutting of the turns when the course is too soft are generally less dangerous and can often be used advantageously.

In order to ski in a very rutted giant slalom course : 1) You must be sure to shape your turns depending on the position of the outside bank of the ruts and not depending on the position of the poles. You should start your turns so that your skis come into contact with the outside bank from the very beginning of the rut. You will be able to break this rule from time to time and to turn on the inside of a rut without slipping to the outside of the turn. However, you must only do so in very special cases, after which you must again use the outside banks. Otherwise, you will slow your skis, lose the rhythm of the course and disturb your balance in rutted giant slaloms which are often true massacres for these very reasons. 2) You must be sure to flex your legs smoothly as soon as you come in contact with the outside bank of the rut, in a slightly seated position, arms spread wide apart, outside pole ready to be planted. Do not try to check under any circumstances. Work like a bobsled. 3) You must be sure to come back into balance over the full length of your skis as soon as the rut ends. In order to do so balance completely on your outside ski and project forward onto your uphill ski with a skating step. When two turns link together without an intermediate traverse, be careful of lateral projection, which will be discussed in the next paragraph. If you do not know how to use it very well yet, you risk throwing yourself from a seated position on the tails of your skis to a position even farther back thus losing your balance over backwards.

Controlling the turn with a flat ski vs. carving the turn

I will not return to the techniques of controlling the arcs of turns already presented in the preceding chapter (pages 138 to 146). I have mentioned the advantage for the amateur racer for practising racing technique systematically while free skiing. This is especially true for controlling the arcs of turns. However, it is also necessary to train a great deal in courses in order to learn to adapt these techniques to the imperatives of racing. In effect, you should work constantly in courses in order to combine a maximum *glissement* with the best possible line. This work will require a constant effort to overcome centrifugal force, to adapt to unexpected changes in terrain, etc... You will probably discover the most effective movement for a given difficulty when presented with it in a course, even though you have been unable to find the solution in free skiing. You will then be able to improve the movement whenever you want, but it is in competition that you will discover other movements which will little by little turn you into a very good skier. We have noticed this fact for the last twenty years in working with our pupils in the University of Grenoble ski programs. From a similar technical level those who race surpass definitively within one season those who do not.

Traditional forms of acceleration

To accelerate by pushing with your arms or legs is only possible at slower speeds. Giant slaloms seem to be becoming faster and faster. The movements to be discussed below should therefore be reserved for the slower parts of courses.

The simple skating step at the end of the turn allows you to balance on your outside (downhill) ski by bending your leg so that you can project yourself forward and uphill by extending this leg. During this projection you displace your inside ski obliquely uphill. You then balance on it in order to place the downhill ski parallel in the traverse.

The skating step with a forward thrust of the uphill leg and a double pole plant is similar to the preceding movement, but after the straightening of your downhill leg you weight your flexed uphill leg and, by extending it, you prolong and amplify the forward projection of your upper body, arms forward, and poles ready to be planted. You then plant both poles and pull on them in order to accelerate while pulling your feet forward, and in order to assume a balance body position either in a traverse or in a turn which can be initiated immediately.

Holding with the inside ski while extending the uphill leg resembles the second part of the above movement very much. You can do this by trying to hold with your inside ski in the last third of your turn. Your outside ski will spread diagonally toward the outside of the turn in a movement resembling its movement in a skating step, but very different because you will not be weighting it. You will have discovered holding with the inside ski at the end of the turn through a flexed position of your inside leg and a transfer of the mass of your body over this ski. At the finish of the turn you will be able to project your upper body and arms forward by straightening this leg. As

Lateral Projection

in the skating movement described above, you can then plant both poles and pull on them in order to launch yourself into the following traverse or more often into the beginning of a new turn.

The new lateral projection with avalement

A new type of projection which allows the skier to dart from one turn into another developed with the appearance of *avalement*. Gustavo Thoeni and Patrick Russel affirmed their indisputable superiority in international competition at the beginning of the 1969-70 season because they were the only racers to possess this technical element. Many believed this movement was only a skating step permitting them to accelerate from one turn into the

other. This analysis was not completely false. Their projection from one foot to the other does allow them to go faster. However, this projection does not actually create the acceleration as it is hardly directed forward at all. The movement is primarily lateral. The secret lies in the movement of *avalement* which follows, resulting in an accelerated forward movement of the skis into the turn being started. In having Patrick Russel repeat this movement thousands of times, I found that it presents several advantages : 1) It forces the skier to remain on his outside ski at the end of the turn, and I noticed that nine times out of ten this fact permits a better control of the third phase of a turn. On the other hand, the traditional skating step with forward projection must be made an instant earlier, and does not allow a perfect and total completion of the arc. 2) It permits a thrust

GIANT SLALOM

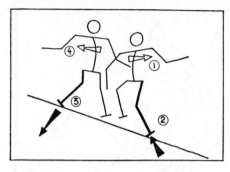

A Schematic Representation of Lateral Projection

You should feel as if the force, generated by the lateral thrust on the downhill leg, were transmitted totally to your uphill ski. In this manner, you will be able to balance on your uphill ski (which is the outside ski of the turn to be initiated) as soon as the turn begins. You thus avoid sideslipping at the beginning of the turn, and you can start carving immediately. A displacement of the upper body accompanies and facilitates the lateral projection. It is a downhill displacement before and at the beginning of the thrust, and uphill during and after the thrust which insures your balance on the outside ski and an early weighting of the outside ski of the new turn. It is actually a movement in two phases: 1) thrust, 2) balance on the displaced ski.

onto the middle of the ski, and as a result there is the least possibility of the tail or tip section of the ski slipping out when maximum pressure is applied.
3) The lateral projection of the skier's upper body allows him to weight and balance on his new outside ski perfectly as soon as its edge has changed and it starts the next turn. Sideslipping at the beginning of the turn resulting from inward lean is thus avoided, or at least decreased.
4) Lateral projection, which is actually an extension of the leg and of the small of the back, prepares the following

avalement muscularly. The uphill ski after being projected laterally uphill is thrust forward through *avalement* and changes edges gradually during this thrust. At the end of his *avalement* movement, the skier is in perfect balance on the tail of his outside ski which controls the beginning of the arc of the next turn.

This lateral projection is the same as the "S" turn with projection from one foot to the other, a turn which you can easily perfect and practise while free skiing.

Starting with a wand

The problems posed by starting with a wand in giant slalom are identical to those in slalom (see page 153).

Training for giant slalom

It might be thought that training for giant slalom would be easier than training for slalom. This is in fact not true. First a giant slalom occupies a great deal more surface area. Most ski areas have prepared only a slalom stadium and do not permit courses elsewhere. In my opinion, this is too bad. I think that it would be interest-

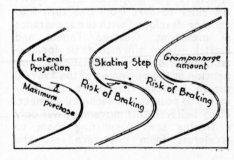

ing for an area to provide a giant slalom run with a course reset each hour by an instructor or a patrolman. Second, instructors and coaches find it easier to observe and correct their racers on a complete course which can be seen from top to bottom. At this point I would like to call to the attention of my colleagues the fact that valuable giant slalom training is possible on a 200 to 300 yard run. All of the suggestions given on page 156 for slalom training are applicable to giant slalom. I have noticed that training in slalom technique improves a racer's giant slalom technique while the opposite is not always true. However, this observation should not lead you to neglect giant slalom training because, while movements are practised better in slalom, the sensitivity to *glissement* is developed more effectively in giant slalom.

Giant slalom tactics

Tactics in giant slalom are very similar to those in slalom (page 156) with two nuances. First in learning the course you must pay more attention to the relief of the terrain. Your increased speed multiplies the effect of the slightest bump, fall-away, or knoll considerably. A fall-away which is negligible at twenty or twenty-five miles per hour can become fearsome at thirty-five to forty. The technical problems in giant slalom should result as much from the use of the terrain as from the placement of the gates. The best way to judge the speed of the course and the problems it poses is to make turns parallel to it. This practice is against the rules but generally tolerated by the organizers of the race. Another special problem in giant slalom is making a good estimate of your probable fatigue at the end of the course. Depending on your physical condition you must decide whether you will be able to project from one foot to the other over the full length of the course, or whether you had better save strength in certain parts of the course in order to concentrate your efforts on the sections where they will be most effective.

It is said that downhill is the king of the alpine ski events, but the number of downhill races organized each year decreases regularly. Why ?

The organizers of downhill races have been unable to change the design of their runs in such a way as to favor the popularization of this discipline. Let me explain. The evolution of ski design, running surfaces, and of techniques for *glissement* have allowed racers to reach much higher speeds on the same runs. Even though safety bindings have limited the dangers of falling at high speeds, these dangers are still great. The proportion of skiers willing to schuss a given run has as a result decreased considerably. In addition those responsible for the downhill runs have made the courses wider in order to avoid the risk of a racer hitting the trees, but in doing so they generally make them straighter as well. However, considering what has just been stated, they should have made the courses more winding in order to limit the possible speeds. Again, in order to limit the risks, bumps have been cut, knolls rounded and fall-aways flattened, all serving to eliminate or decrease the checks required in the past and as a result, to increase the speed which in itself constitutes a danger.

The increase in the number of skiers and the traffic on the slopes has resulted in the growth of mogul fields which make high speeds impossible. Even the best skier cannot continue to absorb beyond a certain rhythm. As a result he must then lock his legs and ricochet over the tops of the moguls. This is only possible for a short distance, perhaps ten yards. In order to set a downhill, it is first necessary to cut down all of the bumps !

In addition, a run devoted to downhill either for training or for a race must be closed to all other skiers. Neither should it intersect another run. These two requirements make it materially impossible for most ski areas to reserve a run for downhill. Many even have great difficulty organizing one downhill race a year as the course must be open for training during two or three days before the race. This problem is even greater during school vacations and as a result collegiate and interscholastic racers have fewer and fewer opportunities to learn to run or to train for this event.

It is a shame that this should be the case because the desire for speed, and possibly for violence, takes hold of everybody at one time or another. Downhill could be a precious outlet and an incomparable mode of education. Downhill is in effect the culmination of the joy of skiing, complete liberty, flying. It is also an unpardoning confrontation of the voluntarily excessive enthusiasm of the racer with hard reality. To enjoy downhill may require being a little crazy, but much more courage, self-control, and sure judgment are necessary. More than a fight against the clock, it is a fight and a victory over oneself. It is, in a few minutes of competition, one of the last "adventures" of modern times. An enriching adventure which the initiated continue to discuss twenty years later...

This section is not only intended for downhill racers but also for any skier who would like to taste the joy of speed even if until now it has always seemed impossible. It is often true that a simple mistake prevents the skier from ever exceeding a certain speed. Among these mistakes are :

● an excessively narrow stance, knees locked together

● an excessively forward body position

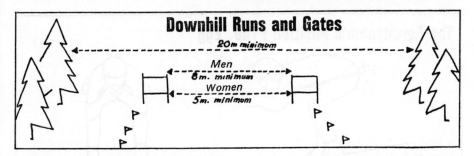

Downhill Runs and Gates

20m minimum

Men
6m. minimum

Women
5m. minimum

Downhill runs must have a minimum width of 20 meters at their narrowest point. The gates are red for men and alternately red and blue for women. Small flags are used to mark the sides of the course, red to the left and green to the right. Yellow flags mark a danger (boulder barely sticking out of the snow, abrupt dip, etc.).
The F.I.S. rule requires a 500 to 1000 meter vertical drop for a men's downhill and a 400 to 700 meter vertical drop for a women's course.

● poor support from the skis due to some morphological problem which could be remedied (see page 183)

● bad, deformed, or poorly adapted skis.
All of these problems have been studied and solutions proposed.
However, even without one of these mistakes you could feel your ability limited in downhill. Either you are over cautious and, consciously or not, you refuse to take the risk, or you feel deep down that your balance is not good enough. Through technical improvement in slalom and giant slalom, you can make up for a mediocre sense of balance, but in downhill, this is much more difficult. This sense of balance, difficult to define clearly or measure, is divided unequally among men just as any other motor talent (like springing which allows one man to high jump over seven feet and another to high jump only a yard)... Nine times out of ten it is sense of balance which determines relaxation, flexibility in the legs, independence of the legs, ease while in the air, and the ability to recover. I do not think that this innate characteristic can be developed after a certain age, but I believe it can be improved in a child if he skis a great deal. If you were not able to learn to ski when you were young, except if you are an exceptional case, limit your ambitions to your real possibilities, and do not try to rush your improvement. In this way you will be able to gain the greatest pleasure in speed.

Schussing

All of the suggestions I gave to beginners and intermediates for straight running are applicable here again : wide or semi-wide stance; ankles, knees, hips, small of the back as flexible hinges; proper position of the pelvis (see page 111); maximum relaxation; independence of each leg; smooth balancing play of shoulders and arms... Balance in downhill depends essentially on the feelings under the feet. Eyesight and correct judgment of the terrain allow the skier to anticipate, to prepare

The Aerodynamic Position : The "Egg"

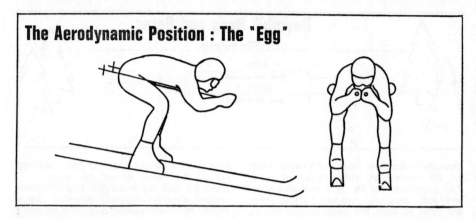

for coming changes, but this preparation is determined ninety-nine per cent of the time by what the skier feels with his feet and legs. Action in downhill is almost always a response to the demands of the run. No matter how fast they go, the greatest downhillers still retain a certain passiveness. Try to feel on the slopes what I have explained here. I think it is the only way you will understand what I mean.

Have you felt what is meant by terminal speed ?

While schussing a long regular slope have you felt the moment when your speed no longer increases ? Wind resistance is neutralizing the acceleration produced by the resultant of gravity. If the slope increases, your speed increases, then becomes stable once again. If you flex your body into a more aerodynamic position, wind resistance decreases, and your speed increases, then becomes stable once more. This game of reaching your terminal speed in a variety of conditions should be your first type of training for downhill. It should eliminate much

of your apprehension, and you will discover the simplest and most effective manner of checking, standing up into a windcheck.

Feel the glissement of your skis

In downhill you should consider yourself the pilot (driver) of your skis. You should try to get the most out

The High Position

of them. In order to do so you must know them perfectly; feel them, perceive the slightest friction, and the slightest vibrations in your tips. All of your movements should be determined by a search for *glissement* of your skis on the snow without, however, neglecting the problem of wind resistance which will be discussed farther on.

The *glissement* of your skis results from their own characteristics : good distribution of flexibility, perfect condition of the base and edges, sufficient damping for avoiding superfluous chattering and vibration, sufficient "life" for holding a line,... It also depends on how you control them through the arcs of turns. As a general rule you should not hold your skis very firmly (especially in a lateral plane) during schusses. On easy runs you should let them run as freely as possible, almost floating, so that they flatten as much as possible on the surface of the snow by themselves, adjusting to the many irregularities in terrain. You allow your skis to "float" by keeping your feet and ankles relaxed. You should even feel a certain lateral mobility in your knees. Any forward or backward lean which would put your foot, ankle, or knee joints under tension and disturb their mobility would disturb that of your skis as a result. Thus, a perfectly balanced body position is essential under any circumstances for obtaining better *glissement*.

Be sensitive to aerodynamics

With the increase in downhill speeds the search for a more aerodynamic position continued until 1960. In 1956 Jean Vuarnet and I described the egg

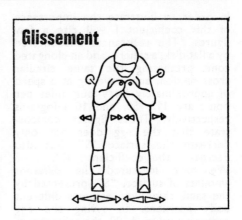

position which has not been improved since and which was one of the most important factors in Vuarnet's victory in the 1960 Olympic downhill at Squaw Valley. Since this date downhill speeds have continued to increase, and in most cases the search for an even greater improvement in aerodynamics would seem to have become superfluous. It seems that at present insufficient attention is paid to aerodynamics in the parts of the run where terminal speed is not attained. Think about this idea when you are racing a downhill. It is in the easier parts of the course that you will be able to gain a few tenths of a second most easily, and a slight improvement in your aerodynamics is often enough to do this.

A few figures concerning wind resistance : The formula for determining wind resistance for speeds exceeding 38 miles per hour is KSV^2. "S" is the surface area opposing forward movement, "V^2" the square of the speed (which means that a speed which is doubled corresponds to a quadrupled wind resistance), and "K" is a coefficient which varies according to the form and the nature of the surface of the moving object.

In order to illustrate the importance of this coefficient I will cite a few figures. The resistances encountered by a flat disk, a sphere, and an elongated cone presenting the same circular cross section, and traveling at a speed of approximately forty-four miles per hour, are 112, 50, and 10 kilograms respectively. These figures demonstrate that the egg does not only decrease the surface "S", but also decreases the coefficient "K".

We have measured the different amounts of surface, "S", presented by the same skier who assumes different body positions. In giving the egg position a value of 100, the corresponding value of a standing position is 165 and for an egg position with arms unfolded, 125. These simple increases in "S" can correspond to decreases in usual terminal speeds in the order of 22 % in the first case and 11 % in the second. On the speed trial run at Alpe d'Huez we found that two skiers who weigh about 165 pounds, who are equipped with the same skis and dressed in the same manner, attain a ceiling speed of 90 miles per hour in the egg position and of 59 miles per hour in a straight body position with arms unfolded.

A wide, semi-wide, or very wide stance

There is no absolute rule for a stance in downhill, as the goal of the skier must be considered : avoiding loss of balance, better *glissement*, better aerodynamics... However, it will be possible to give you a few general hints.

In a straight body position do not spread your skis too far apart. Assume at most what I have called a semi-wide stance. First, this is the only way to keep your skis flat on the snow. (If by chance this is not the case for you, your morphology is special, and you should probably cant your boots. See page 183.) In addition, each change in relief encountered by one ski, if you are in a wide stance, will result in an oblique push which would tend to unbalance you, instead of in a simple upward push of your ski under your body.

In the egg position use a wide stance. The more you bend at the waist, that is, the closer you bring your chest to your thighs, the more your thighs and knees tend to spread. Your tibias should remain vertical when observed

The Super "Egg" : The Bullet

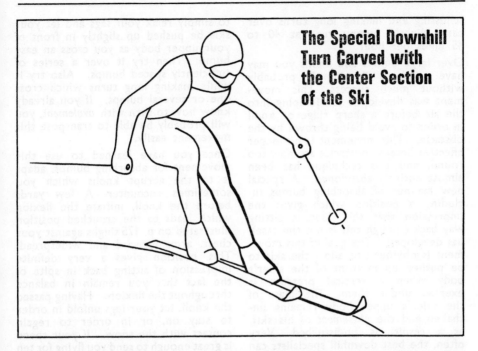

The Special Downhill Turn Carved with the Center Section of the Ski

from the front so that they can oscillate vertically without causing your skis to tip onto their edges. The lower your egg position, the wider your stance should become. Once you have become familiar with the position, you will find your aerodynamics improved because your position is lower. You will find that your balance is better because your knees no longer hit your chest when you ride bumps. Your chest will ride between your legs, allowing them to work more freely for better *glissement*. If in a low position you tend to lose your balance over backwards, elevate the heels of your boots. This might even improve your overall balance on your skis.

Bumps, the seated position

I have already mentioned the current tendency of rounding off or even eliminating most of the bumps which constituted the principal difficulty of most downhill runs in the past. Knolls and transitions are also smoothed. When bulldozers are used to make new runs or to improve old ones, this trend is emphasized. Downhill runs become wide, smooth "boulevards". However, at the high speeds of modern downhill a bump which would have been insignificant in the past will catapult the racers tremendous distances. A resultant evolution in downhill technique has begun.

On small bumps, which have become rare on modern downhills, you will notice very quickly that it is essential to hold a very balanced position over your skis in order to allow your legs to work freely, folding and unfolding, to absorb the changes in relief. You can easily improve this technique by schussing and making long turns over easy, slightly bumpy runs at 40 to 45 miles per hour.

Over large bumps and knolls you may have tried to "prejump", probably without much success. This movement was developed for jumping into the air before a sharp ridge or knoll in order to avoid being thrown by the obstacle. This movement is no longer effective because obstacles are now too round, and this technique has been almost entirely abandoned. A special new manner of absorbing bumps including a position which gives the impression that the skier is sitting way back (though this is not the case), has developed. The goal of this movement is obvious : to allow the skis to be pushed up in front of the skier's body when a vertical pressure is exerted under them. The mass of the skier's upper body remains unshaken and the *glissement* of his skis, as a result, is undisturbed. Very often, the best downhill specialists can be observed using their stomach muscles in order to pull their feet up in front of their upper bodies even more rapidly. When in spite of pulling with their stomach muscles the racers are thrown into the air, one notices that their seemingly back position does not increase. Instead their legs unfold downward like the landing gear of an airplane while their trunk continues forward, and they come back into contact with the snow in a balanced position. This movement resembles *avalement*, the means of starting a turn with maximum *glissement*.

As in *avalement*, the initiation of a forward rebalancing movement of the trunk while the legs are pulled upward underneath, is essential if this movement is to be executed properly. Do not try to learn the manoeuvre by making too ample and too rapid a movement. On the contrary, try first to simply relax your legs and let your skis be pushed up slightly in front of your upper body as you cross an easy bump. Then try it over a series of sufficiently spaced bumps. Also try it while making long turns which cross one or several bumps. If you already know how to turn with *avalement,* you will probably be able to transpose this movement easily.

Once you have learned to use this movement for absorbing bumps, adapt it to the abrupt knolls which you sometimes encounter. A few yards before the knoll, initiate the flexion which leads to the crouched position illustrated on p. 175 thighs against your chest, arms forward and widespread. This position gives a very definite impression of sitting back in spite of the fact that you remain in balance throughout the flexion. Having passed the knoll, let your legs unfold in order to stay on, or in order to regain contact with the snow. If your speed is great enough to send you flying for ten yards or more, and if you want to hold an aerodynamic position while in the air, remain folded for a few tenths of a second by contracting your stomach muscles before unfolding.

A mistake to avoid

The most common mistake, made by novice downhill skiers, and even by some great slalom and giant slalom champions, is to make the same kind of turns used in giant slalom when skiing downhill. It could be thought that the difference in speeds between the slalom events and downhill would not be great enough to require very different techniques. One fact proves the contrary : The best giant slalom specialists can be, and often are, mediocre downhillers. You can be

Turns Made with Inward Knee Push

certain therefore that you must learn to make special turns in order to be effective in downhill.

Turns made while in a low body position

In a low position, especially in the egg, the most common and most effective turn currently used by the greatest downhill specialists is made with an inward push of the outside knee. This inward push of the knee edges the ski which produces the turn as a result of its sidecut and its bend. Centrifugal force weights the outside ski, and the less weighted inside pivots easily into the turn while remaining flat. This type of turn is particularly easy and is very effective in long radius arcs on relatively easy slopes. It can also be used effectively on steep slopes in tighter arcs if the terrain banks slightly. On fall-away terrain, however, it is ineffective. It can be executed perfectly while the skier holds the egg because the upper body is used very little and because it generally disturbs the skier's balance

very little. The turn can also be used when the skier is in a semi-straight body position, holding his arms widespread. It then requires a fair amount of angulation along with the inward push of the knee.

Carved turns in the egg with weight on both skis rarely give maximum glissement. The racers who use them do so most often because they give a feeling of security. Unfortunately, however, it results in a slowing of their skis. This deceleration increases even more if the skier leans forward and holds his feet together. If you are a narrow stance specialist you must be extremely wary of using this type of turn. Of course, it is elegant and permits a very aerodynamic arm position in both a low and a semi-straight body position. It can, however, completely arrest your improvement in downhill.

In a high body position, carve on your outside ski

It is enough to have seen Karl Schranz carve a perfect turn over rough terrain at sixty miles per hour with his inside ski lifted to recognize the superiority of this technique. I think that this type of turn was first perfected by Tony Sailer more than fifteen years ago and that it has remained, at least partially, the speciality of the great Austrian downhillers. The technique is very simple. It is that of carved turns, or more exactly, that of the control of carved arcs, because at downhill speeds the initiation of turns is an almost imperceptible movement. It depends entirely on the perfection of balancing on the outside ski from the very beginning of the arc. At very high speeds the question is no longer one of carving with the tip or the tail of the ski. One must balance perfectly on the center section of the ski so that its forward and backward sections can oscillate freely without disturbing the purchase of the central portion of the ski, which alone seems to establish the arc. In the lateral plane this necessitates a perfectly controlled angulation which places the upper body in exact balance over the head of the femur of the outside leg. During the arc you should feel two support points, your outside hip and the inside edge of your outside ski, constantly. Your outside leg should work perfectly in the plane of your ski. It should be able to flex or extend freely in order to absorb the changes in terrain. The leg remains stable only in the frontal plane in order to control the arc of the turn, as do the oscillating arms which hold the wheels of a car that has a flexible suspension. This balance on the hip, which implies marked angulation (especially if the skier is tall and thin), is almost always used with a wide arm position which favors the lateral balancing indispensable to this kind of turn. When you try this turn, be careful to avoid carving with your tip. Forward pressure can be effective at intermediate speeds and

even at high speeds on easy terrain. However, it does not provide maximum *glissement,* and you would have to weight both skis if you ran into trouble. You would risk losing your balance more easily and the chances of slowing your skis unintentionally would increase. In downhill, efficient carving on one ski is more closely related to carving with the tail as described on page 145 than to carving on the tips, which for years many coaches considered the best technique.

Checking

I will not discuss the most common form of checking, wind checking, which consists simply in unfolding the body, and possibly the arms, in order to increase wind resistance. This can lower your speed ten to twenty per cent so rapidly that you should use it carefully. Another type of checking is a brutal movement which can allow you to stop within twenty, forty, or sixty yards without leaving the axis of the course. This checking method is nothing other than *braquage,* that is the

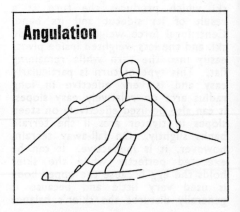

Angulation

The Seated Position for Absorbing Bumps

abrupt pivoting of your skis across the slope which we suggested for athletic beginners during their first hours of skiing (page 27). Without knowing how to check or stop with this technique, you should try to train only on a downhill course which is packed very wide. Most injuries in training result from skiing out of the course when trying to stop.

Typical Silhouette of Present Day Downhillers

Checking on a fall-away is the easiest. This consists in simply sideslipping on the edges with maximum pressure on the tails of your skis, the technique discovered by any energetic beginner who wants to slow down in a traverse. The only skiers who have trouble checking in this manner are those who have learned to associate sideslipping with forward lean. They must discover a truly balanced sideslip in which sitting back slightly compensates for the slowing of the skis. This check is most effective in a fairly wide stance. It results essentially from the gripping of the downhill ski, and frequently this ski stems slightly. Learn to control this check at high speed with your downhill ski. The other ski, spread uphill slightly, is only used to insure your balance.

The braking snowplow is valuable in downhill, or more exactly, during downhill training. The racer who can open a snowplow and slow down before reaching a difficult section without moving out of his line, who can even snowplow through a section of a course in order to establish points of reference, feel out the terrain, and establish his line perfectly, has a very valuable tool at his disposal. The snowplow unfortunately is possible only on smooth parts of the course. With the advent of "boulevard" courses it could be used more often in training than it is. The snowplow does not require a special technique. It simply necessitates strong legs, a perfect sense for the purchase with the tails of the skis, and the ability to use *braquage*. If you have trouble with it, force yourself to snowplow at high speed down the full length of a smooth slope. I know of no better exercise for building your hip muscles and for becoming conscious of the forces which you can exert on the tails of your skis.

Checking while turning is common, but I do not recommend it. The repeated passage of racers through the gates wears the turns and makes ruts, or small steps. Under some conditions it may cause the course to break up or become icy. Checking before the turns is always best. However, you will sometimes find yourself going too fast in a difficult turn, and you will have to check during the arc of the turn. The only rational way to check in this case would be to use *braquage* of your outside leg from a wide stance. In other words you should edge your outside ski and hold it slightly crosswise to your direction of travel in a sideslip. Pushing your outside knee inward and balancing on your oblique outside ski, you will check as effectively as if you were sideslipping on both skis. However, your balance will be better, especially if you bounce over bumps or ruts. In addition your inside ski will be placed advantageously for instantaneous use if you should want to stop checking or to plunge into another turn.

As I stated at the beginning of this chapter, it is increasingly more difficult to train for downhill. The few permanent courses which do exist are either too difficult (when designed for major downhills) or too easy (when designed for ski school standard races). These easy courses, however, are very valuable for getting used to speed. Take advantage of them, especially when they have been rutted or when they are icy. Once you have become accustomed to them, you will be able to adapt to difficult courses more easily.

You could also use a deserted beginner or intermediate slope for a couple of high speed runs. These should be simulated downhill runs with as many schusses and major changes in direction as possible, not a series of high speed long radius turns which you can make while free skiing. Such downhill runs are always more or less risky, but they are perhaps your only means for becoming a real downhill racer.

The course before a downhill race is often in poor shape, good enough for the strong, experienced downhiller to learn it well very quickly, but not for the less experienced racers. During training periods, I spend my time discouraging competitors from losing their precious training time standing next to the course watching the better racers, or trying to learn the tiniest details in the terrain which they will not be able to remember anyway. This is absurd. If you are not already a great downhill specialist, remember that you will only become one by getting as much mileage as possible. Only when you have this mileage should you devote some of your time to observing small details in terrain.

How to learn a downhill course

You must study in stages : 1) Learn the general relief of the course, for example, long easy schuss, long turn into the woods, double S, then long fall-away, rough schuss over a sharp knoll,... At the same time look for places where you will be able to stop easily. You can complete this first stage while the course is being prepared and thus avoid losing training time. 2) As soon as you can, run part of the course in a standing position. Stop, and make mental notes for improving in this section, then run the next section. Limit the number of stops as much as possible. Remind yourself constantly that it is by skiing a downhill course that you will learn it. 3) As soon as possible, link several sections of the course together. If you do not want to take the full course non-stop in order to avoid getting tired, avoid stopping in the same places all the time. Vary your stopping places especially if they correspond to difficult areas... 4) Run the full length of the course repeatedly, criticize your run yourself, and if you do not have a coach, ask your friends their opinion of your runs through one section or another. Before reacting to these opinions, evaluate them thoroughly. During the mandatory non-stop run take the course as if you were racing. Do not count on doing better in the race. It might be possible to do better, but it would probably be dangerous. Instead, wait for the next downhill, and go faster from the very beginning of the training period.

Race tactics

Try to leave as little as possible to chance. You will be more calm at the start, and you will be better able to resist the temptation to change plans drastically at the last minute. You should have already thought about waxing corrections in case the conditions change a great deal at the last minute. You should know where to take a shorter line if the snow is slower or where to check if the snow is faster than in practice. If you have not been able to look at the course in the last few minutes, and if you do not have a coach, ask the officials about the conditions or about any changes, bumps removed, etc... You have already checked your bindings, your boots, poles, and goggles carefully. If necessary, you have put your goggles in a dry place. You should arrive at the start early, but not so early as to allow yourself to cool off too much. You have just skied at least five or six hundred yards at high speed in order to warm up. On some types of snow you may use this warm up run to "ski out" your wax, to make it run faster. On other snows, which might wear your wax or dirty it, you should use a second pair of skis. At the start remain calm and relaxed. Push off with your plan in mind and stick to it.

PREPARE YOURSELF PHYSICALLY

Indispensable physical qualities

Before beginning a physical conditioning program for a particular sport it is essential to know the physical qualities demanded by that particular sport. It is also necessary to determine whether one is preparing for an immediate goal, for a few months later (summer training for example), or for a few years later (aiming for maximum results once you are an adult). In addition, physical conditioning should be adapted to each individual. All of this is very complex, and obviously I can only touch on the subject. This problem still seems to be treated empirically in most national teams. Individualization in training and adaptation of training to the different age groups in both men's and women's national teams seem inadequate. There is a lot to be done before physical conditioning for skiing reaches the level of physical conditioning for track, as an example.

The essentials in physical strength for a competitive skier would seem to me to be : 1) sufficient muscular power and joint strength for his weight, 2) suppleness, which supported by the power already mentioned permits him maximum speed of execution (taking into account his initial neuromotor qualities which are difficult to improve), 3) maximum physical resistance to intense efforts lasting forty seconds to three minutes, 4) endurance, which under favorable circumstances would permit him to last through large doses of training for several consecutive days over a period of several months, and 5) resistance to cold, bad weather, shocks, pain, torn muscles, to loss of energy, to sickness, etc.

The neuro-motor qualities precious to the ski racer are exactly the same as those required by a race car driver. The skier "drives" his skis at speeds over sixty miles per hour. He must have excellent sight, a well developed kinesthetic sense, clear judgment, great decision-and-execution speed, quick but not hasty reflexes, great skill, and great composure which will not let any emotion disturb the functioning of his body. Are these qualities innate, acquired definitely at birth, or can they be improved ? This question will be discussed for a long time, but one fact is certain. Repeatedly subjected to the tests of competition, the racer improves unquestionably in these areas.

How to train for physical conditioning

If you are younger than seventeen, eighteen or nineteen and if you have not finished growing, do not try to develop physically by conditioning exclusively for skiing. The simple fact that you ski often has probably already influenced your physical development. If you are not working for immediate results, try to develop harmoniously without hesitating to develop the qualities which skiing has a tendency to decrease, joint flexibility, spring, muscular relaxation... In the long run you will be better off. Play volleyball, tennis, basketball. Swim, train for track (especially the sprints) and gymnastics. If you are limited materially to running and bicycling, avoid long, monotonous efforts. Vary your efforts with short, or even very short sprints, then relax, and repeat. In any case use the exercises described on page 47, and push your limits. Do not use a single exercise intensively unless you have a weakness, for example, bicycling or running if you lack endurance, muscle building if you are skinny...

If you are a normally developed adult, work equally between : 1) running on varied terrain or bicycling at alternate speeds, first increasing your pulse to 120 or 130 then resting, good soccer or basketball games, or swim training, and 2) muscle building, not for mass, but for quality (the muscles to be developed are essentially those of your legs and hips including your rotators, the small of your back, your abdominal muscles, and your shoulders) and 3) an opposite type of muscle and joint conditioning in order to counter balance the contracting effect of intensive skiing. To make this more comprehensible, a few examples will help : the hops or rope skipping as practised by boxers will loosen your leg muscles, help you to increase their agility and their spring. Volleyball and tennis can do the same thing if not played too intensively. Traditional stretching exercises for legs, arms, and trunk with swinging movements and changes in rhythm also correspond to what we are looking for. The series of four exercises proposed on page 47 are a minimum for a skier who would like to get in shape for racing. They cover the needs already mentioned with the exception of endurance. A weekly run, hike, or bicycle ride should be added to them.

Conditioning through skiing

In my opinion the time spent on skis by all racers, even those of the national teams, is insufficient. The length of time spent training on skis increases each year but will continue to increase in years to come. I base this judgment on personal experience in older sports than skiing. It has only been since 1968 that the French National Team has started to train during the summer, though summer training has been proven successful at the Grenoble University Club since 1953. The decisive advance of the French over the Austrians is probably due to this training. To choose to train dryland when one could be training on snow would definitely be a mistake. Indispensable physical conditioning could take place between training sessions on the snow. Besides, skiing itself is a highly specialized form of physical conditioning especially if the coach is aware of the fact, plans and varies the training with this goal in mind.

Ski training used to be seasonal, but it is becoming a year-round endeavor. When it does so, skiing will take a bound forward similar to that made by the other sports which have made the same change. However, a necessarily slow transformation must take place in the psychology of skiers. Training programs must be carefully planned in order to give the correct doses at different times of the year. This evolution will make the compensation exercises already mentioned even more necessary, especially because skiing by itself does not seem to develop a satisfactory body morphology.

TYPES OF RACES

Races for average skiers

Races for average skiers are regularly
held by ski schools. They are normally
"standard" races set on the same run
each week and forerun by two or
three instructors. The courses are
usually open slaloms or relatively easy
giant slaloms set for the average skier.
Many areas hold NASTAR (for National
Standard Races) giant slaloms. The
courses are set and forerun by an
instructor who has competed in elimi-
nation runs at the beginning of the
year in order to establish a handicap
relative to the other NASTAR "Pace-
setters" all over the country.
Any skier may register for a nominal
fee to race in these standard races.
Once he has raced, his time is computed
relative to that of the forerunner, and
a prize, a gold, silver, or bronze medal
is awarded according to the interval.
In NASTAR, the medal awarded in one
area corresponds more or less closely
to a medal won in another. At the
end of the season regional eliminations
are held between the best racers
from each area, and the winners
participate in a national championship.

TYPES OF RACES

Collegiate and interscholastic competition

A collegiate circuit of races is sanctioned by the NCAA. College teams representing separate institutions compete regionally and nationally. Nordic as well as alpine competition determines the national and regional champions. Interscholastic competition is relatively poorly developed except in advantageously located private schools. Some high school programs do exist, but they are subject to local scholastic transporatation rules, and do not coordinate very well with USSA programs.

USSA competition

The clubs and regional divisions of the United States Ski Association have traditionally held races for amateurs. Open racing may begin soon as well. The major goal of the USSA has been the development and fielding of a national team to represent the United States in international competition. All races are held in accordance with rules established by the Fédération Internationale de Ski (F.I.S.). Age and ability categories determine the classification of each racer and limit the races in which he can participate. Classification races are held by the

divisions at the beginning of the season. Individuals move from "unclassified" into an ability group and work up through the categories depending on their race results.

For further information contact your division office. You will be able to find out about junior programs for children, the normal amateur program for adults, and the veteran races for those twenty-seven years of age or older.

Citadin competition

Citadin competition, that is a race circuit for competitors who do not live in ski areas, unfortunately does not exist in the U.S. These amateur races are organized by individual clubs and serve as eliminations for citadin national teams which compete in citadin world championships every two years. They also serve as a great complement to the normal amateur circuits which are often already over encumbered with ambitious national team aspirants. Those who would compete without ulterior motives are thus gradually forced into poor seedings or classifications. A citadin circuit in the U.S. could give these racers greater opportunities for high level competition in many scenic ski areas and for the development of great friendships and comradeships which are the true pleasures of ski racing.

CANT YOUR BOOTS

It is impossible to ski well without good boots which are well adapted to your feet. Certain morphological peculiarities in feet and legs are a considerable handicap in skiing. Through experiment we have found a remedy, although we cannot guarantee a 100 % correction in every case.

Four problems are particularly common

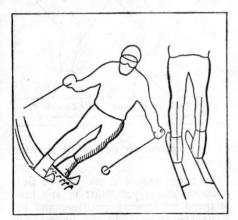

1) Weight distributed onto the outside edges during straight runs and onto the inside ski during turns :

If you have a tendency to catch outside edges when straight running or in very long radius turns; if you tend to weight your inside ski excessively in narrow stance turns; if you feel, or if someone else notices that your

knees are wider apart than your feet when you assume a low position or, especially, when you turn; you are weighting the outer sides of your skis excessively, and you are having trouble weighting the inner sides. Your legs are probably bowed, either over their full length, only in your lower legs, or possibly only when you flex them. The remedy ? A 2, 4, or 6 millimeter cant under the inside edges of the soles of your boots. Thus more of your weight will be distributed automatically onto the inner side of your skis.

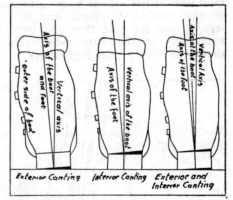

Exterior Canting   Interior Canting   Exterior and Interior Canting

2) Difficulty making edges hold in traverses and edgesets :

If you must push the knee of your weighted leg inward excessively in order to edge effectively on steep, icy slopes, and if in spite of doing so you

183

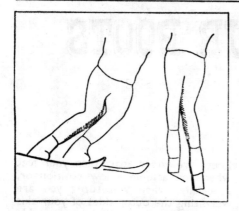

have trouble holding, the solution is the same. The same type of cant as that above will increase your edgeset angle for a given knee position.

3) *Difficulty flexing the legs, excessive bending at the waist :*

If you are unable to flex your legs supplely in spite of knowing that you must learn to use a lower body position or that you must unlock your stiff legs, if you are told that you bend excessively at the waist when you should be flexing your legs, check to

see if you might tend to lose your balance over backwards each time you assume a low position. With your boots on (holding your arms out forward) crouch down until your seat hits your heels. If you lose your balance over backwards, put a 4, 8, or 12 millimeter lift under the heels of your boots. If your boots are a little large, especially around your instep, try to glue lifts on the inside, then complete the canting on the outside.

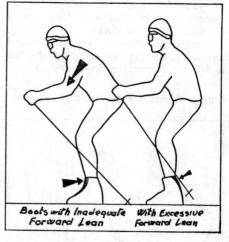

Boots with Inadequate   With Excessive
    Forward Lean   Forward Lean

4) *Your boots do not allow normal flexing :*

Your boots should allow you to flex your ankles, as you must in any low balanced or forward position, and to straighten them as in the up motion for *avalement* for example. The boots should also gradually begin to restrict these movements as they reach extremes where they should provide firm comfortable support points which would make any excessive movements impossible.

These almost divergent requirements have resulted in the design of boots with adjustable forward lean. If your

Lean of the foot
Lean of the boot
Initial lean

Canting in the Boot

Canting Under the Sole

boots disturb your ankle flexions, cant under the back part of your soles. If the support on the fronts of your boots is inadequate when your ankles are bent forward as far as possible, lower the height of your heel or (if this is not possible) cant under the fronts of the boots. The remedy is the same if the back of your boot restricts your ankle bend. In this case you can also hollow out the back of your boot in order to make room for your achilles tendon and make it more comfortable. If your boots are plastic, you can shave the back edge in order to make it more flexible.

Some corrections are more delicate

In the case of bowed legs, if the canting gave good results in straight running but too great an edgeset angle in turns, try another solution. You can have boots custom made with the uppers tilted to the outside. In the case of boots made in two parts riveted together, you can move the rivets in order to lean the uppers to the outside. If your boots have separate inner boots and if there is enough room between them, you can put a plastic or leather wedge between the two on the inside of each boot. Thus, your knee will be pushed outward.

In case 2 discussed above if you feel your ankle "floating" inside your boot and limiting your ability to hold, try to slip a cant between the inside of your ankle and the inside of your boot. This cant could be 2, 3, or 4 millimeters thick and made of leather if you have inner boots. You then place it between the inner and outer boots. If you do not have inner boots, slip a flat piece of soft but firm plastic or very firm foam rubber between your ankles and the inside of your boot tops.

Also in case 2, if you injure the front part of your ankles on the inside against the tops of your boots, modify your cants. If your boots are fairly high, have canted innersoles glued inside your boots in order to lift the insides of your feet over their full length. Cant the outside sole as well if necessary. You can also try the lateral canting discussed in the preceding paragraph.

In cases 3 and 4, depending on the relation between your weight, your power, the length of your lower legs, and the mechanical resistance of your boots to ankle flexion, the solutions I have already suggested will be effective or not. If your boots are too stiff there is no remedy. If they are leather or one piece plastic and not stiff enough, you can reinforce both sides of the uppers or just the inside with fiberglass. If they are plastic and made in two parts, lower and upper riveted together, you can try adding a rivet or two in order to make flexing more difficult.

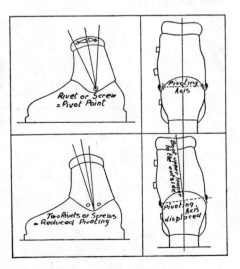

185

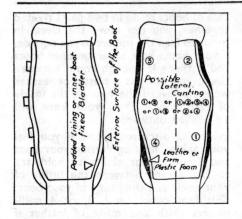

Eliminate sore points in your boots

Some soreness in boots is caused by an incompatibility between the shape of the boots and that of your feet, a bad fit. If a boot is too narrow, for example, there is no remedy. Other sore points result from manufacturing errors, and a good shoe repairman should be able to fix them. Often sore points result from a malformation of the foot frequently resulting from the use of badly fitting boots. These malformations are generally bone spurs, or swelling and hardening in tendons which grow if one is not careful. You can eliminate these sore points by having "bubbles" pressed into your boots at a ski shop. This process is easy in leather boots. For plastic boots, heat must be used. For plastic covered leather boots the process is more delicate. If your sore point corresponds with a very padded point in the boot, you can have some of the padding taken out at this precise point and increased around it. If the point in the boot is not padded, you can make a cant which pads the area around the sore point on your foot. Make the cant from 2, 3, or 4 millimeter thick leather, soft plastic, or firm foam rubber. This type of cant can be glued between inner and outer boots, between the boot and its lining, or put directly on the skin. Sore points also result when a boot is too big. In this case, line them with plastic or foam rubber, or use a sock which is made with a layer of foam rubber around the ankle. Use an innersole as well.

TECHNICAL AND PEDAGOGICAL ANALYSIS

This last chapter is not intended for all my readers. It would be completely useless for those who have confidence in me and who follow my advice. I doubt that it will convince the others of anything. However, at least it might serve to prove that a group of serious researchers has been formed at the University of Grenoble around a large and important ski school and club. It might also serve to prove that this group has not been satisfied by dealing only superficially with the problems posed by skiing in order to present a series of empirical recipes, but that its members possess a coherent general knowledge of all of these specific problems.

This chapter is intended on the one hand for the inquisitive who always want to pursue an idea further, for those enthusiasts who want to know everything. On the other hand and especially, it is intended for instructors and coaches, both professional and amateur who will be spreading their knowledge. This book was obviously not designed for them as the instruction presented is addressed directly to the pupil. As for the intermediary, he should adopt the language of this book, but this implies that he should possess a store of knowledge and experience which will permit him to vary his explanations according to the exact ability of the pupil and eventually to answer often pertinent questions correctly with a complete knowledge of the underlying facts. Unfortunately, it would be impossible to present a full course for instructors and coaches in these few short pages. Such a course is presently being offered at the University of Grenoble "I". A diploma (D.U.T Ski) is given for the completion of one or two years of study in one of three specialties : ski instruction, ski coaching, or ski area management and promotion. More modestly in the following pages, we will touch on some of the practical problems posed by ski teaching. As for technique, I will try only to classify our knowledge methodically, attempt to catalogue it and to establish the relationships between its separate elements. Certain new subjects which should have been discussed thoroughly could not be fully developed here, and I must content myself with merely setting them down. I apologize for this.

TECHNICAL AND PEDAGOGICAL ANALYSIS

I. SKI INSTRUCTION

My goal in writing this book was not to present a teaching method to instructors. Nevertheless, any instructor worthy of the name, should be able to extract the elements necessary to the elaboration of a progression intended for any type of pupil.

National ski schools. The instruction in these schools suffers from three constraints which in my opinion are excessive :
The desire to teach a uniform method in all ski schools in order to permit pupils to move, supposedly with ease, from one school to another slows the evolution of ski teaching method excessively. Though the concern is understandable in the case of ski school classes, personal research and experimentation by instructors giving private lessons and lessons to relatively homogeneous groups over given periods of time should be encouraged.
Clients grouped together for a lesson have different reasons for being in the class. It would be better to separate the groups into two large categories, those who want primarily to improve their skiing, and those who are only looking for a guide and morale booster in the instructor and for a pleasant group of friends among their classmates. The large number of instructors, their rapid training, and the rapid evolution of technique and training method in skiing, a very young sport, makes the introduction of new technical elements very difficult. If it were not for problems of this nature, these new elements would insure a continuous evolution, and the revolutions which now disrupt national ski school could be avoided.

The time lost during a ski lesson. One learns to ski by skiing, not by listening to an instructor speak or by watching other pupils ski. Many ski instructors apparently are not aware of this fact. It must also be recognized that the pupil asks over and over again for useless technical explanations and is often unconsciously satisfied with avoiding the physical work of learning. The early use of easy tows or lifts for beginners, and the "merry-go-round" technique (that is the instructor standing halfway down the hill while the pupils ski by and take the tow repeatedly) are two essential elements for teaching beginners efficiently, and for teaching some important

technical elements to intermediates and experts as well.
It is useless for the pupil to correct his every move especially when a new error appears each time he tries a new movement. I would like to quote one of my colleagues whose words concerning ski instruction for children were greatly appreciated during an international colloquium. "A well chosen ski tow is frequently more effective than the best instructor."

Learning exercises. This book includes very few preparatory exercises. On the contrary, most of the exercises included are immediately effective in skiing. An experienced instructor can make up exercises which will make it easier to acquire the new movement or to correct them. He should be careful, however, because the time spent on a preparatory exercise might better be spent in practising the target movement. Preparatory exercises, often practised at slow speed, sometimes modify the real rhythm of the movement and result in exaggerated movements. They are sometimes even more difficult to learn than the target movement itself. However, some of these exercises (the hops leading to wedeln for example) can be very useful.

Demonstration problems. The instructor often tries to be too elegant while demonstrating in front of his clients, even if they are beginners. The result : the pupils admire him, but because they cannot imitate him, they come up with a thousand subterfuges which they hope will approximate the movement demonstrated but which are actually entirely different. Our experiments prove that pupils learn far more rapidly when the instructor demonstrates using only the technical elements known to the pupil. The new element, as a result, becomes strikingly obvious to the pupil who can see, understand, "feel", and then do it.
It is often more difficult for an instructor to perform an elementary movement than it is for the pupil, especially if the movement is new to the instructor. The knowledge of refined technical elements (more, effective, economical, and easier to perform without intellectual concentration or physical fatigue) makes it difficult to perform move-

ments using only elementary technical elements. Examples are : wide stance vs. narrow stance, *braquage* vs. *vissage*, stemming vs. parallel skiing... The traditional training for instructors has neglected this fundamental element. In addition, instructors often judge the importance of a movement by how easily they themselves can perform it and not by the reaction of their pupils. The reaction of the pupil is obviously the most important, but it can only be properly judged if the movement is explained and demonstrated correctly.

Instructor certification. Certification by the French government for the instruction of skiing for pay was defined by law in 1948. In 1963 a more general law defined the certification of instructors in any sport.
The French Ski Federation trains amateur instructors for its member clubs ; for competition, the Federation holds examinations for club coaches.
The government, through certain universities, starting in 1971, will train professors of physical education who will become specialists in skiing.
The University of Grenoble "I" has created a university diploma in skiing with three possible specialities : instructions coaching, and area management and promotion. The courses last one or two years. The technical and pedagogical levels are equivalent to that of the Professor of physical education specialized in skiing.

Programming of individualized instruction. Many readers, among them an engineer who is a specialist in the subject, criticized our last book for its lack of programming. In writing this book, I have made an effort in this direction by writing chapters especially intended for those learning to ski exclusively from my book (Chapters "Begin" and "Improve"). I have written others for those who already know how to ski, or who are learning to ski in various ski schools, and who want to correct their bad habits. I have also mentioned different peculiarities both favorable and unfavorable, linked to peculiarities in body conformation or to various physical attributes. I did not go farther with this idea for two reasons : First, a precise program is not effective unless perfectly adapted to the problems to be solved, and here the problems are the pupil's physical and psychological peculiarities, his character, background, and goals... Only an intelligent instructor, I should say a true educator, can adapt instruction perfectly to the individual and then only in private lessons. Even in this case, the instructor would have to question the pupil in depth in order to really know him. Second, even if I had categorized several types of skiers, I would have hesitated to meticulously individualize an instruction for each of them for several reasons. Nothing is less interesting than reading an instruction program. Many of my readers would lose interest in the book or would not retain certain essential concepts because they would become bored. I have on the contrary attempted to use an easy-to-read, "journalistic" style. By intentional repetition of words, ideas, and illustrations, I have tried to inculcate my readers by force with certain fundamental ideas. Even lost in the back of the subconscious mind, these ideas will help the skier to improve. Finally, I know my readers, at least my latin readers well enough to know that it would be useless and out of place to impose a program on them. In fact, it is essential for their technical improvement, that they ski for fun without constraints. I can only encourage them to continue to do so. I think, nevertheless, that an organized reader, who would like to develop his own personalized program can find the necessary elements in this book.

AN EXAMPLE INSTRUCTION PROGRAM - THAT OF THE UNIVERSITY OF GRENOBLE SKI SCHOOL

This program was developed for young people between the ages of 17 and 25 who take lessons voluntarily. It was established for the 1970-71 season, and is reworked and reprinted each year according to the observations made the preceding year. Three other columns are normally included with those shown : 1) Adaptation of the Exercises to the Poorly Talented, 2) Adaptation to the Gifted, 3) Learning Exercises.

Gifted and ungifted skiers work side by side, with parallel exercises in the first case and with stem exercises in the other. The first group moves from one level to another more quickly.

The complete program may be obtained at the Secretariat de l'Association des Universitaires Skieurs (A. U. S.), La Pageonnière, 38-Saint-Ismier, France.

Primary Goals	Basic Exercises
A Balance in straight running : in wide stance, in gliding snowplow, on both skis, on one ski	1 — Straight Running (see illustrations pages 19 and 20) In wide stance, low position, and high position 2 — Gliding Snowplow (p. 25) 3 — Stepped Turn on the flat (p. 21) 4 — Use of tows or lifts for beginners
B Learn to Stop (through *braquages*, stem *braquages*, wide stance) First large radius turns	1 — Stops through *braquage* while facing straight downhill (pp. 24 and 27) ◆ in a wide stance ◆ from a slight gliding snowplow 2 — Stops through Down Motion-*Braquage* in a traverse ◆ in a wide stance ◆ from slight gliding snowplow 3 — Large-radius turns through an Uphill Stem (pp. 26, 27) ◆ first emphasizing the uphill stemmed position 4 — Long Turns through Inward Knee Push ◆ not leaving the fall-line by a great deal 5 — Traverses on steeper slopes, Angulation (pp. 30 and 62)
C	1 — First tries at Wedeln (pp. 36 to 41) through successive down motion — *braquages* and gradual change to up motion — *braquages*

2 — Large Radius Turns through uphill stem or inward knee push (pp. 25 and 57)
  — trying to initiate the turn with little or no stem, a sideslip in a narrower stance, and a position of angulation

3 — Short or Intermediate Radius Turns Preceded by a check (pp. 35, 58, 59)
  — check through a downhill stem then initiation of the turn with an uphill stem
  — same exercise with a wide stance

4 — Sideslipping (pp. 32, 33, and 65)
  — between planted poles
  — after downhill stem
  — after a *braquage* in a traverse
  — in garlands

---

1 — Preparation for Counter-Turns
  — by successive downhill stems in a traverse (p. 58)
  — by *braquages* (p. 59)
  — » » with poleplant
  — by rebound garlands with poleplant

2 — Improvement of fairly short-radius turns with counter-turns

3 — Introduction to lateral Recoil in large radius turns : jet-turns (p. 94)

4 — Improvement of Wide Stance Wedeln
  — *braquage*, lateral recoil, and poleplant
  — use of up motion — *braquage* (pp. 66, 67), then

5 — Turns over moguls through down motion — *braquage* (pp. 66, 67), then through *replomement*
  — the *braquage* effort is made with the outside leg of the turn

---

Improvement of large-radius turns,
Introduction to wedeln rhythm (through *braquage* wedeln and stem *braquage* wedeln),
Introduction to short and intermediate-radius turns (through lateral supports and *braquage*).

D

Improvement :
— wide stance wedeln
— short and intermediate radius turns
— long radius turns

E

Same as D

In addition, refinement of technique for transition to:
— true edgesets which allow dynamic counter-turns, real wedeln, quick checking
— precision in the control of the arcs of turns
— adaptation to difficult snows (powder, ice, slush, etc.)
— competition
Introduction to Slalom and Giant Slalom

TECHNICAL AND PEDAGOGICAL ANALYSIS

II. TECHNICAL ELEMENTS AFFECTING THE SKIER'S COMPORTMENT

In pretending to analyse ski technique most people have contented themselves with simply describing and explaining movements through mechanics, while ignoring the possibilities of human joints and the neuro-muscular characteristics of the human body. Even more serious is the fact that certain important factors related to the condition of the snow, the relief of the slope, and the form of the skis have almost always been ignored.

I will try to take into account all of these elements, but unfortunately, I will only be able to touch on these subjects. My two principal goals will be to give you, on the one hand, a general, inclusive view of the problems posed by the comportment of the skier and on the other hand to relate the more or less new technical elements mentioned in this book to these problems. The few brief analyses, which I will present here, have no scientific pretentions and should simply be considered attempts at presenting the material to lay readers.

THE RUN

Snow. All skiing requires a certain exchange of forces between the skis and the slope. Depending on the snow conditions, these exchanges may vary a great deal. Smooth ice resulting from wet snow having been packed and then frozen, or wind-glazed snow (crystals broken down and formed into a conglomerate by the wind) make it difficult for the skier to hold an edge. The edge should be considered a tool used on a hard material. Because the ski does not sink into the snow, it is deformed more in flex and, especially, in torsion during traverses and turns than it would be in soft snow. The hardness of the icy surface increases the risk of vibrations, particularly during runs straight down the fall-line. The difficulty in making the edge bite increases the risk of sideslipping during traverses and turns. The sudden releasing and biting of the edge, which results from the sideslip, causes the ski and the corresponding leg to vibrate. The ski is then said to chatter. This vibration seems to relate to a mechanical characteristic of

the ski and to a locking of the muscles which affix the foot to the leg.

Rough or granular ice : This kind of ice presents either greater irregularities due to inconsistent packing of wet snow, or fine grained irregularities due to the granular nature of the snow (frozen granular spring snow). A uniform granular ice surface allows the edges to hold better than does a smooth ice surface but poses the same kinds of problems. During a sideslip the ski scrapes the surface more than on other snows and the braking action is increased. An uneven, rough granular ice surface poses different problems because the lack of uniformity can cause the skis to be deformed. A hump of frozen snow the size of a fist, a small ridge of snow , the frozen track left by a skier the day before, for example, deforms the ski in flex and in torsion first at the tip and gradually through the full length of the ski. The ski may then be deflected from its original path. At high speed it may vibrate and chatter. Less severe but more numerous irregularities deform the ski in the same manner, but the deformation is not adapted to all the irregularities at the same time. The skis scrape as they would on granular ice but more severely, and the braking action increases even more.

Packed snows. There are two kinds of packed snows in which the ski leaves tracks, packed powder snow and matted snow. The first is made up of more or less star shaped snow crystals. The crystals retain a great deal of mobility in relation to one another. The track is made by the skis without much work during straight running and flat-ski sideslipping. If the skis are edged during sideslipping, more work results and the skis are slowed because the snow accumulates and is compressed under the running surfaces of the skis, thus being hardened slightly before being moved downhill. Flat-ski sideslipping on the other hand displaces unhardened snow.

Matted snows are either slightly humid packed powder or dry snows composed of very fine or broken down crystals. Ie both cases the snow crystals are less mobiln

192

relative to one another. Their displacement both vertically (compression) and horizontally (during sideslipping), or against the tip during forward movement, results in more work, and thus the ski is slowed more than by normal packed powder. Matted snows are normally slower and less slippery, but the correct wax can be used to overcome this problem in part.

Heavy snows. These snows are saturated with water. In addition to their weight, heavy snows are very sticky, and the stickiness increases considerably under the slightest pressure. These characteristics make this type of snow difficult for skiing. The forward slide of the ski tip, as well as that of the full length of the ski in sideslipping, is slowed considerably.

Deep snow. These are the snows into which the skis sink, tips completely submerged. There are two extreme types and all the gradations in between. If deep and dry, the snow shares some of the qualities of packed powder. However, the varying depth of the unpacked snow gives the skis a totally new horizontal instability. Each ski tends to sink, to tip over sideways, and to flex differently depending on how much it is weighted. The resistance encountered by each ski during forward and sideways movement, while straight running, sideslipping, or turning can be very different.

Deep, heavy snows share the same characteristics as those described for heavy snows but are considerably more severe as the increased weight makes it difficult, or sometimes impossible, to jump both skis above the level of the snow or even to lift one ski at a time, or to stem.

Slope variations

I will distinguish between the large variations (knolls and transitions), smaller variations (bumps and moguls), and finally those which the skis encounter while they turn on a uniform slope.

Knolls and transitions. When the steepness of the slope increases, the transition from flat to steep is called a knoll. The speed acquired by the skier on the slope preceding the steep section is oriented parallel to the original slope,

and the orientation will only change progressively downward at the knoll. The vertical pressure on the skis will therefore decrease for a while no matter what the skier does. Ski-snow friction and the resulting braking action will decrease. Transitions, on the other hand, correspond to a flattening of the slope. The direction of the acquired speed must be oriented upward and requires a muscular effort on the part of the skier who must resist the compression. Increased friction and braking action also occurs. The problem of balancing over knolls and through transitions has been discussed very frequently. Actually the problem is not serious, and I will explain it in the paragraph entitled "The Skier's Balance".

Bumps. Bumps can be either natural, a result of the relief of the underlying slope, or of wind action, or artificial, that is a result of skiing. A series of large bumps poses the same problems as do knolls and transitions. Small bumps, on the contrary, do not affect the direction followed by the skier's center of gravity. They simply require upward-downward flexibility in al segments of the skier's body in order to maintain a rectilinear displacement of his center of gravity. The friction between his skis and the snow increases when the skier slides up a bump, that is onto a lesser slope. Friction decreases on the opposite side of the bump where the slope increases. In addition, the skis are flexed when climbing a bump and tend to flap when unweighted after passing the crest of the bump. Bumps of intermediate size pose the problems o both large and small bumps.

Variations in slope resulting from turning the skis. We spent a lot of time on this point in our last book, *How to Ski the New French Way*. Every downhill turn requires the passage from a flat slope (in the traverse) to a maximum slope (at the fall-line), and back to a flatter slope (the new traverse). The skis then encounter increased and decreased friction, and the skier must absorb upward-downward variations by extending and then flexing in order to keep his center of gravity moving parallel to the slope and thus maintaining balance. It should be stated that for rutted turns in competition the variations in slope are amplified as shown by the diagram in our last book. The same is true of turns made on knolls and through transitions.

SKIS

Length. The elongated form of skis is justified, at least it has been for the last thirty years in alpine skiing, because of the difficulties encountered by a skier who attempts to stay in balance during a straight run. The ski, because it is fixed to the skier's foot, serves in effect to lengthen the foot, and the rectangle, which serves the skier as a support base, is as long as the amount of the running surface in contact with the snow. The tip and tail sections also act as levers which increase the resistance of the front and back extremities of the skis to the lateral displacement of the skis on the snow during sideslipping and turning. This resistance results from their inertia and from the friction between the skis and the snow. For similar resistances the manoeuvrability of a turning ski is therefore increased if its length is decreased. However, a shorter ski designed for a skier of a given weight will always exert greater pressure on the ground at its extremities and will serve to decrease or even nullify the above effect. Length not only plays a role in the forward-backward stability of the skier but also in his stability during rectilinear displacements. It also affects the ability of the ski to hold a curve, that is, to maintain a given radius for an already initiated turn. The greater width of the front and back of the ski gives a greater precision to the control of the ski through an arc. As a result, the modification of the lengths of the front and back levers due to a forward or backward displacement of the binding is very important. (A displacement of one centimeter is noticeable.)

Side cut. Seen from above, the sides of a ski form arcs which are concave toward the outside. Sometimes these arcs are perfectly circular, each defined by three points : the first at the point of greatest width at the front of the ski (80 to 90 millimeters at the shovel), the second at the point of greatest width at the back of the ski (75 to 80 millimeters) and the third at the narrowest point in the middle of the ski (65 to 70 millimeters). For the most part, however, these arcs are not perfectly circular but very complex. As a result of its side cut, its concave arc, any weighted ski moving over hard snow in a traverse must bend both lengthwise and torsionally in order to come in contact with the snow over its full length. The ski is deformed more as the angle of edging increases. The line of contact between the ski and the snow is a curve. The lengthwise bending of the ski tends, therefore, to make the ski slide in an uphill curve during a forward sideslip and in a downhill curve when the skier changes edges before moving into a downhill turn. During stem turns the outside ski bends in a similar manner which also tends to make the ski slide in a curve.

Shovel width, tail width. The width of a ski at its widest point in the shovel is generally from eight to ten millimeters greater than the widest point at the tail. This difference has no function in traverses, or turns with edgesets, where only the curved form (the sidecut of the ski) is necessary to the manoeuvre. On the other hand, when the ski is tipped from flat on the snow onto its edge, the bite of the shovel, which is wider, tends to start the ski into the turn more forcefully. Once the turn is initiated, the curve of the sidecut tends to make the ski continue to turn.

Width. Two skis with identical sidecuts, the same difference in width between shovel and tail, and the same length but different widths, differ in two ways. As for speed, the wider ski has a greater area of running surface and exerts less pressure per square centimeter. Depending on the snow conditions, the speed of the wider ski will be faster or slower. In addition, the skier must exert more energy on the wider ski in order to edge it.

The groove. The groove in the running surface is the only rectilinear part of the ski. Its primary function is to help the ski track in straight running. Its second role is to insure a directional effect in addition to that of the scraping of the edges during "flat ski" sideslipping in soft snows where the ski sinks enough for half of the running surface to come into contact with the snow. The effectiveness of the groove depends on its depth, its shape, and on its distance behind the tip. A simple modification in the edges of the groove can modify the performance of the ski in soft snows. Filling the groove with wax can make it easier to turn in deep snows.

Flex. This word encompasses both amplitude under a given force (the ski sitting on two horizontal supports, one under each end, the force exerted on its center) and the distribution of the flexibility over the full length of the ski. The flex, then, refers to the overall line of the ski which bends more or less at different points along its length according to their respective degrees of flexibility. The longitudinal flexibility of the ski affects its *glissement* in straight running by distributing pressures, especially those generated when the slope flattens abruptly in transitions and bumps, over the full running surface. It acts in a similar manner to facilitate forward-backward balancing adjustments. A stiff ski, or one with a stiff tip section, will ram into bumps. If this section is too flexible, the shocks will be too great when the skier's foot hits the bump. Forward-backward balance is also difficult on too flexible a ski because the forward and backward support is not firm enough. Finally, longitudinal flexibility determines how well the ski will hold during a traverse, or in a turn because of the sidecut of the ski which we have already seen. Note : we will discuss lateral flexibility further on. For greater precision longitudinal flexibility should be called frontal flexibility.

Camber. Camber is the bend in each ski which becomes apparent when the skis are placed running surface to running surface. It is not the amplitude of this gap that is necessarily important, but the force needed to flatten the skis against each other. (This force actually is related to the amplitude of the camber. If the camber is increased through heating the skis, the force necessary to flatten the skis increases proportionately.) Due to its camber and the distribution of its flexibility, a ski flattened under the weight of a skier exerts different amounts of pressure under its different sections. In general, the pressure is greatest under the foot and diminishes rapidly toward the ends becoming practically zero. It then increases at the ends, playing an important role in the ability of the ski to track, and in its ability to hold during turns.

Lateral flexibility. A ski placed edgewise on a horizontal surface and subjected to a downward push on its center will flatten (that is the side of the ski in contact with the horizontal surface will form a straight line). The push must have a force of roughly eighty to one hundred kilograms. This kind of deformation (about which nothing has ever been written before) is called side camber deflection and is an important element with the new foam core skis. It affects the shape of the curve established by the contact of the side of a ski with the surface of the snow when the weighted ski is edged in a traverse or a turn.

Torsional flexibility. Because of its wasp waist, a weighted, edged ski is twisted in a double torsion. (A simple torsion would be a single twist, a helix, over the full length of the ski whereas in this case there is a helix in the front and one in the back of the ski in the opposite direction from the first.) These twists in torsion are added to the frontal and lateral bending and affects both of them.

Elasticity, chattering, vibrations, and damping. I will not spend much time on these characteristics though they are important. I must, however, specify that the idea of "liveliness" in a ski comes from the tradition of wood skis in which elasticity was a desired quality. Today, the elasticity of most skis must often be voluntarily decreased. I differentiate between chattering and vibrating by referring in the first case to an oscillation of greater amplitude in the front and tail of the ski. These are visible to the experienced eye most often in straight running and in long turns over regular, smooth bumps. It is even possible to observe certain periods in these oscillations. They disturb the skier's balance, slow him down, and impair the ability of the ski to hold. We call the smaller oscillations, those which must be measured with strain gauges either in the lab or while skiing, vibrations. (In this last case the skier carries a transmitter which sends signals to an oscillograph.) These oscillations are produced not only lengthwise but also torsionally. The damping characteristic of a ski is its capability to make these small vibrations stop more or less rapidly. This quality can be measured in the laboratory. The vibrations impair both the ability of the ski to hold and its ability to slide fast.

Combinations of the above elements. The "personality" of a ski results from a combination of all the above characteristics. It should be noted that different mixtures can give similar results. It would seem, however, that due to the increasing use of quality control machines by ski manufacturers, few mechanical characteristics of the better skis can be kept secret. A certain uniformity in these characteristics should soon be established.

A few figures concerning the above mentioned characteristics (for skis from 205 to 210 centimeters long).
Force necessary to flatten the ski's camber: 9 to 12 kilograms.
Force necessary to flex a ski supported on each end of its running surface to an arc of 5 centimeters: 40 to 50 kilograms.
Force necessary to flex the central zone of the ski (the half of the running surface of the ski located arround its center point) to an arc of 1 centimeter: 90 to 110 kilograms.
Force necessary to flatten the camber of this central zone: 20 to 30 kilograms.
Force necessary to flex the forward zone (quarter of the length of the ski just in front of the bearing surface) in order to lift the tip 3.5 centimeters: 25 to 30 kilograms, for the tail: 23 to 30 kilograms.

THE SKIER

I will only be able to touch on this vast subject.
The human body can be considered a stack of movable segments (leg, thigh, pelvis, vertebrae,...) in contact with one another at the joints. When a man is standing still, these segments can be moved by two forces, gravity on the one hand and muscular force on the other. To these two forces should be added, when the skier is moving, the inertia of each of these body segments. The possible movements at each joint are strictly limited as to direction and amplitude by the nature of the surfaces in contact, by the ligaments which encircle the joints, and by the muscles which join two or several neighboring segments together. The planes in which each joint can move should

be known to sports technicians who can thus avoid erroneous interpretations. For example, to speak of a lateral knee angulation would be absurd because it is impossible. The impression of a lateral movement is in this case given by a double pivoting at the hip and the foot. When contracting, muscles exert an equal traction on both segments to which they are attached. If one of these segments is in a fixed position, the other will be displaced and eventually cause the movement of other segments attached to it. If neither segment is fixed, both will move an amount inversely proportionate to their masses.

On the functional level one should not consider the isolated action of one muscle but that of a number of muscles together, called a muscle group, which contribute to the same movement. One muscle may participate in the movements of different neighboring muscle groups but never in opposing movements. Muscle groups control all of the movements allowed by the joints. The groups are defined by their functions: flexing muscle group of the thigh, rotator of the thigh in the pelvis... Each muscle group is opposed by another which makes the inverse movement, for example: flexing group of the leg on the thigh and extending group of the leg on the thigh, external rotation group of the thigh in the pelvis and internal rotating group... Many movements result from the effect of gravity: for example, the flexing of the legs or of the upper body. The degree of movement is controlled by the muscle group which counteracts the force of gravity and which causes the inverse movement, that is, it slows down, then stops the movement.

The kinetic energy acquired by a segment can also produce its movement relative to another segment without the intervention of the corresponding muscle group and even with the intervention of the opposing muscle group which acts here again as a brake. Thus, the contraction of a muscle group does not necessarily cause the points where the muscles are attached to move closer to one another, but can slow down their spreading caused either by gravity or by inertia. Thus the same muscle group during a prolonged contraction can slow, then stop a movement and immediately cause an inverse movemen . This is the principle of the movement called wind-up and release which play such an important role in athletic movements. For example, let's study the case of the flexing and straightening of the legs. The flexing is produced by a relaxation of the extensors which by resisting the force of gravity allows man to remain in a standing position. This flexing is then slowed down by the extensors which begin their contraction during a phase in which they are extending. These muscles stop the flexing, and if they do not immediately stop contracting, begin extending the legs. This is called down-up motion which would seem to depend on two movements, but which in fact depends only on one, the same muscle contraction. A contrary case: a skier accelerates his flexing to the point of pulling his feet up under his body. Gravity then is not enough; the thigh flexors act on the pelvis, and the legs on the thighs. Then in a second phase, the extensors slow down the fall of the upper body.

A movement of wind-up and release can be purely muscular. A discus thrower pivots first backward and thus prepares the forward pivoting which permits him to throw the discus. Any preceding stretching of a muscle will facilitate and increase the effectiveness of its contraction. In addition, the wind-up, which can be called a preparation, if it is aimed properly, favors the contraction of the muscles resulting in the final movement.

These few concepts make it possible to understand that the real nature of a movement is dependent on its direction and not on the initial position of the segments which must move. For example, the wisting movement, *vissage*, resulting in a position of *vissage*, or in a normal position from *vissage*, or in a position of *vissage* from another position of *vissage* to the opposite side is the same movement in every case if, of course, the displacement of the segments is in the same direction in all three cases.

THE SKIER'S BALANCE

Balance depends on the individual, his skis, the snow, and the slope.

At the neuro-muscular level. The skier balances differently depending on whether he is a beginner or an expert. The beginner reacts solely from the points of support which he finds under his feet: support from the front or the back of the skis for forward-backward balance, support from one foot to the other for lateral balance when he has his weight on both skis or on an edge, or support on the other ski if he has weighted only one. His balance is therefore better on longer, stiffer skis which are spread wider apart (widestance if he has his weight on both skis) or on a wider ski if he is balancing on only one ski. A good skier, on the other hand, uses these supports less after reaching a certain speed and depends more on the supports of his own body segments. Similar to a cat which falls onto its feet when dropped upside down, he depends on the changes in position and the movements of his upper body, arms, thighs, and legs relative to one another in order to stay in balance.

Nevertheless, like the beginner he uses some of the supports under his feet, in particular those which act vertically and laterally. However, under his feet he could not find the points of support which would permit him to displace his whole body forward or backward. A forward lean corresponds to a forward movement of the upper body or to a backward movement of the skis. A backward lean is just the reverse.

Variations in slope pose a problem for balancing. The extreme mobility of skis makes it necessary for the skier to exert forces only perpendicularly to the surface of the slope. The "law of perpendicularity" of the skier to the slope results from this observation. (We will see farther along that friction on the snow and in the air will modify the law slightly.) In order to remain perpendicular to the snow surface over knolls and through transitions, the skier must change the respective positions of his upper body and his feet. The beginner does so by reflex reactions to the feelings of unweighting or pressure which he feels under the fronts of his feet. The advanced skier can readjust even when suspended in the air as his vision can be enough to allow him to judge the relative positions which he should give to the various segments of his body according to the type of slope he is about to reach.

The friction of the snow and the air also have an effect. The effect of the friction between the skis and the snow makes it necessary for the skier to place his center of gravity behind the perpendicular already mentioned. The effect of air friction at high speeds does not necessarily require the inverse. In effect, the resultant of gravity which pulls the skier in a direction parallel to the slope is exerted on the center of gravity of the skier. Air friction resistance is exerted on roughly the central point of the part of the skier's surface area exposed to the direction of the movement. In a moderately low position, arms spread, or in the egg position this central point remains at approximately the same height as that of the center of gravity. Thus, the torque of the unbalancing pivoting action which could exist is negligible. The variations in air friction, therefore, hardly disturb the skier's balance at all.

GLISSEMENT ON THE SNOW AND IN THE AIR

Ski-snow contact. Friction results over the full length of the running surface of the ski each time it slides on the snow. There is a greater amount of friction at the shovel of the ski when the snow is soft enough for the ski to leave a track. The observation of this friction can be made empirically but accurately enough by watching the wearing of a layer of wax on the running surface of the ski. In order to make the effect of this friction more comprehensible, I am going to differentiate between two of its aspects. On the one hand, I will discuss the forces of adhesion between the running surface of the ski and the snow surface. On the other hand, I will discuss the forces absorbed by the ski due to the accumulation of snow under the ski and particularly under the forward zone.

Adhesion. Adhesion depends on the physico-chemical nature of the running surface, its physical aspect (more or less smooth, rough, threaded, stretched,...), the physical condition of the snow and of the slope, and finally the distribution of the pressures due to the weight and the weighting of the ski which affect the different parts of its running surface. This distribution of pressures depends on the respective

flexibilities of the different parts of the ski, of the total surface of the ski, and on the position and movements of the skier in the frontal and lateral planes. It also depends on the relief of the slope which can result in more or less localized increases in pressure at the tip section or over the total length of the ski. Note: These increases in pressure can be absorbed, even completely, with appropriate movements by the skier. It should also be pointed out that steel edges are far slower than the rest of the running surface. The width of the hidden edge exposed to the snow is, therefore, an important factor in determining the speed of the ski.

The compression of the snow accumulated under the tip of the ski and slowing it down. This compression is dependent on the condition of the snow. However, poor distribution of the forces exerted on the skis by the skier both in the forward-backward and lateral directions increases the braking action of the skis. The distribution of the flexibility in the ski also has an effect , especially in the forward zone. The more gradual the accumulation and compression, the less the ski is slowed. The width of the ski also affects its speed in this regard. Accumulation and compression of snow under the forward part of the ski is a factor often forgotten when attempts are made to explain an unusually poor performance by a downhill racer on soft snow. More often, the wax is blamed.

Glissement. In turns, *glissement* poses a very complex problem. Three forces would seem to have an effect in this case, the two forces already mentioned and a third related to the displacement of snow or ice during sideslipping in the turn. Adhesion seems to have greater importance in flat ski turns. On the other hand, such turns do result in some accumulation and compression of snow and sometimes in a slight displacement of the snow. In turns involving a definite setting of the edges, however, the accumulation and compression of snow is fairly great. The displacement of snow is also great if the longitudinal axis of the ski forms a large angle with the ski's real direction of travel. If on the contrary the axis of the skis and their direction of travel correspond more closely, and especially if the flexing of the skis and their sidecut result in an arc similar to that of the turn, the edges make a relatively clean cut in the snow, and the skis are slowed down very little by snow displacement.

Glissement in the air. I discussed this subject at length in the chapter on downhill, and just mentioned it again in regard to a skier's balance. I will simply discuss here the various tests carried out in wind tunnels. Some have been accurate and others blemished with errors. For accurate wind tunnel tests to determine the most aerodynamic position, the skier must be subjected to the same balancing problems as those posed by skiing. If, for example, the skier leans forward to resist the blast of the oncoming air, the positions he assumes become artificial and as a result, lack interest.

III. THE TECHNICAL ELEMENTS OF TURNING
A. The initiation of downhill turns

THE TECHNICAL ELEMENTS INDISPENSABLE IN INITIATING TURNS

Two elements are indispensable to the initiation of any turn : edge change of the skis and **inward** lean of the skier. Edge change does not result in a pivoting of the skis as do other movements which will be discussed later, but due to the shape of the ski it does result indirectly in the initiation of the turn.
We will now study edge change and inward lean respectively, even though the same movements result in both most of the time.

Edge change. Edge change refers to the lateral tipping of the skis which move from the uphill edges to flat on the snow and, then, to the downhill edges, which become the inside edges of the turn which is beginning. Considering the lateral rigidity of ski boots which allow hardly any lateral flexing of the ankles, an edge change must result from an inclination of the lower leg. The greater the slope of the run, the greater must be the angle of inclination of the legs. The legs can assume the same angle as that of the rest of the body. The vertical axis of the skier's body leaning downhill from the traverse, becomes perpendicular to the slope when the skis are flat on the snow, then results in the edge change. The outside leg tips more than his body when the skier angulates. It assumes the same angle as that of the thigh if the angulation is due to a pivoting and lateral tipping at the small of the back and hips, or a still greater angle through an additional pivoting of the hips.
Other technical elements can facilitate the edge change : a jump with a lateral displacement of the skis in jet-turns, and the forward and uphill thrust of the skis in sliding jet-turns and *avalement* turns.
I will only mention the alternating edge changes (uphill ski, then downhill ski) which can be performed from a stem or a wide stance.

Inward lean. The basic means for a man to lean his body laterally are : 1) the relaxation of the extensors of his downhill leg if he wants to lean his entire body, and 2) the same movement as above plus the relaxation of the abductors of his thigh on his pelvis if he desires an accelerated lateral fall from his hips. (An abduction corresponds to a lifting of a leg in the lateral plane of the body.) In this last case inward lean occurs at the same time as angulation. It should also be mentioned that the same muscles are simultaneously abductors and extensors and, as a result, the movements of inclination and angulation share a physiological unity.
In our last book we included a table showing the times necessary for the tipping to different angles of inclination depending on the initial amount of inward lean produced by the relaxation of the skier's weighted leg while he is in a narrow, fairly wide, or wide stance. These times can vary from a half to a full second for a narrow stance, and they confirm that in the traditional forms of initiating a turn the skier must use movements which increase the speed of his inward lean.
The other means available to the skier for accelerating his inward lean are : 1) a slight uphill jump which also results in the edge change (This rather basic movement is actually very complex as it includes : a down-up motion resulting in a jump, a

slight angulation during the theoretically vertical thrust which in fact becomes oblique, and a slight pivoting of the legs under the pelvis during the jump.), 2) a counter-turn (or jet-turn) through a displacement of the skis into a position crosswise to the direction of travel (There is a checking of the speed of the lower body while the upper body continues to move forward and, as a result, towards the inside relative to the new direction of travel of the skis.), and 3) a downhill pivoting and sliding of the skis while the skier's body continues to move in its original direction (as in sliding jet-turns and in the *avalement* turns presented in this book). These three movements combine with movements resulting in the pivoting of the skis. We will see them again further along.

OTHER TECHNICAL ELEMENTS WHICH CAN OCCUR DURING THE INITIATION OF TURNS

Unweighting. The processes of unweighting are very well known, and I will only discuss them briefly. In the example of muscle analysis I explained how unweighting by flexing is very close to unweighting by down-up motion, and how on the other hand it differs a great deal from unweighting by a flexing and traction of the legs (resulting in a lifting of the skis from the snow during the down motion).

Down-up unweighting is itself very similar to unweighting through a simple up motion. This last fact makes the radical separation of the two movements in some instruction methods seem completely absurd. These four types of unweighting last about 0.15 of a second for a vertical displacement of ten centimeters of the center of gravity in the case of a complete unweighting of the skis. If a down motion is linked to a down-up motion, one has an unweighting through down-up-down motion. In this case the movement lasts 0.30 of a second. These very slight lengths of time suggest that all the movements resulting in the pivoting of the unweighted skis must be very quick and perfectly synchronized with the unweighting movement. Finally, it must be remembered that all unweighting causes an increase in pressure preceding the unweighting in the case of up and down-up motion, following the unweighting in down motion, and before

and after the unweighting in down-up-down motion.

What we have called rebound, then, is nothing other than a down-up motion in which the down motion is very dynamic and results in an intense contraction of the muscles during the edgeset. This intense contraction causes the mass of the body to be thrown back upward even before the up motion can be seen. The skier can thus unweight his skis by maintaining a compact, folded position.

Reploiement for turns in bumps is only a traditional down motion, a relaxing of the extensors performed while the bump pushes the skis and the skier's legs upward. *Avalement* is altogether different. Considering only its unweighting effect, it is a type of down motion. However, the flexing is accelerated by traction between the thighs and pelvis and the upper body and pelvis through a violent use of the abdominal muscles, resulting in a "jacknife" movement. In competition or in an athletic wedeln, when short turns are linked together with *avalement*, or in "S" turns, the force exerted on the skis by the extensors immediately preceding the *avalement* makes it an up-down motion. (Here again is the wind-up and release movement.)

Forward and lateral projections. These are also unweighting movements. They are up motions and down-up motions performed from the support on the edge of one ski and oriented not vertically but obliquely uphill in the lateral plane of the body, or downhill and forward.

Movements which result in the pivoting of the skis. The pivoting forces used during the initiation of the turn have often been called "pivoting impulses" by technicians who have thought only of the very brief pivoting efforts made while the skis are unweighted. In fact, we will see that some of these movements can produce a lasting effect not just during the unweighting but also after the unweighting and sometimes even without an unweighting.

Braquage. In defining the expression *braquage*, I described the independen pivoting effort of each leg under the pelvis A complex interaction exerted at the pelvis results from a wide or semi-wide stance in this double pivoting effort without causing an opposite reaction in the upper body. The movement is produced in each leg at the pelvis by the rotators. In the most common type of *braquage* the pivoting effort is produced in each leg. It can also be produced in only one leg at a time if the other leg is weighted. In this case the steering produces the beginning of a stem, which can be very obvious, or imperceptible. The force which can be exerted in *braquage* is considerable. The great advantage of this force is the possibility of exerting it on the skis for several seconds, whereas the pivoting forces resulting from rotation or *vissage* can be exerted only during a few tenths of a second. It should also be pointed out that if a ski is lifted, the movement is no longer *braquage* but is then termed *vissage*.

Rotation. Rotation necessitates a "throwing" movement. From a balanced phase of the turn, the skier throws his upper body (head and shoulders in the Allais technique, upper body and pelvis in the light christy) in the direction of the coming turn, to the right for example. This movement results from the action of the rotators toward the right, of the upper body on the pelvis, and possibly of the pelvis on the legs. It is then slowed by the action of the inverse muscle groups and, as a result, the legs and skis (unweighted) are dragged around by the rotating force generated by the upper body. The force produced by rotation can be very great. The amount of force depends in particular on the speed of the rotation. Its transmission to the legs and skis can be made to last a short time by a gradual braking action with the opposite muscle groups. The pivoting force is transmitted, however, only during a few tenths of a second. It should also be noted that the muscles which make rotation effective are identical to those which would result in a pivoting of the skis through a movement of *vissage*. Thus, *vissage* can be linked perfectly to a rotation in order to complete the effect of the rotation on the skis.

Vissage. This is a movement which insures the simultaneous pivoting of both legs and the skis through the support of the mass of the upper body which acts as a fulcrum. A position of *vissage* can also result when the skier's upper body

is not facing in the same direction as his skis but downhill during traverses or sideslipping and toward the outside during turns. A position in which the body is pivoted in the opposite direction, on the other hand, is called a position of rotation. The hinging point of this movement may be situated in the small of the back or at the hips or, as it is most frequently, in both at the same time. In contrast to rotation which requires momentum, *vissage* requires no support from the surface of the snow. The few elements of muscular mechanics previously described explain why *vissage* results in a pivoting, or at least, a tendency to pivot, of the upper body in the opposite direction of the legs and skis (which are pivoting at the same time). Even if the upper body does not begin pivoting immediately by rotation and even if it is not partially immobilized by a poleplant, it will pivot much less than the skis during a movement of *vissage* (because of its great mass among other reasons). The force of the pivoting depends on the muscular force exerted by the skier. It can be considerable but may last only a brief instant (a few tenths of a second) as it ceases once the skier reaches a position of maximum *vissage*. In actual practice a steering of the outside leg generally follows the *vissage* effort. It should be noted that when the inside ski is lifted this *braquage* of the outside ski actually becomes *vissage*. The reaction of the upper body to this *vissage* is very slight and almost imperceptible. We will see further along that the pivoting effect produced by *vissage* is always accompanied by a lateral thrust produced by angulation. This is why the term *vissage-angulation* is often used.

Anticipation. Anticipation, which is either a pivoted position of the upper body in the direction of a coming turn before its initiation, or a pivoting movement which results in this position, can serve as a preparation phase (the wind-up movement explained in the paragraph on muscle analysis) to *vissage* if the latter is linked immediately to the movement of anticipation. The simple position of anticipation also favors *vissage* by permitting the upper body a more ample counter-rotation... I emphasized in the muscle paragraph the similarity between the pivoting movements (in the same direction) from a position of *vissage* (anticipation) to a normal position and eventually to a position of *vissage* in the opposite direction. It should also be noted that a rapid movement of anticipation is in fact a rotation of the upper body which permits a storing of energy that can then be transmitted to the skis through a *vissage* effort.

I must also point out that from a position of *vissage* (anticipation) any straightening movement or any down motion results automatically in the action of the muscle groups which cause a de-angulation, and thus a pivoting of the feet. This is the case in that particular flexing movement called *avalement*. To the beginning of the pivoting movement, which might be called a release from *vissage*, is generally linked a pivoting produced by the steering of both legs, or only the outside leg.

The downhill pole plant. Before or during the initiation of a turn the pole-plant offers an outside lateral support point which, due to the forward movement of the skis, helps the pivoting of the skier and his skis into the turn. The thrust-into-pivoting (deflection) exerted by the pole from the hand to the skier's feet is transmitted through the trunk by the muscle groups which would be used to begin a turn by *vissage*. This is true even if the skier's upper body does not start into a movement of *vissage* or even into a movement of rotation. When the skier does use a movement of *vissage* or even a movement of rotation, he profits from an additional support on the pole. In effect, his upper body can be considered stabilized by the pole, and the muscle action of *vissage*, as a result, produces only the pivoting of his legs and skis. The force and amplitude of the movement are then increased.

The planted pole also offers a vertical support which facilitates unweighting, a lateral support which helps in lateral thrust (which we will discuss below), and a forward-backward support which aids in *avalement*. During the "jacknife" of

avalement the upper body is partially blocked from forward movement by the pole plant, and the forward movement of the feet is thus increased. We have seen also that the pivoting of the skis is increased by the poleplant in a release from *vissage*.

Lateral thrust. Any lateral thrust exerted on the ski by the skier's foot will tend to make the ski pivot. This fact is explained especially by the greater friction at the tip of the ski than at the heel during a lateral displacement over the snow and by the greater inertia of the forward part of the ski when it is displaced through the air. The mechanical and muscular analysis of the movement of lateral thrust is very complex, and I would not think it necessary to give a full explanation here, as I have emphasized the movement throughout this book. To be explicit, the obvious lateral thrusts which can be made from a stem or from a wide stance, and the lateral projection from one ski to the other are not different in nature from the lateral thrusts which can be made from a narrow stance in jet-turns, sliding jet-turns, or "S" turns. In the case of excellent advanced skiers and "instinctive" skiers, the effect of these lateral movements is frequently added to the movements of *braquage*, *vissage*, or rotation. This is not the case of most of the skiers trained in ski schools which have forgotten to include this technical element in their methods.

Note : In a preceding paragraph I spoke of *vissage* and not of *vissage-angulation* as I have in other works. I did so intentionally in order to distinguish the pivoting of the skis produced by *vissage* from the lateral displacement which can result either from a pure movement of angulation or from the use of angulation during a straightening thrust of the legs. In fact, the movements of *vissage* and angulation are always associated in skiing even when talking simply of a position. The slightly flexed position of the skier's trunk over his legs gives an impression of angulation as soon as *vissage* occurs.

B. The technical elements occurring during the carving of turns

I have emphasized very strongly the importance of the carving phase of turns. Carving is not a simple sideslip controlled by putting the skis crosswise to the direction of travel or by setting the edges and leaning forward or backward in a certain way. Pivoting forces must often be exerted during the turn in order to make the ski continue to follow a certain arc. This is especially true when the initiation of the turn has not been strong enough, or in the case of skis that are difficult to turn. On the other hand, pivoting efforts must be made in the direction opposite to that of the turn, in order to control an initiation which has been too powerful, and which would result in overturning. These pivoting or "counter-pivoting" forces are produced most often by *braquage* of both legs but predominantly the outside leg, or of only the outside leg if the inside ski is lifted (this steering of one leg being mechanically similar to *vissage*).

For the carved control of turns we have seen that forward and backward pressure are determining factors. It must be added that very complex adjustments are made in the feet and legs in order to control the torsional and frontal action of the ski in order to make it carve. Turns passing over knolls, through transitions, over bumps, against favorable banks or across unfavorable fall-away slopes, complicate the problems involved in the control of the arc of a turn both as far as the ski-snow contact and readjustments made by the skier to retain his balance are concerned.

TABLE OF CONTENTS pages IX - X

Imprimé en France

TEXTE ET HÉLIOGRAVURE PAR
SCOP - SADAG — OI - BELLEGARDE
FRANCE

Dépôt légal 4e trimestre 1971
No 972